PRAISE FOR *HOW MINDS CHANGE*

"If you join David McRaney on this journey—a spirited tour that ranges from activists to scientists to cultists—you'll arrive in an unexpected place. He shows us how generous conversations can replace zero-sum debates and how genuine empathy can close deep divisions. *How Minds Change* is the ideal book for our perilous moment."

—Daniel H. Pink, #1 *New York Times* bestselling author of
The Power of Regret, To Sell Is Human, and *Drive*

"A timely, informative, and encouraging case for why the craziness paralyzing our society may not be permanent, and a refreshingly actionable proposal for changing ourselves, among others."

—Douglas Rushkoff, author of *Team Human* and
host of the *Team Human* podcast

"This book is a fascinating journey through the neuroscience and psychology of how we form and update our opinions. *How Minds Change* is the book our society desperately needs right now. David McRaney shows us how to connect, consider, and see the potential for change in others and ourselves."

—Scott Barry Kaufman, founder of the Center for the Science
of Human Potential and author of *Transcend*

"Read this book cover to cover—it will change how you feel about tackling one of the most difficult relationship challenges: Changing the minds of the people we care about, without damaging the relationship itself."

—Tessa West, psychology professor at NYU and author of *Jerks at Work*

"One of the most powerful traits of humanity is our capacity to not only update our own beliefs, but also change the minds of others. David McRaney provides a tour de force on how we can persuade others without relying on coercion."

—Jay Van Bavel, director of the NYU Social Identity and
Morality Lab and author of *The Power of Us*

"That very rare thing—an astonishingly interesting book on a vitally important topic."

—Rory Sutherland, vice chairman at Ogilvy UK and author of *Alchemy:
The Surprising Power of Ideas That Don't Make Sense*

HOW MINDS CHANGE

HOW MINDS CHANGE

*The Surprising Science of
Belief, Opinion, and Persuasion*

DAVID McRANEY

PORTFOLIO • PENGUIN

PORTFOLIO / PENGUIN
An imprint of Penguin Random House LLC
penguinrandomhouse.com

Most Portfolio books are available at a discount when purchased in quantity for sales
promotions or corporate use. Special editions, which include personalized covers, excerpts, and
corporate imprints, can be created when purchased in large quantities. For more information,
please call (212) 572-2232 or e-mail specialmarkets@penguinrandomhouse.com. Your local
bookstore can also assist with discounted bulk purchases using the Penguin Random House
corporate Business-to-Business program. For assistance in locating a participating retailer, e-
mail B2B@penguinrandomhouse.com.

Image credits: p. 73 chart courtesy of Pascal Wallisch;
p. 266 graph courtesy of Peter J. Richerson.

Library of Congress Cataloging-in-Publication Data
Names: McRaney, David, author.
Title: How minds change : the surprising science of belief, opinion, and
persuasion / David McRaney.
Description: New York, NY : Portfolio/Penguin, [2022] |
Includes bibliographical references and index.
Identifiers: LCCN 2022002722 (print) | LCCN 2022002723 (ebook) |
ISBN 9780593190296 (hardcover) | ISBN 9780593190302 (ebook)
Subjects: LCSH: Belief and doubt. | Attitude change. |
Judgment. | Public opinion.
Classification: LCC BF773 .M37 2022 (print) | LCC BF773 (ebook) |
DDC 153.4—dc23/eng/20220302
LC record available at https://lccn.loc.gov/2022002722
LC ebook record available at https://lccn.loc.gov/2022002723

Printed in the United States of America
First Printing

BOOK DESIGN BY FINE DESIGN

PREMIUM ISBN 9780593092507

IN MEMORY OF BLAKE PARKER

Thank you for giving an only child a brother, always leaving me with new stories to tell, and teaching me how to play hooky with the universe.

CONTENTS

INTRODUCTION

We are about to go on a journey together to understand how minds change. By the end of this journey, you will not only be able to use what we learn to change the minds of others, you'll also change your own, I hope, because that's what happened to me, in more ways than one.

After writing two books about cognitive biases and logical fallacies, and then spending several years hosting a podcast about those topics, I had settled into a long and comfy pessimism that you may currently share. Onstage, behind a microphone, in articles, I often said there was no point in trying to change people's minds about topics like politics, superstitions, or conspiracy theories—and especially not a combination of the three.

After all, when was the last time you tried to change someone's mind? How did it go? Thanks to the internet, we have more access to people on the other side of the issues we care about than ever before. So the odds are pretty good you've recently been in an argument with someone who saw things differently, and I bet they didn't change their mind when you presented them with what, to you, seemed like clear evidence of their wrongness. They likely left that argument not only angry, but more convinced than ever they were right and you were wrong.

Growing up in Mississippi, like many in my generation, these kinds of arguments were part of our daily lives long before the internet introduced us to the wider world of disagreement. The people in movies and television shows seemed to routinely disagree with the adults who told us the South would rise again, homosexuality was a sin, and evolution was just a theory. Our families seemed stuck in another era. Whether the issue was a scientific fact, a social norm, or a political stance, the things that seemed obviously true to my friends, the ideas reaching us from far away, created a friction in our home lives and on the holidays that most of us learned to avoid. There was no point in trying to change some people's minds.

Our cynicism wasn't abstract. In the Bible Belt, there were real stakes to breaking taboos, and from time to time we each had to make a choice about how—and when—we'd defy them.

As a teenager, I spent a summer delivering flowers for my uncle, who had bought a florist shop in the middle of our small town with money he had saved working as a paramedic. When the landlord began to bully him, my uncle called my father for help. As he hung up the phone, my dad grabbed his car keys and asked me to join him, and then we raced to the shop. He parked, walked into the middle of the confrontation, made it clear there would be trouble if the intimidation continued, and returned to the car. But the thing that stuck with me was that he said nothing on the ride back, nothing the rest of the day, and never mentioned it to the rest of the family. He didn't need to ask for my silence. I knew why we had to keep it secret, and I did.

A science and science fiction nerd, my cynicism only grew stronger after I left home and began working for local newspapers, and then local television, just as social media entered our lives. Before becoming a science journalist, one of my responsibilities was moderating the Facebook page for the small news operation at WDAM-TV in Ellisville, Mississippi. For years, I spent a portion of every day reading the disheartening comments of angry viewers threatening to boycott the station after any science story that challenged their worldviews.

I realized just how far our viewers were willing to take these arguments when a meteorologist explained on air why climate change was real, and most likely the result of carbon emissions from human activity. The comments overflowed with rage after I used the station's official Facebook account to share links from experts. Like most people, I thought the facts would speak for themselves, but a slew of angry commenters countered my links with links of their own, and I spent the afternoon playing fact-check whack-a-mole. The next day, a man confronted one of our news crews out on assignment and asked who ran our Facebook page. They gave him my name, and then he drove to the station and asked to see me in person. Sensing he was potentially dangerous, the receptionist called the sheriff. The angry viewer drove away before police arrived, and local law enforcement added the station's parking lot to their patrols for the rest of the week, but I spent months looking over my shoulder when entering and leaving the building.

While still at the station, curious about the psychology behind all this, I started a blog about it. That led to a few books, then lectures around the world, and a new career. I launched a podcast to explore all the ways that people refused to accept evidence or empathize with others, and under the brand *You Are Not So Smart*, I made the psychology of motivated reasoning my beat as a science journalist. I was making a decent living telling people that there was no point in trying to change people's minds.

But I was never comfortable with that pessimistic viewpoint, especially after witnessing the sudden shift in opinion about same-sex marriage across the United States. That shift that eventually reached my hometown, allowing my uncle to live as an openly gay man, and my LGBTQ friends to post photos of their weddings.

Though in 2012 the majority of the country was opposed to legalizing same-sex marriage, the very next year, the majority supported it. Around 2010 opposition began to plummet. When the majority opinion flipped, the arguments evaporated. Just a few years earlier, I had been moderating daily arguments about how same-sex marriage would ruin America by destroying its family values. *Clearly*, I thought, *people can change their minds, and quickly. So what was the point of all that arguing in the first place?*

I looked for a scientist who could help me answer a question I had never really considered asking, one that was now making my brain itch. Why do we argue? What purpose does it serve? Is all this bickering online helping or hurting us?

I invited the famed cognitive scientist Hugo Mercier, an expert on human reasoning and argumentation, to be a guest on my show. He explained that we evolved to reach consensus—sometimes on the facts, sometimes on right and wrong, sometimes on what to eat for dinner—by banging our heads together. Groups that did a better job of reaching consensus, by both producing and evaluating arguments, were better at reaching communal goals and out-survived those that didn't. That led to the innate psychology that compels us to persuade others to see things our way when we believe our groups are misguided.

Mercier told me that if we couldn't change our minds or the minds of others, there would be no point in arguing in the first place. He asked me to imagine a world where everyone was deaf. "People would stop talking," he said. The fact that we so often disagree isn't a bug in human reasoning; it's a feature. For examples of how arguing had led to sudden shifts, all I had to do was look at the history of change in America.

I found a book about public opinion by political scientists Benjamin Page and Robert Shapiro that revealed since polling began in the early twentieth century, nearly half of the significant opinion shifts in the United States had been, as in the case of same-sex marriage, abrupt. Opinions about abortion, the war in Vietnam, attitudes about race and women and voting rights and smoking and marijuana and many others were stable for years. In each case, arguing had spread from small groups to large, from homes to the House of Representatives. Then all at once it seemed that stasis shattered. When the tide of public opinion turned on these issues, it shifted so quickly that if people could step into a time machine and go back just a few years, many would likely argue with themselves with the same fervor they argue about wedge issues today.

I started to see the push and pull of our incessant arguing as a form of punctuated equilibrium. That's what they call it in biology. When creatures have the capacity to change but there's little encouragement to do so, they remain mostly the same from one generation to the next. But when the pressure to adapt increases, the pace of evolution increases in response. Over long timescales, a pattern emerges, long stretches of sameness punctuated by periods of rapid change. Looking at the history of social change, revolution, and innovation, it seemed like the same pattern, and I wanted to understand the psychology behind it.

I wondered what was happening inside all those brains before and after they changed their minds. What persuades us, and how? What breaks through resistance so powerfully that we not only see things completely differently, but wonder how we saw it any other way?

How does a person, over the course of a decade, go from being opposed to the "gay agenda" to happily attending a same-sex wedding? How does an entire nation go from smoking on airplanes and in offices to banning smoking in bars and restaurants and daytime television? What makes hemlines go up and down and beards appear and disappear? How did marijuana go from a prescription for madness to a prescription for glaucoma? Why don't you agree with the person who wrote your teenage diary, want or believe the same things, or cut your hair the same way as the person you were just a decade ago? What changed *your* mind? How *do* minds change?

I wanted to understand the psychological alchemy of epiphanies, big and small. I thought if I could explain the mysterious nature of how people do and do not change their minds—and why that change often comes in bursts after long periods of certainty—we could become better at changing them, our own included. And so began the obsession you now hold in your hands.

This is a book about how minds change—and how to change them—not over hundreds of years, but in less than a generation, in less than a decade, or sometimes in a single conversation. In the pages that follow, we will learn what we are doing wrong when we fail to change minds, by exploring the surprising psychology behind how people modify and update their beliefs, attitudes, and values; and how to apply that knowledge to whatever you believe needs changing, whether it's within one mind or a million.

We will meet experts who study this sort of thing, and spend time with people who changed their minds, whether in powerful moments of epiphany or on long walks toward surprising insights. In the final chapters, we will see how these ideas combine to create social change and, in the right circumstances, sweep across entire nations in less than a generation. We will see that the speed of change is inversely proportional to the strength of our certainty, and certainty is a feeling: somewhere between an emotion and a mood, more akin to hunger than to logic. Persuasion, no matter the source, is a force that affects that feeling.

When we wade into the techniques, you might feel some misgivings about the ethics of it all. Even if we feel like our intentions are good or that the facts are on our side, persuasion can seem like a form of manipulation. But it may put you at ease to learn that by its scientific definition, persuasion is the act of changing a mind *without* coercion. As Daniel O'Keefe, a professor of communication, defines it, persuasion is "a successful intentional effort at influencing another's mental state through communication in a circumstance in which the persuadee has some measure of freedom."

More specifically, as psychologist Richard N. Perloff explained years ago in his book *The Dynamics of Persuasion*, we can avoid coercion by sticking to symbolic communication in the form of messages meant to alter another person's attitudes, beliefs, or both via the "voluntary acceptance" of those messages. According to Perloff, you can differentiate coercion from persuasion when "dire consequences" are employed to encourage someone to act "as the coercer wants them to act, and presumably contrary to their preferences." He adds that when people believe they are free to reject the communicator, that's when ethical persuasion is at play. It's only "when individuals perceive that they have no choice but to comply, the influence attempt is better viewed as coercive."

Persuasion is not coercion, and it is also not an attempt to defeat your intellectual opponent with facts or moral superiority, nor is it a debate with a winner or a loser. Persuasion is leading a person along in stages, helping them to better understand their own thinking and how it could align with the message at hand. You can't persuade another person to change their mind if that person doesn't want to do so, and as you will see, the techniques that work best focus on a person's motivations more than their conclusions.

We will learn that, in many ways, persuasion is mostly encouraging people to realize change is possible. All persuasion is self-persuasion. People change or refuse based on their own desires, motivations, and internal counterarguing, and by focusing on these factors, an argument becomes more likely to change minds. As psychologist Joel Whalen once put it, "You can't move a string by pushing it, you have to pull it."

This is why it is so important to share your intentions up front. Not only does that keep you on solid ethical ground, but it also increases your chances of success. If you don't, people will assume your intentions. Whatever they assume will become your "actual" position in their minds, and you run the risk of not having the conversation you intended. If they believe that your position is that they are gullible or stupid or deluded or in the wrong group or a bad person, then of course they will resist, and the facts will now be irrelevant.

Early in the research, I applied some of this with my father in an argument over a conspiracy theory that had made its way into his politics. We were debating the facts—for a long time. Exhausted, I took a breath and asked myself what I actually wanted. Why did I want to change my father's mind?

I said, "I love you, and I'm just worried that you are being misled." The debate ended instantly. We then entered a conversation about who we can trust on the internet. He softened, and admitted he was open to changing his mind about the facts, just wary of where they came from.

When I asked myself why I wanted him to change his mind, my answer was, "I don't trust his sources, and don't want him to trust those sources either." Why? "Because I trust other sources who disagree, and I wish he did too." Why? "I want us to be on the same side." Why? You can keep asking until you are contemplating quarks and gluons, but it's crucial you at least share your intentions for challenging someone's ideas, or else both of your positions will be: "I am right, and I think you are wrong."

I hope you will carry that question—*Why do I want to change their mind?*—in your mental backpack as you travel with me chapter by chapter. And I hope that question will blossom, as it did for me, into a series of questions.

You are reading these words because we each have the power to give up old beliefs, to replace old ignorance with new wisdom, to shift our attitudes in light of new evidence, and to free ourselves from outdated dogma, harmful traditions, and the diminishing returns of defunct politics and practices. The ability to realize we are wrong is baked right into the gooey mess of neurons wobbling around in every human head. But when and what and who should we be trying to change?

What counts as dangerous ignorance or outdated dogma? What qualifies as a malignant tradition, defunct politics, or a misguided practice? What norms are so harmful, what beliefs are so incorrect that, once we know how to change minds, we should take every opportunity to do so? And here's the kicker: How do we know when we are right and they are wrong?

But also, what does the phrase "change your mind" even mean?

We will answer all of these going forward, but I didn't start this journey with these questions in mind. They came later, after a good deal of my own ignorance revealed itself. That's why I think we must ask ourselves these questions here, before we begin, and bring them along to the lessons and conversations ahead.

The ability to change our minds, update our assumptions, and entertain other points of view is one of our greatest strengths, an evolved ability that comes free with every copy of the human brain. You soon will see why, to leverage that strength, we must avoid debate and start having conversations. Debates have winners and losers, and no one wants to be a loser. But if both sides feel safe to explore their reasoning, to think about their own thinking, to explore their motivations, we can each avoid the dead-end goal of winning an argument.

Instead, we can pursue the shared goal of learning the truth.

1

POST-TRUTH

I spotted Charlie Veitch as he rose on an escalator from beneath the London Road entrance to Manchester's Piccadilly train station. He wore a green plaid hoodie, blue jeans, and a backpack. A splotch of white just above his temples stood out from within his otherwise conservative haircut. At the top, he smiled, pivoted, and kept his momentum going as he closed the distance between us.

He said hello while walking and changed direction to enter the flow of pedestrian traffic, his body parting a parade of people walking in the opposite direction. Charlie kept his head turned toward me and abandoned introductions, explaining with wide gestures the architecture and history of the city where he and his partner, Stacey, were now raising three kids. Life was good here, he said, though he still worked under a false name to keep the truthers from finding him.

Charlie is a tall man, so keeping up with his stride took some effort. I felt pulled along as if I had grabbed the back of a bus, my feet suspended in the air like in a Chaplin gag. He had insights he wanted to share on homelessness, the local art and music scenes, modern movie production, the similarities and differences between Manchester and London and Berlin—all before we had reached our third crosswalk, which he would have likely ignored like the others if traffic had permitted.

I wanted to meet Charlie because when he was making a living as a professional conspiracy theorist he had done something incredible, something so rare and unusual that, before I started this book, I thought was impossible—something that had nearly ruined his life.

It all began in June 2011, just ahead of the ten-year anniversary of 9/11, when Charlie boarded a British Airways flight at Heathrow Airport bound for the United States and Ground Zero. He and four other truthers joined a group of cameramen, editors, and sound engineers along with comedian Andrew Maxwell, the host of a TV series called *Conspiracy Road Trip*. Maxwell and his crew would make four programs for the BBC, each dealing with a different conspiratorial community: UFO enthusiasts, evolution deniers, London bombing conspiracy theorists, and truthers, the people who believe the official story of what happened on September 11, 2001, is a lie.*

The premise of the show was to send such people around the world and have them travel by bus to meet experts and eyewitnesses who would challenge their conspiratorial beliefs with undeniable evidence, with facts. Whatever drama that ensued made for great television, arguing and frustration on both sides cut together with playful music and the usual reality show editing. At the end of each show, Maxwell, our host and guide into the world of conspiracy theorists, would sit down

---

*The BBC has taken down the 9/11 episode from the show's official website. It is still available online through a number of streaming services.

with his road trippers to see if the facts presented had persuaded them in any way. That was the hook. People never budged. Maxwell, exasperated, ended every road trip shaking his head, wondering what it would take to reach them.

But Charlie's episode was different.

He and his fellow 9/11 truthers spent ten days in New York, Virginia, and Pennsylvania. They walked the crash sites. They met experts in demolition, explosives, air travel, and construction. They met family members of the victims. They met officials from the government, including one who was at the Pentagon when it was hit and helped with the gory cleanup. They visited the original architects of the World Trade Center. They met the person who was the national operations manager of the FAA at the time of the attacks. They even trained in a commercial airliner flight simulator and took flying lessons over New York City, landing a single-engine airplane with no prior piloting experience. At each step of their journey, they met people who were either at the top of their fields of expertise, saw 9/11 unfold firsthand, or had lost someone that day.

Despite Maxwell's efforts, the truthers doubled down, more certain than ever that there was a conspiracy afoot. If anything, his efforts confirmed it. They all argued with him, suggesting they were being tricked by paid actors, or that the experts were mistaken, or the so-called facts came from dubious sources. All except for one.

At the time, Charlie was a leader in the truther community. His main income for years came from producing hundreds of anarchy- and conspiracy-themed YouTube videos, some receiving a million views or more. He told his fans that the fires of 9/11 couldn't have burned hot enough to melt the World Trade Center's steel beams, and that the buildings fell perfectly into their footprints: it must have been a controlled demolition. He traced out the connections between governments, businesses, militaries, and so on to determine who was truly responsible. He routinely hit the streets with a megaphone in one hand and a camera in the other, working diligently to gain subscribers and wake people up to the truth.

Once it became his full-time job, Charlie traveled the subversive speaker circuit where he regularly appeared at festivals that catered to fellow conspiracy theorists, anarchists, and neo-hippies seeking sex, drugs, and free Wi-Fi. He became friend and collaborator to world-famous histrionic patriot Alex Jones and the interdimensional reptilian investigator David Icke.

For five years, he had paid his dues, even going to jail on several occasions. He was arrested for impersonating a police officer when Russian state television sent him to cover the G20 Summit in Toronto to uncover the machinations of a dystopian new world order. Later, he was arrested on, ironically, suspicion of conspiracy for planning a protest during the royal wedding. Covering his capture, *The Telegraph* described him as a "known anarchist."

A darling of the conspiracy community, a rising star on YouTube, Charlie saw himself as an up-and-coming celebrity provocateur. Hated by some. Beloved by others. He thought the trip to New York would be his big break, the event that would take him mainstream. But once there, at the height of his fame, he did something unbelievable and, as it would turn out, unforgivable.

He changed his mind.

———

At the Eastern Bloc coffee shop, we sat through a few revolutions of customers stopping to eat and talk and laugh, and Charlie seemed to feed off of it, raising his voice so that bystanders could easily hear him explain from within a cloud of American Spirit cigarette smoke why he was no longer a truther.

Early in the filming of his episode, he and the other truthers met a demolition expert named Brent Blanchard, who told them that a controlled demolition would have required a massive crew of people. They would have needed to first demolish the inner walls of the World Trade Center (WTC) towers to expose hundreds of internal columns, then pre-cut each one with jackhammer-type devices, and then insert explosives, Blanchard explained. It would have taken months for workers to rig the WTC towers for a controlled demolition of that size. All the while, they would have been seen going in and out of the building, taking lunch breaks, moving equipment, dealing with debris and construction waste. It would have been impossible to conceal.

Charlie asked: If this was true, why did the buildings fall perfectly into their footprints? Blanchard explained they didn't. He used a prop made of Legos to show Charlie how the top half destroyed itself and everything below it in a chain reaction as it all came crashing down. It blew the debris outward, he explained, not into the buildings' footprints.

Charlie asked: But if it was only jet fuel and not explosives, and jet fuel doesn't burn hot enough to melt steel beams, how could the buildings have collapsed? Blanchard explained that the steel skeleton didn't need to melt. The beams only needed to bend just the slightest bit. Once bent, they couldn't support the entire weight of the building above them and would continue to bend even farther, past the point where they could support the enormous forces pressing down. Charlie didn't argue. He absorbed Blanchard's explanation, unsure what to think.

The group later met the architects of the World Trade Center who patiently explained that it was designed to withstand an airplane of its era, not a modern jet loaded with fuel and traveling at full speed. They met Alice Hoagland, who lost her son, Mark Bingham, whose hijacked flight crashed in a field near Shanksville, Pennsylvania. They met Tom Heidenberger, who lost his wife of thirty years, Michelle, an American Airlines flight attendant who was working on the plane that slammed into the Pentagon. The doubt rushed in on him, filling his head with a swarm of other doubts.

"All of this suddenly, then, bang!" Charlie said, describing his realization. The flight school, the blueprints, the architecture firm, the demolition experts—it had all chipped away at his certainty. It exposed the possibility that he might be wrong, but it was the grieving family members that confirmed it.

But back at the hotel, Charlie was surprised to learn that his epiphany was his alone. The others told him that Hoagland had been brainwashed by the FBI, or worse yet, she was an actress hired by the BBC to trick them all with her "crocodile tears." It shocked Charlie, who had held Hoagland while she sobbed. He said he began hating his companions, thinking, "You fucking animals. You disgusting fucking animals."

While still on the trip, Charlie stood in Times Square and filmed himself explaining what he had learned. He had met experts who showed him how easy it was to fly a plane and land it with little experience, how hard it would be to create a controlled demolition with no one noticing, how the buildings couldn't withstand the impact of a modern jet loaded with fuel, and so on.

"I don't know, man," he said, detailing the specifics. He understood why so many people, like him, had suspected foul play. There had been lies about weapons of mass destruction in Iraq, and wars had been based on those lies. Their anger was justified, their obsessive pursuit for answers understandable.

"We're not gullible," Charlie said. "We're truth seekers in a 9/11 Truth movement just trying to find out the truth about what happened. The mind boggles. This reality, this universe is truly one of smoke screens, illusions, and wrong paths, but also the right path, which is always be committed to the truth. Do not hold on to religious dogma. If you are presented with new evidence, take it on, even if it contradicts what you or your group might be believing or wanting to believe. You have to give the truth the greatest respect, and I do."

A week later, back home, Charlie edited and uploaded a three-minute-and-thirty-three-second confessional intercut with footage from his trip. He titled it: *No Emotional Attachment to 9/11 Theories—The Truth is Most Important.*

He wrote in the video's description that after five years of believing in the conspiracy theory, after appearing on Alex Jones's program several times, after promoting the truther community onstage and on television, he now believed that "America's defenses got caught with their pants around their ankles. I do not think there was high-level complicity in the events of that day. Yes, I have changed my mind." He signed off with, "Honour the truth—Charlie."

The backlash was swift and brutal.

———

At first, people began emailing, asking if he was okay, asking what the government had done to him. Within the first few days, fellow conspiracy theorist Ian R. Crane posted on truther forums that a producer friend told him Charlie had been manipulated by a psychologist who worked closely with mentalist Derren Brown. That explained why Charlie had uploaded that video.

Rumors began to spread that he had been an operative sent by the

FBI or the CIA or the British Secret Service the whole time, sent to in-filtrate the ranks of the truther movement—a plant sent to discredit them. Conspiracy radio host Max Igan said that Charlie was the first person he had ever heard of in the truther movement to change his mind. It just didn't make sense. Commenters to that show's website wrote things like, "they got to him," and "so Charlie how much hush money did the elites give you to shut your mouth?" and "that's like ex-changing the belief in gravity for believing that it doesn't exist."

Hastily shot response videos began to appear online claiming Char-lie had been paid off by the BBC. To explain himself, he appeared on internet conspiracy talk shows. He shared what the experts had told him and why it was so convincing, but his fellow truthers were incred-ulous. Charlie begged in his own response videos for decency. Before long, it became clear he was being excommunicated. The harassment continued for months. His website was hacked. He shut down his com-ment sections. David Icke and Alex Jones cut ties.

Charlie's episode of *Conspiracy Road Trip* eventually aired. At the end, he told Maxwell, "I just need to basically take it on the chin, admit I was wrong, be humble about it, and carry on," but by then the truthers had made that impossible. Charlie told me the most heinous moment in his harassment came when someone discovered he had an unpubli-cized YouTube channel that featured videos of his family and other per-sonal material.

"In one of my videos, my sister had two younger children at the time, and I went to visit her in Cornwall, lovely part of England, and some asshole—" Charlie searched for the right words. "—The channel was called, like, 'Kill Charlie Veitch,' and he Photoshopped nudity on my sister's children. They sent it to my sister."

Charlie's sister called him crying. She couldn't understand how or why it was happening. His mother would call, too. Someone found her email address and sent her thousands of emails, including one that contained child pornography with her grandchildren's faces superimposed. The sender claimed the images were real, and that Charlie had taken them. She contacted Charlie thinking it was true.

"They were out for his blood, like a trophy," explained his partner, Stacey Bluer, who had joined us for breakfast. "When I was pregnant, I started receiving a lot of messages—'Your child is devil's spawn,' all this horrible stuff."

Alex Jones chimed in with a video of his own. He sat in a darkened room, his face illuminated by red light, the camera zoomed in on his eyes, and explained that he knew Charlie was a double agent all along. He ended by saying his fans should remain vigilant because people like Charlie would keep showing up, and they might say they had changed their minds after being in the movement for a while. For Charlie, that was it. He gave up trying to convince anyone of the things he now believed. The truthers had officially cast him out, and so he left the community for good.

In April 2015, Charlie landed his current job, which I won't describe in much detail for the sake of his anonymity, but it involves selling properties around the world.

"I'm very good at it. I can earn good money," he told me, proud that he had finally eluded his haters. "It took a while, but ultimately my six years of YouTube, or having to just rant and speak eloquently about abstract concepts, it was almost like I did six years of training. And I've developed a very thick skin. I think I am a very good salesman."

"That's a good endorsement for how maybe Google won't destroy your career," I told him, considering how troubling a google search for Charlie Veitch would have been for a potential employer.

Charlie told me that, actually, he had posted photos of his new business cards to Facebook when he was first hired, and right away someone emailed his boss and told him Charlie was a child abuser and a criminal. He said he had already come clean about his YouTube past, but not the harassment.

"I told my boss the story that we're talking about now, the whole life change." Then Charlie imitated him: "'It's OK Charlie. These people are cunts, real cunts.'"

Charlie changed his name after that and got new business cards.

———

At first, Charlie's story seemed like a paradox. Charlie Veitch changed his mind in the face of overwhelming evidence. But his fellow truthers saw that same evidence, talked to the same experts, hugged the same widows and widowers, and came away feeling more certain than ever that 9/11 was an inside job. I thought there must be something else at play, something that maybe had very little to do with facts themselves.

For one thing, from writing my previous books, I knew the idea that facts alone could make everyone see things the same way was a venerable misconception. The nineteenth-century rationalist philosophers said that public education would enhance democracy by eliminating all superstitions. Benjamin Franklin wrote that public libraries would make the common man as educated as the aristocracy and thus empower the public to vote for their best interests. Timothy Leary, the psychologist who proselytized mind expansion through psychedelics and later became a champion of the cyberpunk ethos, preached that computers, and later the internet, would remove the need for information gatekeepers and give people "power to the pupil"—the democratic might that comes from being able to put whatever you want into your eyeballs. Each dreamed that one day we would all have access to all the same facts, and then, naturally, we would all agree on what those facts meant.

In science communication, this used to be called the information deficit model, long debated among frustrated academics. When controversial research findings on everything from the theory of evolution to the dangers of leaded gasoline failed to convince the public, they'd contemplate how to best tweak the model so the facts could speak for themselves. But once independent websites, then social media, then podcasts, then YouTube began to speak for the facts and undermine the authority of fact-based professionals like journalists, doctors, and documentary filmmakers, the information deficit model was finally put to rest. In recent years, that has led to a sort of moral panic.

While I was writing this book, in late 2016, the Oxford University Press dictionary named "post-truth" its international word of the year, citing a 2,000 percent increase in its usage during arguments about the Brexit referendum and the United States presidential election. Commenting on the announcement, *The Washington Post* wrote that they weren't surprised. Instead, they lamented, "It's official: Truth is dead. Facts are passé."

Throughout the 2010s, terms like *alternative facts* rose to the top of public consciousness, and across the world the remaining uninitiated became intimately familiar with long-bandied concepts in psychology like filter bubbles and confirmation bias. Apple CEO Tim Cook told the world that fake news was "killing people's minds." Then the term *fake news* mutated from a rebranded way of talking about propaganda to referring to just about anything people refused to believe. This led Brian Greene, a physicist who studies string theory, to tell *Wired*, "We've come to a very strange place in American democracy where there's an assault on some of the features of reality that one would have thought, just a couple years ago, were beyond debate, discussion, or argument."

Social media adapted, leaving behind photos of tacos and babies for arguments over contentious issues that generated more engagement as they grew more intractable. A new cold war began, one based on targeted misinformation, and within months Facebook CEO Mark Zuckerberg was sitting before Congress explaining how Russian trolls were seeding news feeds with weaponized clickbait, not so much to misinform but to encourage the sort of dead-end arguing that makes democratic collaboration difficult.

As the decade came to a close, a *New York Times* op-ed titled "The Age of Post-Truth Politics" argued that democracy itself was now in danger because facts had "lost their ability to support consensus." *The New Yorker* examined "Why Facts Don't Change Our Minds," *The Atlantic* announced, "This Article Won't Change Your Mind," and then came *Time* magazine's ominous black-and-red, bold-print cover featuring a single question that seemed to sum up the moral panic over our growing epistemic chaos: "Is Truth Dead?"

And all of that was before QAnon, "Stop the Steal" rallies, the insurrection, the impeachment of Donald Trump, mobs ripping down 5G towers out of suspicion they may be emitting toxic rays, protests at state capitals claiming COVID-19 was a hoax, the rise of COVID anti-vaxxers, and massive protests over police brutality and systemic racism after the death of George Floyd. In each case, within this new information ecosystem, we desperately tried to change one another's minds, sometimes with videos, sometimes with news articles, sometimes with Wikipedia pages.

But after learning about Charlie Veitch, I couldn't stop wondering: If we now live in a post-truth world, if facts can't change people's minds, then what explained the fact that Charlie *did* change his mind when presented with facts? That's why I traveled to Manchester to meet him, and after hearing his story, I started to feel the same kind of doubts he had felt in New York.

I didn't know it when I first met Charlie Veitch, but the answer to why the facts that changed his mind didn't change the minds of his peers would reveal why so many of us resist some facts and not others. So we will return to his story after we visit activists, neuroscientists, and psychologists to help us understand how we form our beliefs, attitudes, and values in the first place; and how those mental constructs shift, mutate, and change as we move through the world, learning and experiencing things that challenge our preconceived notions and received wisdom.

In a newly flattened, online world, where we are more likely to engage with people who disagree with us than ever before, widespread resistance to change—on issues as wide-ranging as whether Bill Gates wants to use vaccines to put microchips in your blood to whether climate change is real to whether *The Notebook* was a good movie—led us into an age of dangerous cynicism.

Inside this new information ecosystem where everyone had access to facts that seemed to confirm their views, we began to believe we were living in separate realities. We've come to see the people on the other side as unreachable as the truthers who accompanied Charlie to New York. I used to see things this way, too, but in writing this book, I changed my mind.

That all began when I ventured out to meet professional mind changers in Los Angeles.

2

DEEP CANVASSING

From where we parked, the rows of San Gabriel's two-story brick homes seemed endless, as if they stretched to the heart of Los Angeles in one direction and snaked their way to the horizon in the other, disappearing into the nearby mountains separating them from the Mojave Desert far beyond.

Amid a sprawl of scorched lawns and evaporating swimming pools, Steve Deline gathered his gear outside his truck and advised the two UCLA students who rode with us from the staging area to slather themselves in sunscreen. He stuffed their pockets and underarms with water bottles, and then he checked their video camera and traded phone numbers so they could stay in touch by text message. Shielding their eyes with maps, they listened as Steve once again explained their route. Like the other canvassers disembarking across the city, they were to go door-to-door as a pair, one person trying to change a mind and one person recording the effort. On this trip, on our team, Steve would be talking while I worked the camera.

I was sweating in the California sun a few months after the Supreme Court voted to legalize same-sex marriage, because the work Steve and his organization had been doing for years had made headlines around the world, both in mainstream newspapers and in academic journals. Some were saying it was a breakthrough in the art and science of persuasion, something that could change politics and public discourse forever. It seemed to me that if I was going to understand how minds change, and how to change them, this was the best place to start. I sent an email, talked on the phone, explained my interest, and within a week was in California training with Steve's organization, the Leadership LAB.

On most Saturdays, the LAB heads out with a rotating but loyal group of volunteers to talk with people at their front doors. After doing this for more than a decade and having more than fifteen thousand conversations, most recorded so they could pore over each exchange to improve their rhetoric, the LAB had slowly honed a method so fast and reliable, so new, that social scientists began buying plane tickets to study it in person.

They call it deep canvassing. Not every time, but often, people using their technique could get a person to give up a long-held opinion and change their position, especially about a contentious social issue, in less than twenty minutes. I, too, wanted to know how it worked and what it revealed, and so I set out with Steve to see it in action.

The LAB (or Learn Act Build) is the political action arm of the Los Angeles LGBT Center, the largest LGBTQ organization on the planet. With an annual operating budget of more than $100 million, most of the Center's money goes toward providing health care and counseling, but a small percentage goes to the LAB. Their mission for years, they told me, was the "long game": to change minds about LGBTQ issues by developing best practices for shifting public opinion, and then sharing what they learned about how to do that so they could help win elections and ballot measures around the world. The goal, they explained, was to alter policies and change laws in places where prejudice and opposition to LGBTQ issues still flourished.

When they began their work, the debate about same-sex marriage was burning white-hot in the United States. As with any wedge issue today, people daily gathered online to trade arguments and call one another idiots, and the dominant sentiment was that this was a disagreement that could never be settled. We would just have to wait for generational churn. Articles saying as much appeared every week in major newspapers, pundits parroted that resignation nightly on cable news channels, and many people who supported LGBTQ issues in the media had given up trying to persuade their opponents.

In 2014, a year before the Supreme Court decision, the journal *Science* published the findings of a team of political scientists who had studied the LAB's technique, detailing how well it worked. Thanks to faulty research methods, the study would go on to be retracted and then repeated by better scientists using better methods, which we'll come back to. But when *The New York Times* first covered the research, they wrote, "Americans on the left and the right are so entrenched in their beliefs that attempts at persuasion are nearly pointless. But a study in Science this month demonstrates exactly the opposite." Within a few days, the team was appearing in interviews around the world. The implications of a new way to reach out to people, to cut through polarization and change minds, not just about same-sex marriage but any politically charged issue, reverberated across social media. The paper itself was downloaded more than 110,000 times, making it one of the most popular pieces of research ever published.

When I visited the LAB, I joined their efforts to blanket the city with two dozen persuasion brigades as part of new research, an ongoing series of experiments. They suspected deep canvassing could be used to persuade anyone about anything, but had yet to hit on the best way to apply their technique to other wedge issues. We were seeing if it could be used to change minds about abortion among people opposed to its legality. Our assignment, success or failure, was to record our efforts for later review.

—————

After a few knocks and a few refusals, we arrived at an enormous one-story home, twin wings forming a vestibule at its entrance. Steve tucked his rainbow flag cap under his arm as he had before every knock and doorbell press so far, each time revealing his hair more matted. He seemed unfazed by the weather, despite a dark circle growing larger in the center of his back. He checked his paperwork and then loudly rapped on the door.

A stout man with a well-combed, snowy flat-top haircut answered, and when he learned we were interested in his opinions on abortion, he closed the door behind him and joined us outside, eager to share his opinions. The man told us teenagers who don't protect themselves deserved what they got. When Steve asked if he fooled around much as a young man, the man laughed and admitted that he had.

When Steve asked how his life would have turned out differently if had he gotten someone pregnant at a young age, how *her* life would have turned out, the man grew solemn. He said no such thing could have ever happened, because his parents took the time to show him and his siblings the way reproduction works, in their living room with an anatomical chart and a pointer. Later, sitting on the curb, Steve told me he doubted any of it was true, but during the conversation he just listened. After half an hour, having wandered into what Fox News pundits had to say about the issue, Steve thanked the man for his time and parted ways.

People like him, Steve said as he checked the boxes on his documents, weren't unreachable—no one is. We could have gotten past his rehearsed rhetoric eventually, to something deeper, but he suspected there were far more persuadable people in the neighborhood we could meet before the end of the day. As they had explained in the two hours of training that morning, sometimes the work was like trying to urge people to evacuate before a hurricane: in the time it would take to motivate one obstinate holdout, you could persuade a dozen others to pack up and head north.

Steve checked in with the UCLA students canvassing a few streets over. Satisfied they were okay, he consulted his walk sheet to see where we were headed next. On a good day a canvasser can have four or five full conversations, so he was frustrated that we had absorbed more refusals to talk than normal.

At the next house, a woman answered while crafting a large piece of jewelry, and she barely took her eyes away as she spoke. She told Steve she was pro-life, but then, without prompting, as she worked the metal and trinkets in both hands, she said she was afraid that one day overpopulation would force the upper classes to cannibalize poor people. Again, Steve said thank you and moved on.

———

Deep canvassing wasn't invented. It was discovered. That discovery was the result of one man's obsession with answering a single question.

In his sixties, Dave Fleischer comes to work in polo shirts that hug his bulging biceps, and his bald head reveals no discernible wrinkles. He is from a small town in Ohio, graduated from Harvard Law school, and his passion for political activism is part of a weekly routine that includes guitar lessons and turns on stage with his improv group, The Chaperones. With a rich, resonant voice and a carefully modulated cadence, he commands the room whenever he speaks. He explains things in parables, with characters and plots. It often seems like he might be building to a punchline or a reveal, and he usually is.

Though Dave Fleischer is the director of the LAB, he has no office. He finds an empty spot where he can and sets up his computer and notebooks amid the clutter of his team's shared workspace inside The Village, a building with a busy outdoor courtyard, funky '90s angles, and modern exposed ductwork. It is one of seven such facilities the Los Angeles LGBT Center operates across the city, but it is the nicest of the lot according to people who work there.

On most days Fleischer can be found sharing videos with activist groups in one paperwork-piled corner or another. People from around the world visit every day to borrow some of his wisdom, and he often begins with no set agenda, simply saying, "How can I best be of service to you?" He allows lessons to reveal themselves in the back-and-forth, and he takes lots of notes, even during casual chats. He personally reviews many of the conversations the LAB has with voters, so when people ask questions, he often recalls a specific moment from years ago that will illuminate his guests and calls it up on the conference room projector.

I met him on the Friday before a canvass aimed at reducing transphobia. He sat nodding and smiling behind his laptop surrounded by representatives of SURJ, Showing Up for Racial Justice. Earlier in the day his guests were PICO, the Pacific Institute for Community Organization. Tomorrow, transgender rights activists from Houston would be sitting in the same seats, and a few weeks before it was employees of Planned Parenthood, and before them the people behind the hashtag #ShoutYourAbortion.

Fleischer makes no apologies for his bias. He believes people who oppose LGBTQ rights are wrong, and therefore he wants to change their minds. As a professional mind changer for more than thirty years, Fleischer has worked as a campaign manager, community organizer, and adviser to LGBTQ candidates and organizations. He has worked within or closely alongside, by his count, 105 campaigns—most of which were designed to delay, stop, or overcome an anti-LGBTQ ballot measure. In 2007, he created the LGBT Mentoring Project, which would later become part of the Leadership LAB when he became its director.

When we first met, his team still hadn't settled on a name for what they had discovered, but he had granted a number of interviews in which he explained the broad strokes of how it worked. Thanks to his charisma, charm, and prominence as an LGBT rights political strategist, some people in the press were calling what they did the "Fleischer technique," a term he hated.

"Don't get me wrong, I mean, I love myself, David," he said from across the table at a diner near their offices, smiling through a full-throated wheezing laugh that turned heads. "It wasn't as neat and linear as you might hope. It wasn't as if there was this Eureka moment where I jumped out of a bathtub naked into the streets," he laughed. "That was omitted from this learning experience."

Fleischer explained that deep canvassing was discovered after LGBTQ activists in California suffered a crushing loss. They failed, despite great effort, to stop a 2008 ballot measure in California called Proposition 8. Of those who turned out, 52 percent voted to ban same-sex marriage.

"The LGBT community had expected to prevail," said Fleischer. "All the polling showed that our side would prevail. The experience of LGBT people on a day-to-day basis in California is often very positive. People have chosen to live where it is positive. It was a real shock when we lost, and shock almost doesn't do justice to it. People were so furious, and humiliated, and really didn't know what to do."

In the aftermath, the LAB and the network of activists in California who partnered with them settled on the single question they needed to answer before moving forward—*Why* did they vote against us? That's when Fleischer came up with a novel idea: Why don't we just go ask?

At the same time, Fleischer had begun what would become a detailed, five-hundred-page postmortem called *The Prop 8 Report*. It showed the election was too close to call until about six weeks out. But then support grew at a rapid pace until it was clear on the day of the vote what was going to happen. More than half a million voters had flipped from "no" to "yes" in a little over a month, and no one knew why.

At the time, many people blamed African American voters who had heavily opposed same-sex marriage, based on exit polling, but Fleischer didn't believe that explanation. His analysis showed that African American opinions had remained stable. They had not changed their minds, but someone had. Fleischer wanted to know who and why.

That's when he put together the first listening platoons, about seventy-five people each, and had them go out into Los Angeles. They directly asked people who had voted against same-sex marriage what had motivated their decisions.

People wanted to talk. In the parts of Los Angeles County where they had been crushed by two to one or more, Fleischer's team spoke with every voter who answered and found that not only were people willing, they were eager to discuss the recent vote and LGBTQ issues in general. They wanted to be heard and, in some cases, forgiven. So they offered justifications for their behavior.

The LAB soon noticed a pattern in the responses. People's explanations for voting against same-sex marriage clustered around three values: tradition, religion, and the protection of their children. But that pattern disappeared after a few months of canvassing. As time passed, justifications mentioning children faded away, leaving behind only tradition and religion.

The LAB couldn't make sense of it. When protecting their children had been a justification, it had also been their primary justification, and now they were reporting it wasn't a concern at all. That's when Fleischer had his great insight. People's fears about their children had likely disappeared because the anti-gay advertising had ceased. Almost all of those opposition ads had focused on how schools would deal with same-sex marriage. One in particular was very effective. Thirty seconds long, it featured a little girl excitedly telling her mom that she had learned in class she could marry a princess, and a boy could marry a prince. Then the ad explained that if Prop 8 became law, parents would have no right to object to those kinds of lessons.

Fleischer noted that of the 687,000 Californians who supported same-sex marriage but then later flipped, 500,000 were parents with children living at home under the age of eighteen. The answer seemed obvious. Before those ads ran, the people who polled as supporters didn't think of themselves as anti-gay. In fact, the polling showed many of them typically voted liberal and Democrat. They were unaware they harbored a prejudice that could be stoked by the right kind of fear tactic—beware, they want to indoctrinate your children.

To Fleischer, that was actually good news, because it meant that those voters were persuadable. Their values were in conflict between protecting their children and protecting the rights of others. They held both positive and negative attitudes about same-sex marriage, and if they were ambivalent, that meant they might be open to reconsidering their vote.

They knocked on more doors, this time playing the attack ads from the Prop 8 campaign during their conversations, asking people if that was what had persuaded them to vote against same-sex marriage. This was uncharted territory in politics. Most canvasses go out of their way to avoid bringing up the opposition's stance, and no canvassing campaign had ever played the opposition's videos straight to voters in this manner. The reactions were intense, and the conversations began to grow too complex and lengthy to capture with notes, so Fleischer had his team record them.

Video changed everything. With it, they could create a database of reactions, categorize voters, see patterns in their arguments, and see their mistakes, but most importantly, it allowed them to notice when voters openly opposed to same-sex marriage sometimes softened. Those conversations became a shared obsession of the LAB and its volunteers. When a voter shifted, everyone wanted to understand what had happened, like a football team reviewing a game tape to understand every nuance of their performance.

Though this all seemed promising, for years it went nowhere. The successes seemed random, unrepeatable. Steve told me that was because they were operating under a common misconception, one that most people believe when they first try to persuade someone, a tactic that fails so dependably that it leads most people to believe changing another person's mind on issues like these is impossible. It was something they had to change their own minds about before they could change the minds of others about anything.

————

Before I met Steve that morning, under a cloudless, cobalt sky, a swarm of LAB volunteers grabbed clipboards and scripts and name tags from veterans and staff at the tables set up outside the fellowship hall of San Marino Congregational Church and assembled breakfasts from a long makeshift buffet. Greeting, giggling, writing on name tags, they moved inside to drink coffee and munch bagels and gnaw on fruit in circles of folding chairs as they waited for the training presentation to begin.

The LAB was onto something, and word had gotten out. Some had traveled by plane to be here, others had carpooled out from UCLA, and others had driven from their homes for the fifth or fifteenth time. People from around the globe regularly came to spend time with the persuasion experts at the Leadership LAB and train in deep canvassing. Most hoped to bring something home they could apply in their own political campaigns or ongoing activism.

When the crowd was about halfway through their plates, Laura Gardiner, the national mentoring coordinator for the LAB, introduced herself. I'd end up going door-to-door with Laura a few times on subsequent visits, and she was least at ease when sitting in an office or standing silently. All kinetic energy and momentum, keen to do the work or teach it, she seemed both perpetually exhausted and indefatigable, which made her perfect for her role in their organization.

Laura told me she liked to talk to new crowds for a few minutes before getting into specifics, partly to get a feel for their experience with this sort of thing, but mostly to settle their nerves. Their own research had revealed about half of the people they trained in any session had

never participated in anything like this before. She said deep canvassing was an extraordinarily tough skill to master, even if you had experience with public speaking or political canvassing. It can take several
weekends to learn the technique, so the LAB wanted first-timers to return, to try again, to keep improving.

After dozens of these training sessions the team had learned it was
important to spend a lot of time stoking enthusiasm and dampening
anxieties before getting into the particulars of how to talk to strangers about sensitive topics. To that end, they emphasized something
they called "radical hospitality," a form of selfless concern and ener-
getic friendliness akin to what you might experience at a family reunion.
From the moment volunteers arrived at a training until they hugged and
waved goodbye, the team and the veteran volunteers treated each person
as if the day just got better because he or she or they showed up. Radical
hospitality is so important to the process that Laura often tells veterans and staff to take breaks if they feel like they can't maintain a joyous
enthusiasm.

After some improv comedy–style banter with a few other organizers,
Laura walked the audience through some videos showcasing different
aspects of the technique, real conversations recorded during previous
canvasses. The videos were meant to amaze people, show them sudden
changes of heart recorded over the years. They also helped showcase
how veteran canvassers around the room weren't always great at what
they did. The LAB wanted newcomers to see the progress from beginner
to master as much as they wanted to show what a successful deep canvassing looked like.

We watched a few awkward and clunky conversations. Still, most
featured complete reversals by the end of the discussions. People against
schools teaching kids about the historical contributions of LGBTQ

people later said they felt the opposite. Some admitted they had been wrong to ever think otherwise. Opponents of same-sex marriage expressed newfound support. People against abortion reconsidered.

We watched as people started out cautious on their front porches, leaning against cars, standing behind doors cracked just enough to reveal half a face. Once engaged, people tended to emerge, adamant and confident, ready to defend themselves. Canvassers asked where people first heard about the issue at hand. Most quickly realized it was received wisdom—a sermon, something from a talk show when they were a kid, a billboard. Then the canvasser asked if they knew anyone affected by the issue. Invariably they did. People then became extraordinarily open, reliving experiences from their lives that rarely supported the positions they had expressed. By the end, their own opinions seemed alien.

In one, a canvasser asked a woman how she felt about laws that would allow transgender women to use women's restrooms. On a scale of zero to ten, zero being no support at all, she said she was a six. She said she feared for the safety of children. She didn't like the idea of someone who was once a man leering at young girls. When the canvasser asked if she knew anyone transgender, she revealed that she did, a nephew who she used to take care of until he began transitioning. They hadn't been in touch in a long time, and it bothered her.

"With the hair and the lipstick, it's hard," she said. "When I raised him, when he was a baby, he was a boy." She fidgeted, apparently replaying her own words in her head. Her transgender relative could probably tell it made her uncomfortable, she told the canvasser. That's probably why they stopped spending time together, she explained to herself.

She began working it out while the canvasser asked questions and listened, paraphrasing and reflecting back her words. "Now you're making me feel bad," she said, and after a while, the canvasser asked her if, as a black woman, she had ever experienced prejudice. Had she ever been made to feel lesser than or ostracized? Yes, many times, she said. By the end of the conversation, she was totally in favor of less-discriminatory bathroom laws for transgender people. She had been wrong, she said. Now she was a ten.

"It's only right, let a person be who they are," she argued. "Everyone should have the right to be who they want to be."

In another, a canvasser stood in a garage with a voter who the LAB had labeled the Mustang Man, a fellow in his seventies wearing shorts and a dress shirt. He smoked a cigarette and toyed with a Zippo lighter as the two talked about same-sex marriage, which was still illegal in California when the video was recorded.

"I'm not against the gay community," he explained. He just wished they'd stop causing such a ruckus pushing for more rights. The country had enough problems as it is. The canvasser asked the Mustang Man if he had ever been married. Yes, for forty-three years. She passed away eleven years ago, and he knew he was never getting over it. "I was supposed to die first," he said.

He asked the canvasser to help him remove the cover over his late wife's vintage Mustang, which he continued to maintain. It was in perfect condition, he said. She never smoked a day, didn't drink. "She didn't even let me smoke in the car." Then one night she discovered a black spot on her gums. The cancer spread to her throat. Eventually she could no longer speak. She wrote to him on a notepad as she withered. The Mustang Man said that he had learned one thing in life: that riches were irrelevant. Just find happiness with someone, and you've got it made. All the materialistic things are just loaned to you. Happiness like that isn't loaned. It's yours.

The canvasser told the Mustang Man that eleven years seemed like a long time to be alone.

"It gives you an awful lot of time to think," the Mustang Man said. "Sometimes I'll hear a song that happened in our time. I'll cry. Sometimes I'll see something pass by that we used to laugh about, and I'll laugh. I've got some great memories, but also some sores. I've never gotten over her, but that's OK by me. I don't want to get over her."

After a beat, the Mustang Man told the canvasser, "I would want these gay people to be happy too." He pointed to a house across the way with his cigarette hand and told the canvasser that a lesbian couple lived there. The Mustang Man said he allowed them to park in his garage because there was no room in the street. "They're wonderful people. They don't bother nobody. You don't see them, how do you say? Trying to hit on other women or whatever. They're happy, just like I was with my wife."

After some small talk, the canvasser asked how the Mustang Man would vote should same-sex marriage come up on the ballot. He said, "I'd vote for it this time."

Later, I'd spend time in the LAB's video archives watching successes like these. I watched dozens go from *against* to *for*, *opposition* to *support*. You could run the videos from the beginning and hear one opinion, then run them to the end and hear another. I got the sense that if the people on either end of those conversations were to meet, they'd probably argue with each other.

Often, it seemed as if the people who changed their minds during these conversations didn't even realize it. They talked themselves into a new position so smoothly that they were unable to see that their opinions had flipped. At the end of the conversation, when the canvassers asked how they now felt, they expressed frustration, as if the canvasser hadn't been paying close enough attention to what they'd been saying all along.

The longest video I found in the archive ran forty-two minutes, but most only reached twenty or so. Compared with the lengthy political arguments I've had with my family, the brevity of these talks seemed astonishing. I've disagreed with people on Facebook in a single argument that spanned days, and here were people turning cognitive about-faces on deeply held opinions in half the time it takes to bake a cake. I imagined opinions building up for years like barnacles on the side of a ship, every day growing denser, resisting efforts to chip at them. Then one day along comes a stranger with a clipboard who cleanly wipes it all away by just asking some questions and listening.

I couldn't shake the idea that I, too, was probably one conversation away from changing my own mind about something, maybe a lot of things. But I also recalled how many conversations I'd had that only made my convictions stronger. I thought about the truthers and all the conversations they had in New York. I wondered what made these interactions different.

In the training, after the videos, Laura handed things over to Steve, and I got my first clue. He opened by telling the crowd that facts don't work. A serene man with a gentle and patient spirit, Steve put away his persistent smile and raised his voice to address the audience on this point.

"There is no superior argument, no piece of information that we can offer, that is going to change their mind," he said, taking a long pause before continuing. "The only way they are going to change their mind is by changing their *own* mind—by talking themselves through their own thinking, by processing things they've never thought about before, things from their own life that are going to help them see things differently."

He stood by a paper easel on which Laura had drawn a cartoon layer cake. Steve pointed to the smallest portion at the top with a candle sticking out. It was labeled "rapport," the next smallest layer was "our story," and the huge base was "their story." He said to keep that image in mind while standing in front of someone, to remember to spend as little time as possible talking about yourself, just enough to show that you are friendly, that you aren't selling anything. Show you are genuinely interested in what they have to say. That, he said, keeps them from assuming a defensive position. You should share your story, he said, pointing to the portion of the cake that sat on top of the biggest layer, but it's their story that should take up most of the conversation. You want them to think about their own thinking.

The team tossed out lots of metaphors like these. For instance, Steve later said to think of questions as keys on a giant ring. If you keep asking and listening, he told the crowd, one of those keys was bound to unlock the door to a personal experience related to the topic. Once that real, lived memory was out in the open, you could (if done correctly) steer the conversation away from the world of conclusions with their facts googled for support, away from ideological abstractions and into the world of concrete details from that individual's personal experiences. It was there, and only there, he said, that a single conversation could change someone's mind.

———

In one of their media rooms, Steve spun a laptop around to show me a conversation from 2009, one of several that had changed everything about their approach. He explained that I was about to see Dave Fleischer miss something.

Fleischer stood outside talking to a gaunt, leathery, seemingly ancient man that the team called Ed. Fleischer caught Ed backing out of his drive-way in a boat of a car, and after some small talk he asked if Ed had voted to ban same-sex marriage. He said he had, and when Fleischer asked why, Ed told him, "I just believe in it." After some thought, Ed added, "I was in the Navy, and things were different back then." He then went on to share how he grew up in what he called a "hick town," Rochester, so when he went through psychiatric evaluations for the Navy in New York City, it was his first time to hear about gay people. "I learned an awful lot about life in New York City in the Brooklyn Naval Yard," he said.

Fleischer waited for Ed to finish his story, and then moved the con-versation back to present, to the vote, to same-sex marriage, to facts about the Constitution, medical decisions for spouses, civil unions, and so on. They argued for a while, and Fleischer dumped a mountain of information into the conversation to counter Ed's conclusions. After listening to all this, Ed told him matter-of-factly, "I still would vote no on marriage."

Steve tapped the spacebar and stopped the video, but I couldn't fig-ure out what I was supposed to be seeing. I thought Fleischer was mak-ing great points in front of a stubborn old man.

Steve explained that Fleischer was asking Ed to accept the evidence, to bow down to the facts, for his process of reaching conclusions to go to the same places Fleischer's had. When Ed countered by producing a bevy of different interpretations of that same evidence, Fleischer coun-tered with interpretations of his own. "It's all intellectual, logical," Steve said dismissively.

I nodded, still unsure why facts and logic were such a bad idea.

Steve explained that after thousands of recorded conversations they had found that battling over differing interpretations of the evidence kept the people they met from exploring *why* they felt so strongly one way or the other. People could remain in the logic space doing battle with the canvasser's facts for hours and never leave, safe and unable to tap into why those facts evoked such powerful feelings. The LAB tried arguing the facts for years, and it had long proved a waste of time.

"Doing this work has taught me that people make their decisions about issues like this, in their life and when they're voting, at a really emotional, visceral level," said Steve. "What I envision when I'm standing in front of a voter is that people have this intellectual, logical reasoning process. That's one part of how they process the world and make decisions. But they have this almost entirely separate emotional reasoning process which is based on feelings and things they've experienced."

Steve said they used to hand-hold people and try to walk them through why certain facts should be compelling, why they should obviously change their minds, but his hunch now is that it will never work. A canvasser's reasoning can't be copied and pasted into another person. The facts that matter to them probably won't matter to the other person at all.

Steve returned to the video and played back the portion where Ed said in boot camp he went through psychiatric evaluations. Back then he didn't know what gay was, but he "learned an awful lot about life in New York City in the Brooklyn Naval Yard."

Steve paused the video and looked at me. I looked back, unaware of the import of Ed's statement. He said that at the time when Ed was first filmed, they didn't get it either. They thought that what he was talking about didn't bear directly on same-sex marriage, so the whole team ignored that part when they reviewed the conversation. Now they use the full twenty-five-minute video in training to show exactly what Fleischer did not notice, things that today any one of their most-skilled canvassers would immediately seize upon.

"It's hard for me to describe," said Steve, "because I've gone to the other side of this. I'm on the other side of this barrier now where I look back, and I'm like, 'Holy shit.' There's this huge thing that sails by in the night that Dave doesn't touch: What happened in the Brooklyn Navy Yard!?" Steve shook his hands at the screen as if Ed could hear him. "What did you experience? What did you learn about gay people? We can assume that in boot camp for the psychological profiling you learn that being gay is a mental disorder because they were checking to make sure who was gay. That was the first time you learned what gay was!"

Getting Ed to process those memories out loud would have taken the conversation away from the facts that seemed to support his argument and into his motivations for bringing up those facts instead. A deep canvasser could have helped him unpack his life experiences and discover how they had shaped his opinions. Once people see where their ideas come from, they become aware that they come from somewhere. They can then ask themselves if they've learned anything new in the time since they last considered them. Maybe those ideas need updating in some way. Deep canvassing is about gaining access to that emotional space, Steve explained, to "help them unload some baggage," because that's where mind change happens.

"It's in *his* experiences, not *ours*," Steve said. "The path is helping him talk through them whether they seem relevant. Then saying, 'OK, huh, what conclusions have you drawn based on those experiences?'"

The LAB noticed this route to persuasion was superior when, on three separate occasions, after the canvasser had hardly said a word, voters changed their minds about same-sex marriage on their own. Each time, the canvasser had come out, shared how the vote affected them personally, and then let people argue themselves out of their own positions.

"In the LGBT community, the idea of coming out and telling our story is incredibly powerful. It's been part of the LGBT community since Stonewall, and it has been a really smart thing," said Fleischer. "We were clear about the value of it, and there was this sense that telling our story would be an important thing, but somewhere around the time of those conversations we realized, 'Wow, what if that is the second-most-important thing?'" He raised a flat palm above us, indicating the voter's story. "This is at the hundredth floor." Then he indicated his own story, just above the table. "This is at the third floor." Then he lowered his hand underneath and said, laughing, "And intellectual arguments are in the basement."

I kept taking notes with marginalia that reminded me to ask *why* all this worked. Clearly, they had hit on some rules to follow, some steps to take that delivered results. But what were the psychological ingredients in their strange persuasive alchemy? Despite the intensity of the training, Steve and Laura never really explained any specifics about what was happening inside the heads of the strangers they met. After the training, I asked Steve and Laura if they knew, and they said that maybe they didn't, not fully, but I could interview the scientists studying them that week, once I got a chance to see deep canvassing work in person.

———

After a full day of frustration, his back to the sun and his shirt soaked, Steve finally made a breakthrough at the last house on our route.

Martha, seventy-two, said she was strongly opposed to abortion and tried to politely return to however she had been spending her Saturday before we interrupted. She said Steve couldn't come inside because of her protective dog. A common deflection, Steve would tell me later. He told her not to worry, we didn't want to come inside. We just wanted to ask some questions and hear her opinions. Martha softened and agreed to share them. Steve asked, on abortion rights, where she saw herself on a scale of zero to ten, zero being a belief that there should be no legal access to abortion in any way, and ten being support for complete, full, easy access. Without hesitation, Martha said she was a five.

Steve raised his clipboard and made a mark while nodding. Then he asked Martha why that number felt right to her. Martha told us everyone had the right to their own bodies, but she had a problem with women who "have one after the other."

Steve would tell me later that they had learned over many conversations that reasons, justifications, and explanations for maintaining one's existing opinion can be endless, spawning like heads of a hydra. If you cut away one, two more would appear to take its place. Deep canvassers want to avoid that unwinnable fight. To do that, they allow a person's justifications to remain unchallenged. They nod and listen. The idea is to move forward, make the person feel heard and respected, avoid arguing over a person's conclusions, and instead work to discover the motivations behind them. To that end, the next step is to evoke a person's emotional response to the issue.

Steve said he'd love to get Martha's opinion about a video and pulled out his phone with a clip already playing. In it, a woman told the camera that she got pregnant at twenty-two despite using birth control. She said she knew right away she wanted an abortion, that she didn't want to spend the rest of her life with the man she was dating. She wanted to further her education before she had kids.

Martha seemed uneasy. After evoking negative emotions like this, canvassers ask people if their opinion has changed, and they re-ask them where they are on the scale of zero to ten. Sampling their newly salient feelings, people often move a few numbers. Martha said she was definitely still a five. If she *had* moved, he would have asked her why. But since she didn't, he asked her what the video made her think. She said she believed the woman should have discussed her feelings about kids with her partner before they had sex, and that they should have used protection.

In the training, they said it was here in the conversation that a deep canvasser must perform their most delicate work. Even if a person's ratings don't move, the canvasser knows people have begun to think about their emotions and wonder, "Why *do* I feel this way?" After a twinge of unresolved introspection, people become highly motivated to sort out their feelings. They will then produce a new set of justifications, weaker perhaps than before. That encourages a conversation. Instead of arguing, the canvasser listens, helping the voter untangle their thoughts by asking questions and reflecting back their answers to make certain they are hearing them correctly. If people feel heard, they further articulate their opinions and often begin to question them.

"It's like we are solving a mystery together," Steve would later tell me. As people explain themselves, they begin to produce fresh insights into why they feel one way or another. This indicates they've engaged in active processing. Instead of defending, they begin contemplating, and once a person is contemplating, they often produce their own counterarguments, and a newfound ambivalence washes over them. If enough counterarguments stack up, the balance may tip in favor of change.

Steve moved to the next stage. According to the training, if he could evoke a memory from her own life that contradicted the reasoning she had shared, she might notice the conflict without him having to point it out. It would remain private, and she wouldn't feel like Steve was challenging her. She'd be challenging herself. And if he threw his support behind the conflicting thoughts that favored the opinion he was there to champion, she might shift in the direction he wanted. But as the training emphasized, it's a delicate maneuver because she might resolve the conflict in the other direction by further justifying her existing position instead.

Steve asked if Martha had ever talked to anyone openly about abortion. She said she had talked about it with her daughters when she urged them to begin birth control. He then asked if there had been any unplanned pregnancies in Martha's family, and she revealed that there had. Then he asked when she had first heard of abortion. She said in her twenties.

"How did it come up?"

"I knew a girl who had an abortion by someone who didn't know what they were doing."

And there it was: what Steve had been looking for—a real, lived experience, one that was especially laden with emotion. Steve asked a few more questions and slowly drew from Martha a fifty-year-old memory of a friend who came to her house in desperate need of a doctor. She was bleeding out after a botched backdoor surgery. Martha filled in the details, and then soberly added, "She didn't have a choice."

Her friend couldn't turn to family. They would have disowned her. "That was fifty years ago," she explained. "You just didn't do that." Her friend knew Martha was more open-minded than most, so she reached out to her for help. Steve listened, providing space for Martha to tell the story at length, and then drew the conversation to a close by asking a series of leading questions, reflecting back how her friend didn't have a choice and how Martha was open-minded.

He asked, had Martha ever judged her friend for what she did? Did she think her friend had been irresponsible? And so on. Martha explained that she just "didn't want her to die."

Then she told us with all the access people have to birth control, everyone should be more responsible these days. Steve agreed, but added that in the heat of the moment, people make mistakes. In the training they called this "modeling vulnerability," and the idea was that if you open up, so will they. He told her as a young gay man, he didn't take proper precautions his first time, even though he was well aware of the dangers. He asked if Martha had ever been less than careful because of something like that.

"I'm seventy-two years old, and I'm not a nun."

They laughed together, and then Martha apologized because she couldn't stand any longer. The LAB was still developing the script for having conversations about abortion, so in the materials provided there were no further instructions as to how to proceed.

If they had been discussing transgender bathroom laws, the script would have had Steve return to her initial concerns and ask if she still felt that way. He might have experimented with something like that, but Martha was visibly tired, so Steve said before he left that he believed all women should be able to choose for themselves without judgment. This moment is heavily emphasized in the training. They call it "connecting on values." Before you wrap up, you must make it clear where you stand, but in a way that shows you and the other person may agree on what is important at the core of the discussion. If you've done your job, the other side will know you aren't aiming for a fight. Your position can be seen as just your perspective, perhaps one worth considering.

Steve asked where she stood on that scale now, zero to ten?

"I think they should have access to it, if that's what they choose. Go up to seven."

When we departed to the curb so he could fill out his paperwork, Steve said he was sure Martha would vote *for* abortion rights in the future. She'd be thinking about it. It wasn't a slam dunk, but she had discovered she was conflicted. She would notice things she didn't before. She had moved from neutral to somewhat supportive, and that counted as change. Given time, that change might grow stronger.

He checked back in with the UCLA students. They were ready for water and shade and air conditioning, and we were too, but Steve knew his truck was parked along the curb a hike away. As he stood and stretched, the students texted back with the news they had completed full conversations with three people. Steve told them he completed just one, but it was a good one. Waiting, lying in the grass under the shade of a parked car, drenched in sweat, woozy and thirsty and listening to a mix of birds and dogs and lawnmowers, I realized the full depth of what Steve had mentioned earlier as we made small talk walking in the suburban streets of San Gabriel.

"This is why most politicians don't do this," he said. "It takes a lot more effort than just shoving a flyer in someone's hands or leaving it on their doorstep."

———

Once the LAB abandoned fact-based arguing for this approach, everything seemed to fall into place. The more Fleischer's team talked with people, the better they got at flipping them, and with a video database of their successes they could accelerate that improvement. The LAB added scripts with guidelines to help canvassers open up and elicit stories from people, and they added intense training sessions to spread the word and quickly bring new volunteers into the fold.

"The result was that over time we had gotten to a point where we were pretty sure we were having an impact," said Fleischer.

That's when he decided it was time to bring in some scientists. That decision would lead to a torrent of publicity that nearly destroyed everything Fleischer had worked for since the LAB knocked on its first door.

Before scientists began researching the Leadership LAB's technique, few studies supported the possibility that campaigns could change voters' views on polarized, partisan, politically controversial issues, especially not with door-to-door canvassing.

The academic literature in political science is aggressively pessimistic in this regard. In their book *Get Out the Vote!*, political scientists Donald Green and Alan Gerber examined more than one hundred published papers detailing attempts to influence voters' opinions with mailouts, canvassing, phone calls, and television ads. Green and Gerber concluded it was highly unlikely any of them made any impact. Zero. In the rare instances in which a communication technique did alter people's opinions, people tended to revert back to their original position within a few days after their social networks reasserted their influence.

Fleischer paid Donald Green a visit at Columbia University and showed him what the LAB had been up to over the last few years. After seeing some of the videos, Green was astonished.

"One day, Dave announced to me that he thought that he had had this insight," Green told me. "He had found what was lying behind resistance to same-sex marriage and what kinds of things could encourage a change of opinion. I, being the skeptical sort that I am, said that you really need to test it rigorously before I, or anyone else, is going to believe you."

Green cautioned Fleischer that if he put together a study to measure deep canvassing like he had with other techniques, they might discover it produced a weak effect that didn't last, or worse than that, it might show that it didn't work at all. All his effort might have been for nothing.

Dave told him, "'Well that's fine, Don, let's just find out.'"

Donald Green sent over a grad student he was advising, Michael LaCour, to do the grunt work, to quantify the LAB's success rate and crunch the numbers. The two coordinated to produce a paper based on Michael's observations in late 2014.

The big reveal? Published in the journal *Science* under the title "When Contact Changes Minds," their research showed that the LAB's technique worked, really well, in ways that were difficult to explain. Nonetheless, the bottom line was that the data showed it reliably changed the opinions of people opposed to same-sex marriage, often flipping them at their front doors after just one conversation.

That's how I first learned of their work. It was everywhere I turned, and the paper became a sensation for two reasons. One, this kind of real-world research was unusual for social science, especially when it came to the study of political behavior. When trying to understand prejudice, most social scientists had been forced to depend on observational studies: looking at connections and friendships, noting strong attitudes and how they cluster, modeling networks, and so on. Or laboratory studies that might try tactics like bringing employees of a company into diversity training workshops every day for a year to record their effects on employee attitudes. Second, at that time the debate about same-sex marriage was the most discussed, most argued wedge issue of the day. If you could change people's minds about this, you could change their minds about anything.

In the wake of this attention, two political scientists, David Broockman and Josh Kalla, planned to run an extension of the study after learning Fleischer's team was setting up shop in Florida. A new law aimed at preventing transgender bathroom discrimination was in danger, and transgender issues had yet to gain the kind of attention or support as same-sex marriage. The LAB planned to teach deep canvassing to

Miami activists to help them shift opinions in the area, and Broockman and Kalla thought it would be a perfect opportunity to extend the now-famous research by LaCour and Green. Basically, they'd use the same design and methods on the application of deep canvassing to a new issue. But when they began looking for subjects, they ran into a strange problem.

To keep people unaware they were taking part in a study about changing minds, they asked them to take part in unrelated, long-term surveys for small cash incentives, just as LaCour the grad student had done. But only about 2 percent of people agreed. In LaCour's research, more than 12 percent of people had agreed. In social science, that's an alarming disparity, so Broockman and Kalla contacted the survey company to see what they were doing wrong. The survey company was confused. They said they hadn't done any previous work like that. Stranger still, the person LaCour listed as a contact at the company didn't exist. After some searching, they found the same numbers in another study. For reasons that are still unknown, it appeared LaCour copied and pasted his old survey data. Broockman and Kalla published their findings, and Donald Green confronted LaCour, along with a witness. LaCour denied any wrongdoing, but soon after, Green asked for a retraction that *Science* quickly provided.

This led to another frenzy of media attention, except this time everyone commented on how they always knew it had been too good to be true, and we all should have known better. It was wishful thinking to imagine you could ever change anyone's mind on issues like same-sex marriage or transgender rights or politics in general. LaCour disappeared from political science after Princeton rescinded their offer of a professorship. Green lost his Carnegie fellowship.

I was still compiling my notes from my visits to the LAB the morning the news hit, and I called Fleischer and Steve, who said they didn't know what to make of it. Then I called Green. He expressed great sadness and embarrassment, both about not watching over his grad student and not being rigorous with the data. He told me that he felt the people most hurt were the people at the LAB, who had opened up their lives to him and agreed to be researched by someone they trusted.

I feared I had been led astray by wishful thinking, but when I spoke with Broockman and Kalla, they said to hold judgment. At this point other scientists, fearing the taint of scandal, would likely have stayed away, but Broockman and Kalla wanted to push forward. As far as they were concerned, the original research was faulty, but just the research. It said nothing positive or negative about the LAB's methods. The problem was how the method had been measured, not the method itself. Someone still needed to scientifically settle whether deep canvassing worked, and they were poised to make the breakthrough LaCour had failed to produce. They headed to Miami and met with the LAB to pick up where they left off, and I waited to hear back.

Careful to meticulously record their data, Broockman and Kalla both participated in the new canvassing and measured the impact of the LAB on voters opposed to transgender bathroom rights. They framed the research like a medical trial. After getting a large group of voters to agree to take part in a supposedly unrelated survey that would track them for several months, they then divided those people into two groups. Half of the households received the intervention—a conversation by LAB-trained and -supervised canvassers using scripts and materials created by the LAB—and the other half received a placebo, a conversation about recycling. Broockman and Kalla recorded any shifts in attitudes, and then tracked those attitudes for months using those sneaky surveys to see if the mind changes stuck.

What did they find? In short, it worked. When it was all said and done, the overall shift Broockman and Kalla measured in Miami was greater than "the opinion change that occurred from 1998 to 2012 towards gay men and lesbians in the United States." In one conversation, one in ten people opposed to transgender rights changed their views, and on average, they changed that view by 10 points on a 101-point "feelings thermometer," as they called it, catching up to and surpassing the shift that had taken place in the general public over the last fourteen years.

If one in ten doesn't sound like much, you're neither a politician nor a political scientist. It is huge. And before this research, after a single conversation, it was inconceivable. Kalla said a mind change of much less than that could easily rewrite laws, win a swing state, or turn the tide of an election. More than that, a shift of 1 percent had the potential to set in motion a cascade of attitude change that could change public opinion in less than a generation. This was one conversation with people who mostly had limited experience with the technique, and in Miami those conversations lasted about ten minutes each. Had the canvassers been experts, had they continued having conversations over several weeks, had those conversations been longer, the evidence suggests the impact would have been enormous.

Writing about Broockman and Kalla's paper, Princeton psychologist Betsy Levy Paluck said the implications were colossal. She said that as scientists pick apart deep canvassing over the next decade, those efforts have the potential to forever change the way political science and psychology view persuasion and attitude change.

"What do social scientists know about reducing prejudice in the world? In short, very little," she wrote in *Science*, noting that less than 11 percent of the research conducted in the field involved measuring people's attitudes outside of a controlled setting, and even less focused on adults or long-term effects. In her analysis, she said that every effort should be made to understand why deep canvassing works, adding that scientists had already spent long enough figuring out what didn't. The buzz in the social sciences was that a group of activists working to reduce prejudice door-to-door may have pushed our understanding of how minds change ahead in a way that would take generations in the laboratory.

Kalla told me the most exciting aspect of their research was that the effect seemed permanent. They continue to track the households, and so far the people who changed their minds show no signs of backtracking into their former attitudes, something almost unheard of in political science research.

Their paper was published in *Science* in 2016, and the headlines said it all: "No, Wait, Short Conversations Really Can Reduce Prejudice," wrote *The Atlantic*. "How Do You Change Voters' Minds? Have a Conversation," wrote *The New York Times*. This time the science was sound and the data legitimate. After the third wave of media attention, Fleischer and his team said they finally felt validated. All those years of work now had the backing of science, and reporters and academics were once again flying out to Los Angeles to dig into their database and observe their process, including me. I returned soon after their study was published and trained one more time with Broockman and Kalla, who then went out with the rest of us, this time to talk about transgender issues, as part of their continuing research.

With the controversy fading in the public's mind, scientists went to work doing as Paluck suggested, and more studies are forthcoming. Deep canvassers are now experimenting with issues like health-care reform, criminal justice, climate change, immigration, vaccine hesitancy, and racism—in Los Angeles as well as the Midwest, Chicago, and the Deep South.

With satellite groups crisscrossing the country, the core team at the LAB turned their attention to conflicted Trump supporters. In 2020, People's Action, a group that focuses its efforts on rural and low-income voters, spent a summer using deep canvassing on hundreds of thousands of Trump supporters in the battleground states of Michigan, Minnesota, New Hampshire, North Carolina, Pennsylvania, and Wisconsin. Broockman and Kalla studied their efforts and found that they were able to produce, on average, a 3.1-point swing in favor of Joe Biden.

Once again, deep canvassing made headlines across the country. Covering the first time it had been used in a presidential election, *Rolling Stone* reported, "In other words, for every 100 completed phone calls, three votes were added to Biden's vote margin after they received a deep canvassing call." Altogether, Broockman and Kalla found that deep canvassing was 102 times more effective than traditional canvassing, television, radio, direct mail, and phone banking combined.

———

When I first met Broockman and Kalla, and for us going forward, the question wasn't *if* deep canvassing worked, but *how* does it work, scientifically. To answer that question, they said, we would all need to spend some time with some neuroscientists and psychologists.

"It's sort of like if you start off and there's this old wisdom from 2,500 years ago that if you would chew on this one tree bark, then you wouldn't get headaches," Broockman told me. "Later, we realized that was aspirin, and then we distilled aspirin. Now we know, it's actually a particular chemical in aspirin. We're at the tree bark stage right now. If you do this thing, you get effects, but we have no idea what's doing the work or why, or what the underlying chemistry is. Now the real work begins."

We will return to Broockman and Kalla later, after we look at the science of how minds do and do not change. For instance, I'd later find research that helped explain the phenomenon I saw in the archives, something psychologists call belief-change blindness: when people seemed unaware that their arguments from the beginning of the conversation didn't match the ones they shared at the end.

A series of experiments conducted by psychologists Michael Wolfe and Todd J. Williams in 2017 captured this process in action. They asked college students whether spanking, a relatively neutral topic for that age group, was effective as a disciplinary tool. Some said yes, some no, but whatever subjects said they believed, the scientists then presented them with an essay that outlined strong arguments to the contrary. When they brought the subjects back into the lab after some time had passed, they asked about their spanking beliefs a second time. A portion of the group returned to Wolfe and Williams with changed opinions. Considering the persuasive essays, if they were pro-spanking before, they had become anti-spanking in the time since, and vice versa. But when Wolfe and Williams pulled those subjects aside and asked them to recall how they had originally answered at the beginning of the research, most reported that their answers hadn't changed. Though the researchers had proof of it, the subjects themselves had no awareness of their own flips.

The research of Wolfe and Williams is consistent with the literature on something psychologists call consistency bias: our tendency, when uncertain, to assume our present self has always held the opinions it holds today. In one of the landmark papers on the topic, researchers asked the opinions of high school students about topics like the legalization of drugs, the rights of prisoners, and other contentious issues. They returned to those subjects a decade later, and then again a decade after that. They found that among those who had changed their perspectives, only 30 percent were aware. The rest said they saw the issue today the way they had always seen it.

Since this a normal, constant, yet subjectively invisible process, we are more likely to notice it when it happens in others than in ourselves. That can lead to a third-person effect in which we see ourselves as resolute, but see politicians or other public figures as hypocritical or lacking conviction. In one of the most famous instances, in 2004, when John Kerry was running for president, many of the attack ads called him a flip-flopper for saying he voted for an appropriations bill before he realized it was a mistake and then later voted against it. For updating his opinion in light of new evidence, the opposition said he couldn't be trusted. People even brought flip-flops to the Republican national convention and chanted, "Flip-flop, flip-flop!" But the research is clear: the people brandishing casual footwear in anger had changed their minds like Kerry had, many times. We all have, it's just that unlike John Kerry, our changes weren't recorded for posterity.

Broockman and Kalla said their work was made harder by the fact that the team that may have cracked the code on how to rapidly change people's attitudes on divisive social issues didn't base their work on any existing psychological concepts. In fact, as the LAB members told me, they didn't even know psychological studies into persuasion existed until years into their work. Yet, as I would later learn, in many ways deep canvassing is the application of a patchwork of hypotheses that have remained trapped in papers for decades: studies of college students conducted in laboratory settings and untested ideas that might have been tested through the kind of field work the LAB does—if psychologists had millions of dollars, thousands of volunteers, and years they could devote to a hunch, even after failing over and over again to prove there was any point to keep going.

When I asked Broockman and Kalla for a lead or two, they said to look deeper into something psychologists call elaboration, a state of active learning in which a person unpacks a new idea by relating to something they already understand. For example, on first viewing, you might describe *Alien* as "*Jaws* in space," but, if you saw *Alien* first, you might describe *Jaws* as "*Alien* in the ocean." Most of the time, when on autopilot or performing routine tasks, we see the world as we expect to see it, and most of the time that's fine; but the brain often gets things wrong because it prefers to sacrifice accuracy for speed. When we stop ourselves from going with our first instincts, or our "guts," when we are thinking about our own thinking, we become more open to elaborating, to adding something new to ourselves by reaching a deeper understanding of something we thought we already understood quite well. In short, deep canvassing likely encourages elaboration by offering people an opportunity to stop and think.

Dave Fleischer told me that people don't get a chance to reflect like this very often. Daily concerns take up people's cognitive resources: providing lunch money for their kids, evaluating their performance at work, planning who will take the car to get repaired. Without a chance to introspect, we remain overconfident in our understanding of the issues about which we are most passionate. That overconfidence translates to certainty, and we use that certainty to support extreme views.

One of the most striking examples of this comes from experiments into what psychologists call the illusion of explanatory depth. When scientists asked subjects to rate how well they understood things like zippers, toilets, and combination locks, most people tended to say they had a pretty good grasp of their mechanics. But when experimenters asked those same subjects to explain how they worked in detail, people tended to go back and update their answers, admitting they had pretty much no idea how those things worked. The same was true for political issues. When asked to provide opinions on health-care reform, a flat tax, carbon emissions, and so on, many subjects held extreme views. When experimenters asked people to provide reasons for their opinions, they did so with ease. But if asked to explain those issues in mechanistic detail, they became flustered and realized they knew far less about the policies than they thought they did. As a result, their opinions became less extreme.

Broockman and Kalla also suspected that deep canvassing also encouraged analogic perspective taking, a key moment in human cognitive development. The idea goes all the way back to Piaget, who first observed that small children couldn't do it. It's the discovery that other minds perceive, think, and believe things differently than ourselves. Until that ability develops, we live in a world of only one mind—our own. To demonstrate this, in one experiment researchers showed children a crayon box and asked what they believed was inside. They, of course, answered that it was full of crayons. The scientists then revealed it actually contained birthday candles. When asked what another child who had not yet seen what was inside would say, children under four believed others would now also say candles.

When we gain a theory of mind, we also gain the ability to imagine what it must be like to be another person, to see and feel things as they do, to have different opinions because of different exposure to different experiences. That's analogic perspective taking, a higher-level cognition that takes a lot of effort. We don't often attempt it unless prompted.

When I asked the late psychologist Lee Ross about it, he told me that when he worked on conflict resolution in Northern Ireland and in talks between Israel and Palestine, where the stakes were very high, people rarely considered the other side's perspective until asked to do so. In his experience both parties were only ever interested in communicating their own perspectives. Not once, he said, in forty years of doing conflict negotiation had anyone ever arrived eager to learn how others saw the issues at hand.

Giving up your own viewpoint for a while and trying on someone else's is difficult, and we don't do it by default. Research into perspective taking shows that people opposed to affirmative action, for example, often blame income disparity on a lack of willpower or strong work ethic instead of widespread prejudice or institutional racism. Yet, when experimenters asked those same people to look at a photo of a black man and write an essay about a day in his life, including as much vivid detail as possible about his thoughts and feelings, subjects reported a strong shift in attitudes concerning affirmative action. By empathizing, even hypothetically, people softened their positions—something subjects could have done at any time but, until prompted, never considered.

Broockman and Kalla said people rarely engage in perspective taking, which is what makes it such a powerful persuasion tool in the hands of a deep canvasser.

"Perspective taking is not just getting someone to feel sad, and therefore you change their minds," said Kalla. Everyone already knows that prejudice is bad. Deep canvassers evoke memories charged with emotion so that people recall what it is like to be ostracized or judged or made to feel lesser than, and it challenges their categorization of otherness. "Now all of a sudden when I say discrimination is wrong, I'm feeling that in a different way," said Broockman. "I can now understand, 'Oh yeah, it's really awful to be discriminated against and treated dif-

ferently. I can see what it might be like to be that person.' It becomes difficult to justify making a fellow human being feel that way."

By the time I left the LAB, I felt as though jumping into the science of
persuasion was getting ahead of myself. Their hypotheses about why
deep canvassing worked all sounded plausible, but I still didn't understand what tied all these ideas together. I needed to resolve a question
that my time with the LAB had only made more mysterious. If facts don't
work on some people—if in fact they can make it less likely to change
their minds—that would explain why the truthers didn't change their
minds when presented with evidence; but why was it that those same
facts *did* convince Charlie Veitch? It seemed to me that there was a lot
missing from all this, and if I was going to make sense of it, I'd need to
look into the science that the deep canvassers had not, the science Broockman and Kalla were about to wade into. In the following chapter, that's
where we will head as well, starting with some neuroscientists who study
disagreement itself.

Fleischer asked me to check back when I knew more. He, too, was
interested in the science behind how it worked, but he wanted to be
clear: in the end, their secret was just open and honest communication
with people who rarely get a chance to engage in it.

"Well, it's funny, in a way it's not new at all. We did not invent the
concept that one human being can talk with another human being," he
told me, laughing. "So in a way, there's nothing original here at all, and
yet it is very original, because it is so much against the grain of the
dominant political culture."

He recalled a conversation years ago with a man who rushed out on
to his porch when Fleischer explained why he was visiting. "The guy
jumps out, he's so eager to tell me how against gay marriage he is."

He was in his seventies, and he excitedly told Fleischer how terrible it would be for the country to make same-sex marriage legal. Fleischer asked if he knew anyone who was gay, and the man said, "Absolutely!" He and his wife had visited Disneyland recently, and to their dismay they had gone on Gay Day. "There were all these gays there, including this guy we saw wearing a big feather boa!" he told Fleischer.

Fleischer asked if the man had a conversation with any of the gay people he saw that day, and he said that of course he hadn't. Why would he?

Fleischer told him, "Well, I forgot my boa today," and the man laughed. Then they talked for a long while. It was likely the first conversation he had ever had with a member of the LGBTQ community.

"He could see that he and I could have a good time talking, even if we didn't agree. I didn't need him to agree, right? I didn't wag my finger at him and say, 'Now you've got to change your mind,' but over the course of the conversation he *did* begin to change his mind. I think that's what changing your mind looks like."

3

SOCKS AND CROCS

I was sitting at the Knickerbocker restaurant in New York City, reaching for the butter, when a soft-faced, bearded man to my left slid between my notebook and the basket of bread a photo of a fried egg, sunny-side up, its yolk a shimmering shade of neon green.

"At first," he explained, the image hovering, "we tried green eggs. You know, green eggs and ham? Not ham though, just eggs. But we couldn't get it to work. Because people know that eggs are supposed to be yellow."

Semi-shouting above the lunchtime bustle, the neuroscientist to my right opened his palms wide and added, "So what do we do? What is something that is both familiar but that has no distinct color?"

I struggled to come up with an answer. My first thought was . . . *A pickup truck?* Then I thought, *Towels, hammers, bicycles, maybe boxes of tissue?* But after spending the weekend with Pascal Wallisch, a frenetic genius determined to build, in his words, "the cognitive equivalent of the nuclear bomb," I felt like this was probably another rhetorical question meant to set up another lesson that would, once again, move too fast for me to take appropriate notes; so instead I pushed a piece of bread into my mouth and thoughtfully chewed.

"Crocs!" shouted Pascal, startling the waiter as he placed a salad in front of him, which would go uneaten. When you imagine Crocs, he explained, those foam-resin shoe things popular with nurses and gardeners and retirees, no particular color comes to mind.

Try it, he said. What do you see when you close your eyes? Are they white, gray, orange, camouflage? Everyone sees something different. I told him mine were no color at all, or maybe every color. I couldn't tell.

"Interesting," he said, delighted, turning to see the reaction of his colleague on my left, cognitive scientist Michael Karlovich, who was putting away his phone. Karlovich looked up and smiled, then explained it was totally understandable if nothing had come to mind. That was why they were so excited when they hit on Crocs. Combined with socks, they said, under the right kind of light, the two items become a single "perceptually ambiguous color object," something they had been hoping to find for months as they tried to get to the bottom of a neuroscientific mystery that had nearly broken the internet a few years back. You may recall it simply as *The Dress*.

———

I had traveled to New York to meet Pascal and Karlovich because if I wanted to understand why the evidence that changed Charlie Veitch's mind didn't change the minds of the other truthers, I needed to first answer, scientifically, *how* minds change. That question seemed inextricably linked to another question: What is it that is *changing* when we use that phrase? Both of those questions seemed wrapped inside an even larger question: How is that thing, whatever it is that we call a mind, made in the first place? That is, how does our understanding of the world get baked into the goop wiggling around inside our skulls? So I wanted to take a step back, a few thousand steps back actually, all the way to neurons.

Before traveling to New York, I asked a few scientists these questions in a few different ways. The answers that came back tended to include a warning or two: This was dangerous territory, they seemed to say, the bleeding edge of both the social and brain sciences. Asking how we make up our minds, and then do or do not change them, is not that distant from asking, *What is the very nature of consciousness itself?*—a question that may not even have an answer, at least not yet, not in the confines of our current scientific understanding, nor the language we use to communicate it. No matter what, they said, I was joining an ongoing investigation that was only just recently gaining ground.

So in addition to chatting with David Eagleman, who studies brain plasticity and consciousness, I decided to seek out a neuroscientist who was more focused on why, in a post-internet world, large numbers of people shared fundamental disagreements on matters of certainty in which other people have no issue seeing eye to eye. Pascal, with Karlovich's help, had inadvertently become an expert on that very topic after devoting years to studying why people freaked out over *The Dress*, a photograph that went viral in 2015 after millions of people separated into two opposing camps, arguing online over reality itself, because they *literally* couldn't see eye to eye.

If you don't recall *The Dress*, here's some background. Back in 2015, before Brexit, before Trump, before Macedonian internet trolls, before QAnon and COVID conspiracy theories, before fake news and alternative facts, one NPR affiliate called the disagreement over *The Dress* "the debate that broke the internet," and *The Washington Post* referred to it as "the drama that divided the planet."

The Dress was a meme, a viral photo that appeared all across social media for a few months. For some, when they looked at this photo, they saw a dress that appeared black and blue. For others, the dress appeared white and gold. Whatever people saw, it was impossible to see it differently. If not for the social aspect of social media, you might have never known that some people did see it differently. But since social media *is* social, learning the fact that millions saw a different dress than you did created a widespread, visceral response. The people who saw a different *The Dress* seemed clearly, obviously mistaken and quite possibly deranged. When *The Dress* started circling the internet, a tangible sense of dread about the nature of what is and is not real went as viral as the image itself.

This particular epistemic crisis entered our lives when Cecilia Bleasdale was preparing for her daughter Grace's wedding. A week before, she took a photo of a $77 dress at a London shopping mall. Thinking she might wear it to the event, she snapped the now legendary photo and sent it to her daughter to get her opinion. Upon seeing it, Grace and her soon-to-be-husband, Kier, could not agree on what they saw, and so they asked their friends to settle an argument. What color do *you* see? Instead, the argument spread to their friends, then their friends' friends, and on and on. Some people saw black and blue, others saw white and gold, no one could agree, and everyone was confused as to why.

Scan this QR code to see *The Dress* and other examples from this chapter.

A week later a musician close to the family posted the image on Tumblr to see if the world at large could settle all this, but it only spread the confusion to the internet, and then the internet started arguing over what it was seeing. Within days, *The Dress* hit Buzzfeed, and then the rest of social media.

At times, so many people were sharing this perceptual conundrum, and arguing about it, that Twitter couldn't load on their devices. The hashtag #TheDress appeared in 11,000 tweets per minute, and the definitive article about the meme, published on *Wired* magazine's website, received 32.8 million unique views within the first few days.

Actress Mindy Kaling spoke for team black and blue on Twitter, writing, "IT'S A BLUE AND BLACK DRESS! ARE YOU FUCKING KIDDING ME." The Kardashians argued for team white and gold, politicians chimed in on both sides, the local news in hometowns around the world ended their shows with it, and for a little while *The Dress* was the centerpiece of pop culture. Wherever items trended, it was far and away the most trending item.

For many, it was an introduction to something neuroscience has understood for a long while, which is also the main subject of this chapter: the fact that reality itself, as we experience it, isn't a perfect one-to-one account of the world around us. The world, as you experience it, is a simulation running inside your skull, a waking dream. We each live in a virtual landscape of perpetual imagination and self-generated illusion, a hallucination informed over our lifetimes by our senses and thoughts about them, updated continuously as we bring in new experiences via those senses and think new thoughts about what we have sensed. If you didn't know this, for many *The Dress* demanded you either take to your keyboard to shout into the abyss or take a seat and ponder your place in the grand scheme of things.

The scientific study of how brains generate reality has always been a bit trippy. That trip began back in the early 1900s when a German biologist couldn't shake the implication that the inner lives of animals must be radically different from those of humans.

Jakob Johann von Uexküll was fascinated by jellyfish and urchins and spiders and bugs, and he wondered how their squishy nervous systems gave rise to their private perceptions. Noting that the sense organs of sea creatures and insects could perceive things that ours could not, he realized that giant portions of reality must therefore be missing from their subjective experiences, which suggested that the same was probably true of us. In other words, most ticks can't enjoy an Andrew Lloyd Webber musical because, among other reasons, they don't have eyes. They can't see the stage, not even from the front row. On the other hand, unlike ticks, most humans can't smell butyric acid wafting on the breeze. And this, according to Uexküll, is why no matter where you sit in the audience, smell is not an essential, or intended, element of a Broadway performance of *Cats*.

Uexküll realized the subjective experience of every living thing was confined to a private sensory world he called an "umwelt": different sense organs, different umwelt, distinctive from that of another animal in the same environment. Each creature, therefore, was tuned to take in only a small portion of the total picture. Not that any animal would likely know that, which was Uexküll's other big idea. Because no organism can perceive the totality of objective reality, each animal likely assumes that what it can perceive is all that *can* be perceived. Objective reality, whatever it is, can never be fully experienced by any one creature. Each umwelt is a private universe, a different subjective experience fitted to its niche, a perceptually bounded internal world. The umwelten of all of Earth's creatures are like a sea filled with a panoply of sensory realities floating past one another, each unaware that it is unaware and none knowing what it does not know.

Uexküll's ideas weren't completely new. Philosophers had wondered about the differences between subjective and objective reality going back to Plato's cave, and are still wondering. When the philosopher Thomas Nagel famously asked "What is it like to be a bat?" he suggested there could be no answer to that question because it would be impossible to think in that way. Bat sonar, he said, is nothing like anything we possess, "and there is no reason to suppose that it is subjectively like anything we *can* experience or imagine."

The extension of this idea is that if different animals live in different realities, then maybe different people live in different realities, too. It's a centerpiece of the writings of many psychonaut thinkers, from Timothy

Leary with his "reality tunnels" and J. J. Gibson's "ecological optics" to psychologist Charles Tart and his "consensus trances." From the Wachowskis' *Matrix* to Kant's "noumenon" to Daniel Dennett's "conscious robots," to every episode of *Black Mirror* and every novel by Philip K. Dick, we've been wondering about these questions for a very long time. You too, I suspect, have stumbled on these problems, at some point asking something along the lines of, "Do you think we all see the same colors?" The answer, as *The Dress* demonstrates, is no.

So this idea that subjective reality and objective reality are not the same, that what we experience inside our minds is a representation of the outside world, a model and not a replica, has been brewing among people who think about thinking for a very long time, but Uexküll brought it into a new academic silo—biology. In doing so, he generated lines of academic research into neuroscience and the nature of consciousness that are still going today. One of those studies is going to seem a bit icky, so bear with me, because it will illustrate something important.

In 1970, physiologists Colin Blakemore and Grahame F. Cooper raised a group of cats in an environment without any horizontal lines. Outside of that environment, when Blakemore and Cooper held a stick vertically and wiggled it around, all the cats' heads bobbed in unison and turned together to follow the stick as the scientists darted it about. But as soon as the stick turned sideways, the cats looked away in different directions, and then they lost interest and wandered off. The vertical stick was fascinating, but the horizontal stick was not, because in their shared internal reality horizontal *did not exist*.

In their laboratory at Cambridge University, Blakemore and Cooper painted the insides of large glass cylinders white, then they added black stripes inside running in vertical columns. The rims of the cylinders curved upward to form rounded walls. The entire design was created so that the cats never witnessed horizontal edges, and to make sure of this, the kittens wore little cowls, a bit like those that veterinarians send home to prevent licking after a surgery. They then raised a series of kittens born in complete darkness who, at two weeks old, started spending five hours a day in a world of vertical stripes. The kittens sat in the cylinders doing the things normal kittens do, and then, five months later, Blakemore and Cooper took their cats out and allowed them to spend time in a room with a table and some chairs to see how they would react.

They noticed right away that the cats had problems with what physiologists call visual placing. As they lowered them toward flat surfaces like the floor or a table, the cats seemed unable to make sense of it. A cat raised in a normal environment will reach out to plant its paws as it comes close to a plane. Blakemore and Cooper's cats couldn't do that. They bumped into tables as if they were transparent. When they walked along a high surface and reached the side, they became confused. Horizontal edges had no meaning for them. If Blakemore and Cooper shoved a horizontal object close to their faces or thrust the cats forward toward it, the cats didn't startle, because for them it simply wasn't there. When they slowly brought a sheet of Plexiglas painted with horizontal lines closer and closer, the cats would be shoved backward as if hit by a force field, unable to perceive the wall closing in until it pressed against their faces.

Blakemore and Cooper repeated all this with another group of cats raised in cylinders with horizontal rings and found the same effect. For that group, the cats couldn't perceive *vertical* edges. And if the scientists played with a mix of the two groups, one group would run after a horizontal stick and paw at it until it was turned upward and then stop their chase as if it had vanished. The other group would, at that moment, spring into action and take over the chase as if the stick had appeared out of thin air.

But these deficiencies didn't last. After about ten hours of playing around in the room, sensing and interacting with horizontal objects, the cats' brains started to add horizontal to their realities. The neurons that had never been exposed to this novel aspect of the outside world began to crackle in response and wire up appropriately. Soon they could jump up and down onto the chairs and tables with ease. They began to reach out when placed down, and as the walls closed in, they moved away. Their internal worlds grew more complex, adding a previously unexplored element of the outside world to the simulation running in their skulls.

Surgeons working for nonprofits in India who perform cataract surgery for people who have been blind since birth have found similar effects in humans. When the bandages fall away, people don't suddenly see the people around them. Instead, they see only shapes and colors, like an infant. After a few weeks, though, they can reach out for objects and tell them apart, but at first they can't tell whether those objects are near or far. They need years of experiences conjuring the third dimension before they can competently operate within it. Their neurons need time, just like those of babies, to learn how to make sense of the new sensory information.

Similarly, when people who have been deaf for life receive implants that allow them to hear, they at first experience only static. If such procedures take place when a person is young, the brain eventually makes use of the noise, notices the patterns within, and converts them into signals it can distinguish from others. But with older people, the bombardment of new sensory experiences can feel unwelcome. They've been making sense of the world without sound for so long that they some-times return the implants so they may return to the silent, yet manage-able, reality they've always known.

For brains, everything is noise at first. Then brains notice the patterns in the static, and they move up a level, noticing patterns in how those patterns interact. Then they move up another level, noticing pat-terns in how sets of interacting patterns interact with other sets, and on and on it goes. Layers of pattern recognition built on top of simpler layers become a rough understanding of what to expect from the world around us, and their interactions become our sense of cause and effect. The roundness of a ball, the hard edge of a table, the soft elbow of a stuffed animal, each object excites certain neural pathways and not others, and each exposure strengthens their connections until the brain comes to expect those elements of the world and becomes better at mak-ing sense of them in context. Likewise, as causes regularly lead to effects, our innate pattern recognition takes notice and forms expectations—Mom will come when I cry at night; mashed potatoes will make me happy; bees hurt when they sting. We start our lives awash in unpredict-able chaos, but the regularity of our perceptions becomes the expecta-tions we use to turn that chaos into predictable order.

But when novel information arrives via the senses, something unusual or ambiguous, it doesn't get added to subjective reality right away. It re-mains noise if it doesn't seem to match a pattern in that layered archive of prediction. The brain needs some repeated experience with it, like the horizontal lines for those sensory-deprived cats and the shapes and col-ors for the patients in India. And since all reality is subjective, an umwelt bounded by the senses available to that creature, the patterns that never get noticed never become part of that animal's internal world. If you can't sense ultraviolet, you could live your entire life never knowing it existed, and so the private universe of a mantis shrimp is painted with colors humans can never see nor imagine.

What research like this demonstrates is that each and every brain enters the world trapped in a dark vault of a skull, unable to witness firsthand what is happening outside. Thanks to brain plasticity, through repeated experience, when inputs are regular and repeating, neurons quickly get burned into the reciprocal patterns of activation. It creates a unique predictive model in each individual nervous system, a sort of bespoke resting potential for those same networks to light up in the same way in similar circumstances.

Together, they form an internal representation, an artificial model within that darkness of what the outside world must be like, via the regular and recurring information arriving from the senses. As Bertrand Russell put it, "The observer, when he seems to himself to be observing a stone, is really, if physics is to be believed, observing the effects of the stone upon himself."

The neuroscientist V. S. Ramachandran told me that he likes to think of it like a general deep in a bunker directing a battle using a big table covered with miniature tanks and soldiers. The brain, like that general, depends on scouts to send reports from the battlefield to know how to update the model. The general never sees the world outside, only the simplified representation on the table in the bunker. In between reports, he can only use the existing representation in front of him to make sense of the present situation outside. Whatever is on that model, at the moment, that's what he uses to plan, make judgments, and settle on goals and commit to decisions about the future. If his scouts don't or can't bring in updates, the model remains unchanged, representing a world that may now be far different beyond the bunker. And if the scouts have never brought in certain information about the outside world, it doesn't appear on the model at all.

———

Before *The Dress*, it was well understood in neuroscience that all reality is virtual; therefore consensus realities are mostly the result of geography. People who grow up in similar environments around similar people tend to have similar brains and thus similar virtual realities. If they do disagree, it's usually over ideas, not the raw truth of their perceptions. After *The Dress*, well—enter Pascal, a neuroscientist who studies consciousness and perception.

When Pascal first saw *The Dress*, it seemed to him like it was obviously white and gold, but when he showed it to his wife, she saw something different. She said that it was obviously black and blue. "All that night I was up, thinking what could possibly explain this."

Thanks to years of research into photoreceptors in the retina and the neurons to which they connect, he thought he understood the roughly thirty steps in the chain of visual processing, but "all of that was blown wide open in February of 2015 when *The Dress* surfaced on social media." As a scientist who studies this sort of thing, he felt like a biologist learning that doctors had just discovered a new organ in the body.

Pascal explained his confusion. The spectrum of light we can see—the primary colors we call red, green, and blue—are specific wavelengths of electromagnetic energy. These wavelengths of energy emanate from some source, like the sun, a lamp, a candle. When that light collides with, say, a lemon, the lemon absorbs some of those wavelengths and the rest bounce off. Whatever is left behind goes through a hole in our heads called the pupil and strikes the retinas at the back of the eyes where it all gets translated into the electrochemical buzz of neurons that the brain then uses to construct the subjective experience of seeing colors. Because most natural light is red, green, and blue combined and a lemon absorbs the blue wavelengths, it leaves behind the red and green to hit our retinas, which the brain then combines into the subjective experience of seeing a yellow lemon. The color, though, exists only in the mind. In consciousness, yellow is a figment of the imagination. The reason we tend to agree that lemons are yellow (and lemons) is because all our brains pretty much create the same figment of the imagination when light hits lemons and then bounces into our heads.

If we do disagree over what we see, it's usually because the image is ambiguous in some way, and the brain of one person is disambiguating the image in a way another person is not. Pascal said that in neuroscience the go-to examples of disambiguation are called intrapersonal bistable visual illusions—bistable because each brain settles on one interpretation at a time, and intrapersonal because every brain settles on the same two interpretations. You've likely seen a few of these: the duckrabbit for example, which sometimes looks like a duck and sometimes looks like a rabbit. Or the Rubin vase, which sometimes looks like a vase and sometimes looks like two people facing in silhouette.

Like all two-dimensional images, whether blobs of paint or pixels on a screen, if the lines and shapes seem similar enough to things we've seen in the past, we disambiguate them into the *Mona Lisa*, or a sailboat, or in the case of a bistable image, either a duck or a rabbit. But *The Dress* was something new, an *interjacent* bistable visual illusion—bistable because each brain settles on one interpretation at a time, but

The Duckrabbit originally appeared, unattributed, as a drawing in an 1892 issue of *Fliegende Blätter*, a German magazine, with a caption asking which two animals are most alike. It was later popularized by philosopher Ludwig Wittgenstein to illustrate the difference between perception and interpretation. He wrote, "We find certain things about seeing puzzling, because we do not find the whole business about seeing puzzling enough."

interjacent because each brain settles on only one of two possible interpretations. That's what made *The Dress* so confusing to Pascal. The same light was going into everyone's eyes, and every brain was interpreting the lines and shapes as a dress, yet somehow all those brains weren't converting that dress into the same colors. Something was happening between perception and consciousness, and he wanted to know what that was. So he acquired some funding and shifted the focus of his lab at NYU to tackling the mystery of *The Dress* while it was still going viral.

The Rubin vase is named for the Danish psychologist Edgar Rubin, who introduced it in his 1915 doctoral thesis to illustrate what happens when two images share a border. If the brain traces inner borders of Rubin's vase, the silhouettes stand out, but when it traces the outer borders, the vase emerges. The image here was created in 2007 by John Smithson.

Pascal's hunch was that different people saw different dresses because when we aren't sure what we are seeing, when we are in unfamiliar and ambiguous territory, we disambiguate using our priors, short for "prior probabilities"—the layers of pattern recognition generated by neural pathways, burned in by experiences with regularities in the external world. The term originates from statistics and has come to mean any assumption the brain carries about how the world outside should appear given how it has appeared in the past. But the brain goes further than this: in situations of what Pascal and Karlovich call "substantial uncertainty," the brain will use its experience to create illusions of what *ought* to be there but isn't. In other words, in novel situations the brain usually sees what it expects to see.

Pascal said this was well understood in color vision. We can tell a sweater is green when our closet is very dark, or a car is blue under a cloudy night sky, because the brain does a little Photoshopping to help us in situations where differing lighting conditions alter the appearance of familiar objects. We each possess a correction mechanism that recalibrates our visual systems to "discount the illuminant and achieve color constancy to preserve object identity in the face of changing illuminations." It does that by altering what we experience to match what we've

Scan this QR code to see the strawberries and other examples from this chapter.

experienced before. There's a great example of this in an illusion created by vision researcher Akiyoshi Kitaoka.

It looks like a bowl of red strawberries, but the image contains zero red pixels. When you look at the photo, no red light enters your eye.

Instead, the brain assumes the image is overexposed by blue light. It turns down the contrast a bit and adds a little color where it was just removed, which means the red you experience when you look at those strawberries isn't coming from the image. If you've grown up eating strawberries and spent a lifetime seeing strawberries as red, when you see the familiar shape of a strawberry, your brain assumes they *should* be red. The red you see in Kitaoka's illusion is generated internally, an assumption made after the fact and without your knowledge, a lie told to you by your visual system to provide you with what ought to be the truth.

Pascal figured the photo of *The Dress* must have been a rare, naturally occurring version of the same phenomenon. The image must have been overexposed, which made the truth ambiguous; people's brains were disambiguating it by "discounting the illuminant" they assumed was present, all without their knowledge.

The photo had been taken on a dreary day. It was taken with a cheap phone. One portion of the image was bright, and the other was dim. Pascal rushed through these details in a frenzied staccato, then asked, "So what does that tell us?"

"The lighting was ambiguous?" I offered.

"Exactly!" Pascal said, pushing on. He explained that the color that appeared in each brain was different depending on how each brain disambiguated the lighting conditions. For some, it disambiguated the ambiguous as black and blue and for others, white and gold. As with the strawberries, people's brains accomplished this by lying to them, by creating a lighting condition that wasn't there. What made this image different, he said, was that different brains told different lies, dividing people into two camps with incompatible subjective realities. But why were they so different?

Chasing that hypothesis, Pascal thought he had an answer. After two years of research with more than 10,000 participants, Pascal discovered a clear pattern among his subjects. The more time a person had spent exposed to artificial light (which is predominantly yellow)—typically a person who works indoors or at night—the more likely they were to say *The Dress* was black and blue. That was because they assumed, unconsciously, at the level of visual processing, that it was artificially lit, and thus their brains subtracted the yellow, leaving behind the darker, bluish shades. However, the more time a person had spent exposed to natural light—someone who works during the day, outside, or near windows—the more likely they were to subtract the blue and see it as white and gold. Either way—and this is the important point for us going forward—the ambiguity *never registered.*

Whatever colors people saw subjectively, the image never seemed ambiguous because consciously people experienced only the output of their processes, and the output differed depending on a person's prior experiences with light. The result was a lie told to them by their brains that felt obviously true.

Pascal's lab came up with a term for this. They call it SURFPAD. When you combine Substantial Uncertainty with Ramified (which means branching) or Forked Priors or Assumptions, you will get Disagreement.

In other words, when the truth is uncertain, our brains resolve that uncertainty without our knowledge by creating the most likely reality they can imagine based on our prior experiences. People whose brains remove that uncertainty in similar ways will find themselves in agreement, like those who saw the dress as black and blue. Others whose brains resolve that uncertainty in a different way will also find themselves in agreement, like those who saw the dress as white and gold. The essence of SURFPAD is that these two groups each feel certain, and among the

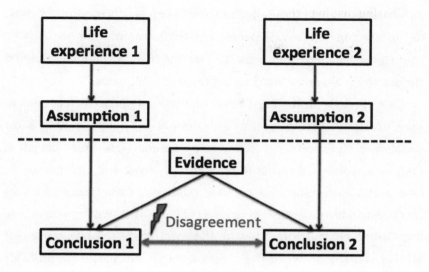

"Conclusions can be anything that the brain makes available to our conscious experience—percepts, decisions, interpretation[s]. Objects above [the] dashed line are often not consciously considered when evaluating the conclusions. Some of them might not be consciously accessible. Note that this is not the only possible difference between individuals. Arguably, it might be that the brains are also different from the very beginning. That is probably true, but we know next to nothing about that. Note that differing assumptions are sufficient to bring about differences in conclusions in this framework. That doesn't mean other factors couldn't matter as well. Also note that we consider two individuals here. Once more than two are involved, the situation would be more complicated yet."

(FROM *PASCAL'S PENSÉES*: HTTPS://PENSEES.PASCALLISCH.NET/?P=2153)

like-minded it seems those who disagree, no matter their numbers, must be mistaken. In both groups, people then begin searching for reasons why so many people in other groups can't see the truth without entertaining the possibility that they aren't seeing the truth themselves.

One example of SURFPAD in action was the different reactions to the COVID-19 vaccines as they rolled out to the public in 2020. Most people weren't experts on vaccines or epidemiology, so the information on how it worked and what to do was both novel and ambiguous. To resolve that uncertainty, people used their prior experiences with vaccines and doctors, their existing levels of trust in scientific institutions, and their current attitudes toward the government to make sense of it all. For some, that led to the conclusion that vaccines were probably safe and effective. For others, it led to a hesitancy that matured into suspicions of conspiracy. For both, the people who saw things differently seemed blind to the truth.

When we encounter novel information that seems ambiguous, we unknowingly disambiguate it based on what we've experienced in the past. But starting at the level of perception, different life experiences can lead to very different disambiguations, and thus very different subjective realities. When that happens in the presence of substantial uncertainty, we may vehemently disagree over reality itself—but since no one on either side is aware of the brain processes leading up to that disagreement, it makes the people who see things differently seem, in a word, wrong.

———

After his initial research into the effects of differing priors on the perception of ambiguous images, Pascal set out to test SURFPAD by recreating the phenomenon he had observed with *The Dress*.

In Pascal's home office, he showed me the crawlspace where he and his colleague Michael Karlovich conducted their research, a blacked-out area filled with Crocs of all colors, tube socks, various LED strips, and piles of paperwork, all evidence of the eureka moment that led to their mad dash through New York to find the raw materials they needed to build their cognitive nuclear bomb.

Swiveling in his office chair, he told me he called it a nuclear bomb because on the ladder of scientific understanding we always go from *description* to *explanation* to *prediction* to *creation*. For example, when it comes to grass, we first describe the types of grasses found in arid places, then create a taxonomy of them, then explain why they appear that way, and then we use that to predict what we might find in an as yet unexplored arid region. The final stage, creation, is only possible when we understand something so fully that we can re-create it in the lab.

We can't yet create grass from scratch, but we *can* create nuclear bombs. To summon something like a nuclear reaction, we had to truly understand the science behind its principles: *description* to *explanation* to *prediction* to *creation*. That's not to say there isn't still more to learn. There always is. But what it does say is that physics, in that regard, has gone way past prediction, which is not something you can say about much of psychology.

Pascal was passionate about this. He wanted the social sciences to go back to the beginning and conduct research in the same way that physics designs experiments. He thought the whole endeavor needed a reboot, a return to first principles. *The Dress* was an opportunity to do just that because it was only one, very unique image: Pascal was describing something that happened in a specific and possibly rare condition. To truly test his hypothesis, he would have to go up a level of scientific understanding.

And so, with the description and explanation of the science behind *The Dress* accomplished, he moved on to prediction and creation. He and Karlovich would build the cognitive equivalent of a nuclear bomb, with socks and Crocs.

To replicate *The Dress*, they needed to take a photo of something whose color was ambiguous: if you saw a black-and-white image of it, you would recognize it, but you would have to guess its color based on your unconscious priors. Then they needed some way to differentially cue people with lighting. Different experiences with light, different guesses, different realities. Karlovich's research background was in color vision, so he hypothesized that if they paired an ambiguously colored object with another whose color seemed obvious, people would use the seemingly unambiguous color as a lighting cue to disambiguate the other.

Karlovich spent weeks trying to find an object that could satisfy both ideas. He tried all sorts of things, from eggs—thinking, thanks to Dr. Seuss, some people would assume they were yellow and others green—to fake flamingos, which maybe some people would see as white and others as pink. Nothing worked, until one day he remembered a time in grad school when he was helping a friend grow some plants in a grow house lit only by green-tinted grow lights.

Karlovich explained that green plants absorb most of the wavelengths of visible light, but reflect back some of the ones that the brain interprets as green, which bounce back into the eyes. So if you use a green light of a specific wavelength to grow them, green plants react as if they were in darkness. Green plants can't "see" green. That way, you can work under green lights during an artificial nighttime without disturbing the plants' circadian rhythms. He had been hanging out with someone doing just that when he noticed something unusual. His friend was wearing Crocs that Karlovich assumed were gray because they appeared gray under the green grow house lights. But outside in the sunlight they appeared pink. The weird thing, the thing that boggled his mind, was that when they went back inside, they *now looked pink*! He could no longer see them the way he had just minutes before, and they never switched back.

As a color scientist, he had a solid guess as to what was happening. If you illuminate pink Crocs in only green light, they will appear gray. That's because they aren't bouncing back any pink light. Under sunlight though, which contains pink wavelengths, you see their true color. The fact that the Crocs didn't go back to gray in his mind when he went back inside the grow house meant that although objective reality hadn't changed, his subjective reality had. The in-between steps in his processing were doing something new. Like with the strawberries illusion, because he now expected the Crocs to be pink, he *saw* them as pink even though those wavelengths of light weren't actually entering his eyes. While looking for an object that could stand in for *The Dress*, something equally perceptually ambiguous, he recalled the weirdness of his grow house experience, and the answer seemed obvious. Visit a local Walmart or Home Depot and you'll see socks paired with Crocs, and most people wear white socks. That was the solution: socks. But not socks alone, socks and Crocs combined.

This was the idea: if they got some pink Crocs and paired them with white socks, then illuminated both with green light, the Crocs would appear gray, like they had in the grow house; but the socks would reflect the green light back and appear green. If you thought the socks had been dyed green, you would surmise nothing was amiss with the lighting and accept the image without editing it. However, if you expected the socks to be white and saw them as such, your brain, without your knowledge, would then edit the image by subtracting the green-tinted overexposure while adding back the pink hues to the shoes. If Karlovich and Pascal were right, depending on what people unconsciously assumed, they would disagree on what they saw.

Once they settled on this hypothesis, they went store to store all over Manhattan buying what they needed, then took everything to Pascal's crawlspace where Karlovich donned the socks and Crocs while Pascal photographed them under green grow lights. They then showed the photos to subjects and asked them what they saw. The results? It worked exactly as they thought it would. Some people saw gray Crocs and green socks, and others saw pink Crocs and white socks. Like with *The Dress*, if subjects saw it one way, they couldn't see it the other.

They had their nuclear bomb. They had created from scratch something that before that moment only appeared in nature in about one in ten billion photographs. That alone would be a triumph, as far as scientific methodology and experimental design are concerned, but for Pascal and Karlovich this was evidence, at the level of neurons, that SURFPAD was true, because there was something deeper in the data: older people were more likely to see the Crocs as pink, and younger people were more likely to see them as gray.

Why? Because older people have had more life experiences with white socks, so that's what they expected to see. That's what socks are *supposed* to look like, and so they disambiguated the ambiguous to make them so. Their brains then assumed the lighting was green, which meant the Crocs must be pink in real life. Since younger people have had more experiences with colored socks, their priors told them the socks *actually were green*, and so they saw the image without any unconscious editing.

Pascal brought up the image on a giant television hanging from a wall above his treadmill deck in his office at NYU and said, "If you take what is hitting your retina at face value, you see gray, but older people say, 'Oh no. I know what these are! I've seen these before, they must be white! This light must be white. So, they unconsciously subtract green from the entire image, and it turns the Crocs pink in their minds."

Complicating all this is the fact that the Crocs *are* pink in natural light, so the people who saw them as pink were seeing the actual truth *behind the image*. But since there are no pink pixels *in* the image, the people who saw them as gray were seeing the truth *of the photo*. Same image, two truths, depending on your prior experiences with tube socks. So which subjective truth would we consider the truest truth out of the two?

Pascal was feverish about the implications. Neither side was right nor wrong, so arguing for only one side or the other wouldn't arrive at a deeper understanding: that objective reality and subjective realities can differ. Only the two truths combined, the combination of shared perspectives, would alert people there was a deeper truth, and only through conversation would they have any hope of solving the mystery.

"One's beliefs can demonstrably color perception," he cheekily explained when writing about the research. "We derived a principle underlying the nature of disagreement," he added, allowing scientists to create disagreements like these in the future, "and—in turn—understand how disagreement comes about in general." The white sock group didn't update their priors; instead, they made what they saw fit into their existing model. They saw what they expected to see. If anything, the socks and Crocs illusion strengthened their assumptions.

Pascal spent the better half of my final afternoon with him and Karlovich running through why what they proved with socks and Crocs was vital to understanding how and why people do and do not change their minds when presented with evidence alone. They believe it literally sheds light on other kinds of polarized disagreements surrounding politics, conspiracy theories, current events, and science denial.

"There are more than thirty steps in visual processing before an image reaches consciousness," Pascal said. You are only aware of the result, not the processes. At no point in processing the image of *The Dress* did anyone feel the uncertainty that led to their disambiguation. It's the fact that uncertainty is eliminated so stealthily—that these processes are both unconscious and undebatable—that leads to our most intractable disputes. When our differing experiences and motivations cause us to disambiguate differently, we can't help but disagree with great certainty. But when we disagree in this way we don't know *why* we are disagreeing. The result is that we argue endlessly over our subjectivity to convince one another of something that doesn't feel subjective; it feels like the raw, unfiltered, unassailable truth.

In psychology, there's a term for this cognitive blind spot, for when your disambiguations feel undeniably true. It's called naive realism, and it's the belief that you perceive the world as it truly is, free from assumption, interpretation, bias, or the limitations of your senses. The late psychologist Lee Ross, who helped popularize the term, told me that it leads many of us to believe we arrived at our beliefs, attitudes, and values after careful, rational analysis through unmediated thoughts and perceptions. Unaware that different priors can lead to different disambiguations, you believe you've been mainlining pure reality for years, and it was your intense study of the bare facts that naturally led to all of your conclusions. According to Ross, this is why people on each side of any debate believe their side is the only one rooted in reality.

When disambiguations collide, like with *The Dress*, people find it difficult to understand how the other side could possibly see things differently when the evidence seems obvious they should.

———

Pascal and Karlovich explained in one of their papers why this work was so important: "The degree of polarization concerning current events is at an all-time high." A study by Pew Research confirms this. According to its findings, "Republicans and Democrats are more divided along ideological lines—and partisan antipathy is deeper and more extensive—than at any point in the last two decades."

From climate change to fracking to election fraud to health-care reform, it can feel like people are living in completely separate realities. Nowhere has this been more starkly represented than in the partisan divide over COVID-19. According to polling by Pew in the United States, nearly 75 percent of Republicans said the government had done a great job handling the pandemic during the worst months of the outbreak, whereas only 30 percent of Democrats and independents agreed. Once Democrats took over the White House, anti-maskers would literally clash with mask supporters, and the vaccine-hesitant argued with those pushing for vaccination, sometimes on their deathbeds, over their differing interpretations of reality itself.

Discussing the implications of their research, Pascal and Karlovich said that science needed "to understand disagreement better in order to avoid disagreeable results." The problem with studying political disagreement, however, is that even though the result seems simple—two ideological camps on two ends of a spectrum of belief—the many nested systems of human interaction that produce that result are immensely complex. The full explanation for interpretation polarization requires a gestalt understanding of not just politics, but the psychology of reasoning, motivation, social rewards, social costs, norms, beliefs, attitudes, and values, not just at the level of the human interaction, but within individual brains, right down to neurons, hormones, and ganglia.

"One viable research strategy to circumvent this problem is to explore perceptual disagreements instead," wrote Pascal and Karlovich in their socks and Crocs research. "These are arguably sufficiently free of preconceptions—innocent enough—that people are open-minded to the outcomes of such research. Fortuitously, we were blessed with *The Dress*—an image that evokes vehement disagreement about perception."

———

The first lesson of *The Dress* is that our disagreements begin at the level of perceptual assumptions, because all reality is virtual; but it doesn't stop at perceptual disagreement. As Pascal said, since the world inside a person's head is a collection of their experiences in the world so far, a hierarchy of increasingly illusory abstractions we call beliefs, attitudes, and values, "the same principles that govern perception are those that underlie conceptual disagreement."

It was here that one of the central mysteries began to seem much less mysterious, why the facts that worked on Charlie Veitch didn't work on the other truthers—or the conspiratorial community that eventually excommunicated him. It would become even more clear when, as you will see in coming pages, I began to understand how cultural forces and motivated cognition are at play when people with different models meet and try to disambiguate something they both find ambiguous.

When faced with uncertainty, we often don't notice we are uncertain, and when we attempt to resolve that uncertainty, we don't just fall back on our different perceptual priors; we reach for them, motivated by identity and belonging needs, social costs, issues of trust and reputation, and so on.

Psychologists call this a frame contest when the facts are agreed upon (mass shootings are a problem) but the interpretation of those facts is not (it's because of X / no, it's because of Y).

As SURFPAD predicts, this is why we so often disagree on matters that, on both sides, seem obvious. Unaware of the processing that leads to such disagreement, it will feel like a battle over reality itself, over the truth of our own eyes. Disagreements like these often turn into disagreements between groups because people with broadly similar experiences and motivations tend to disambiguate in broadly similar ways, and whether they find one another online or in person, the fact that trusted peers see things their way can feel like all the proof they need: they are right and the other side is wrong factually, morally, or otherwise.

"Introducing challenging evidence does not change their beliefs. If anything, it strengthens them," explained Pascal. "This might appear puzzling, but makes complete sense in a SURFPAD framework." He said to imagine a trusted news source continuously paints a political figure in a bad light. If another news source paints them in a positive light, the brain doesn't update. Instead, it would do just as it did with his white socks. It will assume the lighting is off and delete it, and subjectively it will feel like objectivity.

That leads us to the second lesson. Since subjectivity feels like objectivity, naive realism makes it seem as though the way to change people's minds is to show them the facts that support your view, because anyone else who has read the things you have read or seen the things you have seen will naturally see things your way, given that they've pondered the matter as thoughtfully as you have. Therefore, you assume that anyone who disagrees with your conclusions probably just doesn't have all the facts yet. If they did, they'd already be seeing the world like you do. This is why you continue to ineffectually copy and paste links from all our most trusted sources when arguing your points with those who seem misguided, crazy, uninformed, and just plain wrong. The problem is that this is exactly what the other side thinks will work on you.

The truth is that we are always reaching our conclusions through disambiguation, but all of that work is done in our different brains without us knowing it. We just experience, in consciousness, the result. You think you are experiencing the world as it truly is, and when a lot of people are sure their version of reality is the really real version at the same time that a lot of other people are sure that no, in fact, *their* version is, you get arguments that break the internet (like *The Dress*), but also the Inquisition, the Hundred Years' War, QAnon, and anti-mask protests during global pandemics.

———

In his office, Pascal let me hold *The Dress*. I could see in person that it was obviously black and blue, but I now wasn't so sure. Pascal was happy that I wasn't sure anymore. He considered it a form of enlightenment.

A man of science, Pascal is a person for whom conclusions based on supporting evidence are the only conclusions worth considering. Being open to the fact that our current models could be wrong, that the current interpretation is just that, an interpretation, leaves people open to changing their mind when new evidence calls our current understanding into question.

But Pascal also shares his namesake with Blaise Pascal, the seventeenth-century philosopher whose quips about arguing were published posthumously in a book called *Pensées*. In one, he wrote, "Now, no one is offended at not seeing everything; but one does not like to be mistaken, and that perhaps arises from the fact that man naturally cannot see everything, and that naturally he cannot err in the side he looks at, since the perceptions of our senses are always true." Then he added, "People are generally better persuaded by the reasons which they have themselves discovered than by those which have come into the mind of others."

Pascal agrees with Pascal. In fact, he named his own personal blog *Pascal's Pensées* in his honor.

"We need a SURFPADified discourse, a culture where everyone understands, or at least many understand, what's going on," he said, folding up *The Dress* and retrieving the pair of pink Crocs they used in their research. "Did you know that we can't perceive the third dimension?" I knew it was a rhetorical question, so I set down the Crocs and opened my notebook.

Pascal explained that the surface of the retina is two-dimensional, a flat sheet. We receive light in only two dimensions, and then the brain constructs the third dimension from familiar cues, from all the experiences in childhood when we reached out for distant objects, bumped our head on near ones, and so on. Like the yellow of a lemon, the third dimension is always an illusion. It has always been, and always will be, all in our heads. It's why we can watch 3D movies and make realistic paintings. Artists re-create familiar visual cues, and our experience helps us construct a representation inside our minds, all of which, in essence, is a lie that the brain uses to tell us the truth.

The brain must make assumptions to navigate an uncertain world, Pascal said. That usually serves us well; in fact, it has served us well for millions of years. The problems arise when we over-apply those assumptions. He compared it to blindly accepting whatever autocorrect suggested while typing out a text.

"We need to transcend that. We need to be able to say, 'I am subject to SURFPAD, you are subject to SURFPAD.' If we can do that, we go to a meta level. 'What are my priors? What are my assumptions? Do we have different priors? Do we have different assumptions?' And maybe then we can come to some kind of understanding where that person is coming from. Because I used to see a lot of, quite frankly, shocking takes on social media. But now instead of engaging with them, I don't say anything, because when I did try to engage, I made them even worse. So, I think we need a new culture of disagreement. A culture of SURFPAD."

I think Pascal is onto something. After all, scientific ideas like these have changed our conception of ourselves many times. The Copernican Revolution, evolution by natural selection, the germ theory of disease, moving the seat of consciousness from the soul to the brain, the advent of psychology itself making us aware of unconscious forces driving our thinking, feeling, and behavior—have all provided us with the tools to second-guess our most useful, but sometimes very wrong, assumptions. In my most Pollyanna moments I can imagine some future version of ourselves in which SURFPADification could improve our discourse in an always on, always connected, flattened world where all the information is always available all the time, making everything uncertain and everything ambiguous. A world where the truth exists, but trust is hard to come by.

Pascal and Karlovich's research suggests that simply presenting challenging evidence is not enough. We must meet in ways that allow us to ask and understand how people arrived at their conclusions. We must see that other people are using different priors and processes, so that we can see what seems certain to us seems certain to others in a different way. We must accept that we live in different communities, even online, with different problems and goals and motivations and concerns, and most of all, we have had different experiences. We must admit if we had experienced what others have, we might even agree with them.

Contentious issues are contentious because we are disambiguating them differently, unconsciously, and not by choice. If we can see that, it can lead to something Pascal and others at NYU are calling "cognitive empathy": an understanding that what others experience as the truth arrives in their minds unconsciously, so arguments over conclusions are often a waste of time. The better path, they said, would be for both parties to focus on their processing, on *how* and *why* they see what they see, not *what*. The science behind how brains go about updating their priors suggests this is true; in fact, it's how we've overcome every hurdle our species has ever faced. It's literally how minds change. But there's a catch, and that's what we are going to explore in the next chapter.

Pascal and Karlovich's next experiment will be trying to see if the people who see white socks and pink Crocs are given some other information ahead of time, will that allow them to see the image as it truly is? They want to see if people can be taught to see the Crocs differently, to circumvent their own assumptions—in other words, they are going to try to change people's minds by exposing them to new things. They hypothesize that it shouldn't take an entire lifetime of new experiences to realize you might be wrong, to realize you need to update your priors and gain a new perspective. Pascal said, "They need to experience something that will make it unambiguously clear what the light is."

I told Pascal that I was planning on spending some time with former members of cults, hate groups, and conspiracy theory communities.

Based on what I'd read, people often leave groups like those not because their beliefs are directly challenged, but because something totally outside of the ideology causes them to see it differently.

Pascal interrupted. "So that's the strategy, then. You have to open the crack to let in the light."

4

DISEQUILIBRIUM

After spending time with Pascal Wallisch and the neuroscientists at NYU, I believed I had an adequate grasp of how minds form. The brain, trapped in a black box, slowly, effortfully constructs a model of reality that over time gets better at predicting and explaining the regularities in its environment that have excited some neural pathways and not others. Our experiences in the world begin with shapes and sounds and colors, and as we become increasingly better at perceiving them, we interact with objects around us and begin to categorize them. Later, when we are old enough, with the help of others who have already gone through this process, we add language. At first, we associate the currently agreed-upon sounds with the aspects of reality they describe, and then we learn lines that represent those sounds on paper, and off we go learning about things we may never directly experience, except through books about Paraguay and podcasts about serial killers and movies about teddy bears that can talk.

But what happens when we realize that what we thought was true is, in fact, false? What happens when we learn something new that contradicts something old? What happens when we confront arguments that disagree with our worldviews? What happens when we experience something that calls into question an attitude that once guided our values? Now that I had a better understanding how minds are made, I wanted to understand how minds *change*.

———

How we settle on what is and is not true is a two-thousand-year-old conversation, one that has led people smarter than me to set aside the pursuit and go live in cabins where they could focus on needlepoint and perfecting their pancakes.

To avoid that, instead of getting deep into the philosophy of knowledge, we will focus mostly on psychology and neuroscience. That's not to say that philosophy isn't worth our time; it's just that if you've ever picked up a book on epistemology, the study of how we know things, it might take several hundred pages to explore how we determine whether free will is an illusion and yet still not reach a satisfying conclusion. We can escape the semantics, somewhat, by spending more time looking at how brains generate the foundations of those semantics.

As we touched on earlier, information encoded in the brain is the on-and-off firing of neurons. It's written onto a living substrate, but zoomed in it's as neutral as words printed on a page.

When we say the brain stores information, it just means that when the brain interacts with the outside world through its senses, or when it interacts with itself through thinking, the process at the deepest level is physical. Chemical and electrical activity rearranges molecules and atoms in your head, and the brain before an interaction is physically different than a brain after. When you listen to a song, meet a dog, have an argument about mustard, connections between neurons are strengthened, weakened, pruned, and altered so that the brain is no longer the same shape and arrangement of very tiny parts as it was before those events.

How does that translate to information? Just as when you press a mark on a page with a pen or press an emblem into a wax, the physical form of that which is shaped changes. As senses respond to the natural world, they deliver signals to the brain, and those signals alter the brain's physical structure. Like a foot pressed into mud or a mark burned into wood, a cause leads to an effect, and the effect carries with it information. Add some biological machines to notice the information, some others to notice the patterns within it, some others to notice the patterns in the patterns, and you have the making of a mind.

These patterns can also help us to discover truths hidden between them. Psychologist Steven Pinker created a thought experiment to demonstrate this.

Imagine sawing down a tree, Pinker begins, then imagine a machine that could sense the rings in the stump. For each ring, it makes a mark. Five rings, five marks. The pattern in the rings is now encoded elsewhere.

He then asks us to imagine a second machine that could produce truth without "thinking." Here is how it would work: the second machine would sense the rings on a stump and make a mark for each one. Five rings, five marks. Then it senses the rings on a second, smaller stump. Three rings, three marks.

If we added a feature to the machine so that for each ring it sensed on the smaller stump it would then sand off the marks it had made for the larger one, we'd have subtraction. Five rings minus three rings leaves behind two rings. And this purely mechanical process would produce a hidden truth.

The rings correspond to years, the marks correspond to rings, so the two marks after subtraction correspond to how old the larger tree was when the smaller tree was planted: two years old. But we can go further. Since the rings are also a cause left behind by an effect, in this case the dark and light circles left behind as a tree grows fatter over the course of a single orbit of the Earth around the sun, the marks also correspond with two orbits. After the first tree was planted, the Earth traveled around the sun two times before the second tree sprouted. All of this would be true not because the machine was "itself intelligent or rational" but because it produced a "chain of ordinary physical events, whose first link was a configuration of matter that carries information."

That's what is happening in the brain. It continuously "burns marks" into neurons to match the patterns it senses in the world outside, along with a continuous sanding away of those marks as it recognizes other patterns. The brain encompasses many biological machines, and each can translate the correlations they discover into changes within a shared network of neurons. It then alters its behavior based on those internal changes. If those behaviors make it more successful, the neural patterns get stronger; if not, they get weaker.

Over time, the forces of natural selection favored biological machines that could better sense correlations and respond to them. In short, creatures with nervous systems that encode information, then compare and contrast correlations, became better at using that information to survive, thrive, and reproduce. Stimulus and response organisms like spiders and worms emerged from single-celled and free-floating jelly predecessors that moved toward rewards and away from danger.

Generation after generation, that process produced even better biological machines with even better senses and even better responses.

In time, second-order machines rose out of the first-order. They could read the information inside themselves as if noticing patterns in the outside world. And they could make use of those patterns on different levels, translating correlations into inferences and predictions, both of which led to better success when searching for resources and avoiding threats.

On it went, until the first complex nervous systems emerged. As the biological machines built on top of one another shared and cross-referenced information, a complexity materialized that gave rise to intelligence, evaluation, and planning. Entities emerged that could, in pursuit of goals like not starving and not getting eaten, make decisions and judgments in moments of uncertainty based on how novel information compared to information already encoded. In other words, life *learned* how to *learn*. According to neuroscience, that's what mind change really is: a learning machine incessantly and simultaneously burning in and sanding away encoded information.

In complex organisms, survival depends on predicting what will happen next based on what happened before. It may seem odd, but our ability to notice errors in those predictions depends on dopamine, a neurotransmitter crucial for regulating motivation. As neuroscientist Mark Humphries puts it, the brain rests in a "soup" of dopamine, and from one moment to the next the concentration of the soup influences how motivated you feel to remain on task or abandon it for another. When the chemistry in our brains that keeps us at work, keeps us studying, keeps us watching a movie or standing in line or holding up our end of a conversation shifts, we then feel unmotivated and ready to move to something else. Or, in the case of something like scrolling social media or playing a video game or gambling, we may feel a motivation to stay on task at the expense of other motivations, keeping us focused and engaged.

Within this system for motivation, dopamine affects the feelings that arise when outcomes don't match our expectations, and varying dopamine levels then motivate us to notice, learn, and adjust our predictions going forward.

For instance, if you took a flight to Iceland, and at the baggage claim you learned the airport offers free ice cream for arriving passengers, a spike in dopamine would bring your attention to an unexpected positive outcome. You become motivated to add a new behavior to your routines and choose that airport in the future. But if you had chosen that airport before and chose it again specifically for their complimentary ice cream at baggage claim, your dopamine would remain stable. Since your experience matched your predictions, you would likely maintain that behavior. However, if you had expected ice cream, and you learned upon arrival that the airport had discontinued the service, you would experience a dip in dopamine thanks to the unexpected negative outcome, and as a result you might not choose that airport again.

As psychologist Michael Rousell told me, when experiences don't match our expectations, a spike in dopamine lasting about a millisecond motivates us to stop whatever we were doing and pay attention. After the surprise, we become motivated to learn from the new experience so we can be less wrong in the future. For our ancestors, he said, "surprise meant imminent danger or enormous opportunity, but thinking about it instead of acting on it meant you might succumb to the danger or miss out on the opportunity, and either could remove you from the gene pool."

When our models don't match our experiences, whether it's an unexpected party waiting behind our front door or a missing hamburger in our take-out bag, surprises encourage us to update our behaviors. They change our minds without us noticing as the brain quietly updates our predictive schemas, hopefully eliminating the surprise by making it more predictable in the future.

All subjective reality is constructed in this way, in layers of patterns and predictive schemas, but thanks to brain plasticity, that construction project never ends. Like neuronal masons constantly adding rooms to a cathedral of confidence, our brains are continuously deconstructing and rebuilding our models of reality from one moment to the next to make sense of novelty and surprise. Our minds are always changing and updating, writing and editing. And thanks to this plasticity, so much of what we consider real and unreal, true and untrue, good and bad, moral and immoral, changes as we learn things we didn't know we didn't know.

As *you* will learn in this chapter, the brain isn't just a jangling bag of beliefs and associations. This process of burning and sanding may start at the senses, but it leads to a hierarchy of abstractions. At the bottom, raw sensations like shapes and sounds and colors. In the middle, concrete constructs like caterpillars and calliopes. At the top, higher concepts like humility and hurricanes. Each level depends on the levels beneath to make sense of the levels above.

Most of the time when we learn new things, we merely tidy up this hierarchy, but on occasion the ongoing project demands major expansions. For instance, if you learn a new way to cook chicken, you merely add the recipe to your repertoire. You *assimilate* what you've learned and then apply it to other recipes, including those that don't pertain to poultry.

The hierarchy remains as it was before, with some minor updates. But if you visit a factory farm and witness chickens with extra legs eating chickens with no legs at all, you may feel compelled to make a major update to *accommodate* what you've witnessed.

It's these two processes, assimilation and accommodation, that drive all mind change, and we have the great psychologist Jean Piaget to thank for this way of making sense of how brains create and interact with knowledge. But before we can dig into them, it seems appropriate to back up one more time before we move on and run through a quick refresher on what it means to *know*, well, anything.

———

In philosophy, the idea of "knowing" something doesn't mean *believing* that you know something. It means knowing something that also happens to be true. For instance, if you believe that if you simultaneously flush one toilet in Australia and another in Canada the two waters will spin in opposite directions, well, that's not knowledge, because it's not true. The spin of a flush is always the result of where the water first starts flowing in that particular bowl, so if you believe otherwise, it doesn't count as knowledge, just belief. To philosophers, beliefs and knowledge are separate, because you can believe things that are false.

The problem with trying to answer the question of how we determine whether something is the truth comes from the fact that we must answer how we determine our definition of truth itself is true. This is why there are about 2,600 ways to parse the verb *know*, and by the time you finish a degree in philosophy, you can't help but see a chair as more of a collection of beliefs and ideas than an arrangement of wood and upholstery.

This is where the term *post-truth* starts to seem rather silly, because philosophically for about two thousand years or so no one has been able to agree on what the word *truth* even means. We can't be in a post-truth world if we never lived in a truth-filled paradise to begin with. And for millennia we've been debating not only what *is* the truth, but how we go about determining it. The only way out of this loop has been to study how we come to agree on facts in general, the academic discipline known as epistemology.

Epistemology is the study of knowledge itself—facts, fictions, rationalizations, justifications, rationality, logic—all of it. Well before we had a word for it, this was the central concern of philosophy itself. Before we had microscopes and lasers, one could make a living by thinking deeply about the matter until you had created yet another epistemology to add to others in open competition for the best way to identify a fact. That's what an epistemology is: a framework for sorting out what is true. Given how difficult this can be, one can empathize with people who get locked into arguments online about whether hotdogs are sandwiches and, by extension, with people who argue over whether the Earth is flat, or that 9/11 was an inside job.

Most psychological and philosophical musings on the topic agree that knowledge comes in roughly two forms. We can know *that*. Pudding exists and trees are tall, yesterday it rained, tomorrow is Sunday. This is declarative knowledge. We can also know *how*: the method behind break dancing or changing a tire. This is procedural knowledge. In either case, if someone makes a claim to some form of knowledge, the way that claim was tested for a very long time was through the use of propositions.

Propositions are neither true nor false, just claims that could go either way. Someone uses a sentence to state something that could be true, such as "Patrick Swayze played James Bond in *A View to a Kill*." Then that proposition is challenged by asking for its justification. In this case, the evidence suggests that James Bond was played by several actors, none of which was Swayze. Then by the standards of propositions, this one is not justified. Therefore, it is false.

Propositions also allow for what is called propositional logic. "There are 1.2 million stray dogs in Houston. Houston is a city in Texas. Therefore, there are more than 1.2 million stray dogs in Texas." Sometimes, however, even when the evidence presented is verifiable and the logic is sound, you can't depend on a proposition to reach a definite conclusion. For instance, if you claim that all swans are white, and if your justification is that all the swans you've ever seen have been that color, all it would take is one black swan to prove your claim false. In this case, your claim would still be a belief, one you might hold in high confidence, but since there might be a black swan out there you've never seen, it doesn't count as knowledge, philosophically speaking.

In the end, epistemology is about translating evidence into confidence. By taking what we believe and then sorting through some kind of system for arranging, organizing, and classifying it against the available evidence, our certainty in a truth should go up or down. But some ways of sorting out what the hell is going on are better than others, depending on what it is you want to know. In one epistemological framework, we might reach a degree of confidence that suggests the moon controls the tides. In another, we might grow ever more certain it controls our dreams.

Thankfully for us, when it comes to the empirical truth, the epistemology called science seems to have won out, since it is the only one that can build iPhones and vaccines. Sometime in the 1600s, we developed the scientific method to test our fact-based beliefs and reach consensus on what is empirically true among what is observable and measurable. In science, you treat all your conclusions as maybes, and instead of thinking deeply using propositions or meditating using peyote, you spend time creating tightly controlled experiments. Then you use the outcomes to create piles of evidence for your many competing hypotheses. The piles that grow very large become theories, and together they become models that predict how future experiments will turn out. As long as those experiments continue to turn out the same way, the models hold. When they don't, you update the model.

Science, as an epistemology, is great for things that depend on facts alone. Why is the sky blue? Where does oil come from? When it comes to questions about the best policies and politics, about morality and ethics, science can only advise other epistemologies. But the philosophy of the scientific method works in those domains as well, from its insistence that we should always work to disconfirm our conclusions and those of others instead of confirming them, which is what we would usually rather do.

Before we explore the science behind why we would rather confirm our conclusions, I want to look again at the overlap of philosophy, psychology, and neuroscience. In these matters, where they seem to overlap is that raw sensory information, and the thoughts we think about it, doesn't really count as knowledge until we think in terms of conditions.

Conditions allow us to create rules not only for what is true, but also for what isn't true, and that offers us the ability to use a very important word: *wrong*. With conditions, we can be wrong about all sorts of things, not just geometry and how to make lasagna, but what is good and bad, just and unjust.

For instance, we can't refer to something as a square until we agree on what conditions must be met to call it that. We might say something like, "If a two-dimensional figure has four equal sides and four right angles, then it is square." Now if someone looks at a triangle and tells us it is a square, we can say they are wrong. More importantly, we can move up a level from a square by having it serve as a feature in a more complex idea. Once you have a definition for four equal sides in two dimensions, you can then refer to a cube as an object comprised of six equal squares in three dimensions.

Once you have cubes, you can use them as building blocks of other objects in the third dimension and lay down an entirely new layer of agreed-upon concepts. Those concepts become parts of larger concepts, and eventually you can debate abstractions like justice and make sense of phenomena like tectonic plates. At the highest levels, each idea depends on the layers of agreed-upon sets of conditions that support it, and each layer itself depends on layers below as evidence that they are factually correct and, therefore, knowledge.

The only problem is that, after doing all this for so long, we know a whole lot, but we still don't know how much we don't know. Worse still, we also don't know that we don't know that we don't know. Since we can only create a consensus reality out of what we *do* know, or *believe* we know, when wildly incorrect we often have no way of knowing. In both individual minds and groups of minds that agree, to paraphrase the Pulitzer Prize–winning science writer Kathryn Schulz, until we know we are wrong, being wrong feels exactly like being right.

———

Since the brain doesn't know what it doesn't know, when it constructs causal narratives it fills holes in reality with provisional explanations.

The problem is that when a group of brains all uses the same place-holder, good-enough-for-now construal to plug such a hole, over time that shared provisional explanation can turn into consensus—a *common* sense of what is and is not true. This tendency has led to a lot of strange shared beliefs over the centuries, consensus realities that today seem preposterous. For instance, for a very long time most people believed that geese grew on trees.

Centuries ago, people often found a certain type of barnacle floating on driftwood. It featured a long tube that extended out of a white shell

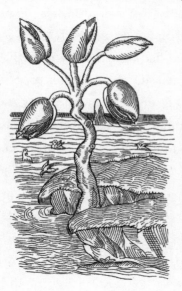

with a smidge of yellow streaked down the side, and for at least seven hundred years, people across medieval Europe thought that this barnacle was some kind of proto-goose, because it looked somewhat like the necks and heads of the familiar geese that lived in the same area where the barnacles regularly appeared. Nature texts going back to the 1100s describe mysterious goose trees with odd fruits from which, they said, birds would form, hatch, dangle, detach, and fly away.

Of course, geese don't grow on trees. So why did just about everyone believe they did for such a long time? The answer is that they didn't know what they didn't know, and what they didn't know in particular was that some of the geese that lived along the marshes in Britain migrated to breed and lay their eggs. For the people of the 1100s and earlier, migration was still an unknown unknown. They didn't even consider it as an option. Since we can build models of reality only out of the materials at hand, they built a model out of what they *did* know, or at least what they thought they knew. They made a leap, one that seemed perfectly realistic at the time. They reasoned that the drift-wood must have come from a fallen branch. They inferred that the weird stuff attached must have been a goose bud that wasn't finished growing into a full-grown goose when it fell from the goose tree.

At the time, spontaneous generation was an accepted truth, a part of everyone's shared model of reality. People believed that rotting meat gave birth to flies and that piles of dirty rags could transform into mice and that burning logs created salamanders. Most everything else came from slime or muck. A tree that sprouted bird buds seemed reasonable, especially if after five hundred years you had never seen any of that bird's eggs. Learned monks who had supposedly recorded this process further solidified the belief. To prove it, they drew the mysterious goose trees and the strange growth process in illustrations that made it into some very nice-looking books. Those same monks also claimed you could eat a barnacle goose during Lent because it wasn't a bird. The belief was well-established and quite popular because in 1215 Pope Innocent III announced that, although everyone knew they grew on trees, the church still strictly prohibited the eating of barnacle geese, effectively closing the loophole created by those wily monks.

Most people had no personal evidence for goose trees, so they trusted the authorities on the matter. It was received wisdom. They were wrong, but being wrong didn't really affect their lives in any meaningful way, so the myth persisted until sometime in the 1600s when explorers in Greenland discovered the birds' nesting sites. That was the first anomaly. Then, when people started poking around inside the weird buds, a second set of anomalies appeared. Ray Lankester writes in his 1915 book *Diversions of a Naturalist* that the belief died out at the beginning of the seventeenth century "when the structure of the barnacle lying within its shell was examined without prejudice, and it was seen to have only the most remote resemblance to a bird." Today we call these two creatures the barnacle goose and the goose barnacle, remnants of a belief that once lived in every brain in that region but today exists in none.

Old consensus realities—great wolves that chase the sun and moon into the horizon; the humeric model of medicine in which all health was the result of a proper balance of black bile, yellow bile, blood, and phlegm; the geocentric model of the universe with a sky enclosed in concentric, celestial, crystal spheres that explained how the sun, moon, stars, and planets moved; the miasmic theory of disease, in which all illness was the result of over-smelling the noxious vapors of things that stink—these didn't seem unreasonable from the inside. Like any outdated worldview, they seem nonsensical only in hindsight, and like all worldviews, though wrong, the people who used them to navigate their daily lives refused to give them up without a fight.

The belief in the barnacle goose didn't immediately evaporate because a few naturalists found evidence to the contrary. At first, people assimilated. They interpreted the evidence as confirmation of what they already thought they understood. It took the addition of novel, disconfirmatory information, a series of anomalies from multiple sources that couldn't be explained by the existing model, before beliefs like goose trees gave way to new explanations.

Perusing the history of science, the philosopher Thomas Kuhn and cognitive psychologist Jean Piaget both noticed, at around the same time, that superseded scientific theories like goose trees revealed something fundamental about how minds do and do not change, which led to two mental models to explain mental models themselves. For Kuhn, "the paradigm shift." For Piaget, the two psychological mechanisms mentioned earlier, "assimilation" and "accommodation." I favor Piaget, but both will guide our exploration for the rest of this book. To understand them, let's look at how this same sort of anomaly overload takes place in the minds of individuals.

———

In 1949, two psychologists at Harvard, Jerome S. Bruner and Leo Postman, created an experiment using playing cards to test people's ability to update their models.

They flashed single images of single cards on a screen. For each slide, the scientists asked the subject to identify the cards they saw, to name each one out loud, then press a button to move to the next slide, revealing another. "Black ace of clubs." *Click.* "Red three of diamonds." *Click.* And so on.

The subjects didn't know that mixed into those cards the scientists had planted some anomalies, cards they had never seen before. Occasionally, the color and suit were switched, black hearts and red spades, for example. At first, subjects didn't notice the novel cards. They called out their names as if they were normal and familiar. But unbeknownst to the subjects, their brains noticed something was off, and their response times grew longer and longer the more often an anomalous card appeared.

The scientists gradually increased the number of anomalies as they ran the subjects through more cards, shuffling a greater number of fake ones into the mix. Most subjects continued to misidentify the anomalies as normal, but they also began to mention feeling some discomfort. Upon viewing a wrong-color card, they often said it seemed grayish brown, blackish red, or even purple. They felt like something was off, but they couldn't put their fingers on what, and their response times began to stall as they pondered their confusion.

When the scientists mixed in even more wrong-color cards, some subjects began to experience what the scientists called a "perceptual crisis." When a fake card appeared, half of the subjects said things like "I'll be damned if I know now whether it's red or what!" or "It didn't even look like a card that time" or "I'm not even sure now what a spade looks like! My God!"

Finally, after some extended cognitive squirming, the subjects reached what Bruner and Postman called "the shock of recognition." In a sudden, thrilling epiphany, they realized that some of the cards had been manipulated. That's why they seemed so strange. They sighed in relief. "Oh! The cards are the wrong color!" And from that point on, instead of trying to make the anomalies match their expectations, they changed their expectations to account for the new kind of card. Once they accepted that the colors *could* be wrong, they were able to see them for what they were. They then instantly and effortlessly identified each one in subsequent runs of the experiment, and their response times returned to normal.

In his book *The Structure of Scientific Revolutions*, Thomas Kuhn said that the Bruner and Postman experiment perfectly illustrated how minds change, both inside and outside of science. At first, the wrong-color cards were invisible. But when the anomalies became too numer-ous to ignore, they tried to assimilate them into their existing models. They suggested the cards existed in some perceptual middle ground, not quite red, not quite black. When assimilation failed them, their brains gave in and created a new perpetual category: cards manipulated to be an alternate color.

When we first suspect we may be wrong, when expectations don't

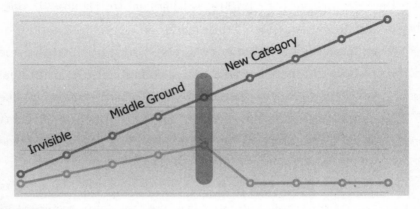

■ Number of Anomalies
□ Response Time

match experience, we feel viscerally uncomfortable and resist accommodation by trying to apply our current models of reality to the situation. It's only when the brain accepts that its existing models will never resolve the incongruences that it updates the model itself by creating a new layer of abstraction to accommodate the novelty. The result is an epiphany, and like all epiphanies it is the conscious realization that our minds have changed that startles us, not the change itself.

Kuhn wrote that "novelty emerges only with difficulty, manifested by resistance, against a background provided by expectation." In other words, when we don't know what we don't know, at first we see only what we expect to see, even when what we see doesn't match our expectations. When we get that "I might be wrong" feeling, we initially try to explain it away, interpreting novelty as confirmation, looking for evidence that our models are still correct, creating narratives that justify holding on to our preconceived notions. Unless grandly subverted, our models must fail us a few times before we begin to accommodate.

When this happens in science, Kuhn called it a "paradigm shift," that moment when a model that can't incorporate its anomalies is retired for one that can. As examples of how quickly this can happen, he pointed to optical illusions that can be seen in two different ways—a box that seems to be facing in two different directions, or one of those bistable visual illusions like the duckrabbit, which looks like a duck when viewed one way and a rabbit when viewed another. Kuhn was suggesting that when we update, it isn't the evidence that changes, but our interpretation of it. The natural world remains the same from one paradigm to the next, but as anomalies in our explanations build up over time, they require us to seek different explanations for what we previously thought was settled and understood. At a certain point, Kuhn said, "what were ducks in the scientist's world before the revolution are rabbits afterwards."

Jean Piaget agreed with much of what Kuhn had to say, but he disagreed on one major point. His research into the development of

children through stages suggested that the old models are never tossed out; instead, we build upon them. He saw mind change as a sort of Ship of Theseus, replacing things bit by bit while at sea so as to never risk sinking the vessel.

There's enough overlap of these two views that one could argue they are basically the same, but Kuhn was talking about how paradigms shift in science, and Piaget was talking about how change occurs in individuals. Together, we can see that, yes, we do sometimes realize our old models are, in a word, wrong, but we never toss them into some sort of cognitive dumpster and start over. What Kuhn called a revolution, or a paradigm shift, Piaget saw as a moment of integration, not replacement. He wrote that all knowledge, "no matter how novel, is never at first, totally independent of previous knowledge. It is only a reorganization, adjustment, correction, or addition with respect to existing knowledge. Even experimental data unknown up to a certain time must be integrated with existing knowledge. But this does not happen by itself; it takes an effort of assimilation and accommodation."

Piaget spent most of his lifetime writing about how brains create knowledge from experience. We tend to think of him as the psychologist who established the stages of child development and object permanence. He created all those fun experiments to find out when children learn that when you pour juice from a small glass to a tall one, it doesn't magically create more juice. But all of that work was in service of understanding assimilation and accommodation, what he called "genetic epistemology." As such, Piaget was adamant that the creation of our subjective reality, and thus our understanding of the world, of knowledge itself, was an active process and not a state.

For instance, when a child first sees a small animal with four legs and a tail, and a parent says to them, "Dog!" the child then creates a category for nonhuman animals with four legs. Later, when that same child sees a horse and exclaims, "Dog!" the parent must correct them. "No, that's a horse." At that moment, the child abandons assimilation for accommodation, revising the old category that once held all four-legged creatures and creating a new one with space for more.

Piaget introduced these two concepts, assimilation and accommodation, as part of his theory of constructivism, which is widely used today in education to develop modern lesson plans informed by the science of human development. Where Kuhn saw mind change as akin to punctuated equilibrium in evolution, long periods of stasis and resistance punctuated by bursts of sudden and often traumatic change, Piaget saw it as continuous and balanced. For Piaget, organisms continuously adapt in the pursuit of making their environment optimal until they feel like they have sufficiently mastered that environment. At that point, they've reached what he called "equilibration."

Equilibration is both assimilation, "integrating new information into pre-existing structures," and accommodation, "changing and building new structures to understand information." As one researcher put it, "When there is a balance between these two processes, there is adaptation, and a level of equilibrium is achieved."

The key to synthesizing the ideas of Kuhn and Piaget is what Piaget called "disequilibrium."

The brain is a plastic entity, always learning, always updating, but carefully so, at a pace that avoids danger by favoring neither stasis nor chaos. In those moments when this careful pace is interrupted, in moments of extreme environmental change or overwhelming uncertainty, we experience an excruciating disequilibrium. We become motivated to bring assimilation and accommodation out of the background of our mental lives. We focus on it consciously, purposefully, even obsessively. It is in those moments that we witness the greatest change of all.

———

When a person's core expectations are massively subverted in a way that makes steady change impossible, they may experience intense, inescapable psychological trauma that results in the collapse of the entire model of reality they once used to make sense of the world.

Psychologists who study this kind of trauma have discovered that afterward people tend to take one of two paths. Some go down a maladaptive spiral, turning to drugs or other kinds of self-destructive behavior, circling lower and lower until they hit a dark stasis. For people on this path, extreme psychological distress often becomes a catalyst for the development of new psychiatric issues, or it exacerbates existing latent tendencies that had yet to be activated in any significant way. However, if their social support system is strong, this is not the path most people take. Most people intuitively and immediately go searching among friends, family, and the internet for new information, new perspectives, raw material for rebuilding themselves.

Throughout the late 1990s and early 2000s, psychologists like Richard G. Tedeschi and Lawrence G. Calhoun gathered evidence for a new theory about how people deal with extreme change. They found that for most individuals, surviving a trauma leads to an *adaptive* spiral of *positive* development, an awakening of a new self through what they call "posttraumatic growth."

In one of their studies, Tedeschi and Calhoun interviewed a musician who had become permanently paralyzed, unable to play, and like many of their subjects, he told them it was "the best thing that ever happened to me." He said even if he could alter the way that things had turned out, he wouldn't. Before, he was an alcoholic with no clear purpose, no plans beyond the next gig and the next bar. He said he would rather be paralyzed as his new self than have his life as a self-destructive musician returned along with his incorrect assumptions and widespread ignorance. The same holds true of their subjects who one day found their lives turned upside down by plane crashes, house fires, the loss of limbs, and so on. As they explain, in "the frightening and confusing aftermath of trauma, where fundamental assumptions are severely challenged," people must update "their understanding of the world and their place in it." If they don't, the brain goes into a panic, unable to make sense of reality. The resolution of that panic necessitates new behavior, new thoughts, new beliefs, and a new self-concept.

Not everyone shares the musician's sentiment that they'd never change a thing, but Tedeschi and Calhoun's research shows that after being diagnosed with terminal cancer, after losing a child, after a crushing divorce, after surviving a car accident or a war or a heart attack, people routinely report that the inescapable negative circumstances they endured left them better people. They shed a slew of outdated assumptions that, until the trauma, they never had any reason to question, and thus never knew were wrong. People report that it feels like unexplored spaces inside their minds have opened up, ready to be filled with new knowledge derived from new experiences.

Despite the potential benefits, it can take something like a plane crash or a cancer diagnosis to go through this kind of transition because we avoid at all costs the catastrophic results of nonchalantly tossing out our old worldviews and identities. Without a strong lattice, our beliefs, attitudes, and values fall away. We lose our sense of meaning and find ourselves standing naked before the world in total bewilderment.

Still, total reboots of the self are sometimes unavoidable, and when that happens, in the aftermath, daily life can be intensely traumatic. In such a crisis, everything seems anomalous. Tedeschi and Calhoun write that a "psychologically seismic event" can "reduce to rubble many of the schematic structures that have guided understanding, decision making, and meaningfulness." The traumatic event so contradicts and, in some cases, nullifies the understanding a person counts on for context and prediction that it calls into question the "general purpose and meaning of a person's existence."

Extending that metaphor, Tedeschi and Calhoun say that the cognitive rebuilding process that takes place after such a traumatic event is akin to the reconstruction that follows an earthquake. Only the strongest structures survive, the ones that we slowly learn are still useful. Anything reduced to rubble won't be rebuilt in the same, unreliable way again. The result is a new worldview that is "far more resistant to being shattered." In crisis, we become radically open to changing our minds.

Posttraumatic growth is an accelerated version of the normally invisible, continuous, and gradual process of updating our priors, that collection of conjectures that don't feel like conjectures. Psychologist Colin Murray Parkes calls them our "assumptive world": a constellation of mental phenomena that provides us with our notions of predictability and control, much of which is inherited and internalized from our cultures—a set of knowledge, beliefs, and attitudes that guides our actions, helps us understand the causes and reasons for what happens, and forms the self that gives a sense of belonging, meaning, and purpose.

The assumptive world serves us in three main ways. First, it puts the immediate present into context. It tells us the *who, what, when, where,* and *why* of our second-by-second existence. Who is my mother? When should I go to sleep? Where is my mailbox? Why did the egg shatter against the floor?

This assumptive world also provides us with a library of if–then statements. These causal narratives tell us what will happen in the future when we interact with the world in a certain way. In the short term, we know if we turn the key, the ignition will fire. If we drop an egg, it will make a mess. If we slap our boss, we won't get that bonus. The assumptive world allows us to create plans to reach goals now, next week, and decades in the future. In the long term, we assume if we stay in school, we will get a degree; if we keep eating cake, we will need new clothes; it's a good idea to save for retirement, and we will live long enough to enjoy it.

And the third way the assumptive world aids our understanding of reality is it tells us how we ought to behave if we want to maintain our social support networks. If we want to keep our friends, spouses, lovers, and family members close, we engage in the behaviors we assume we must and refrain from the rest.

Posttraumatic growth is the rapid mind change that comes to a person after a sudden, far-reaching challenge to the accuracy of their assumptive world. When our assumptions completely fail us, the brain enters a state of epistemic emergency. To move forward, to regain a sense of control and certainty, you realize some of your knowledge, beliefs, and attitudes must change, but you aren't sure which. What is clear, however, is there's no option to continue as if your current models are true, so you enter a state of active learning in which you immediately and constantly consider other perspectives, honestly assess your weaknesses, and work to change your behaviors to resolve the crisis. In the end, so many of the facts, beliefs, and attitudes that populated your old models of reality are replaced that your very *self* changes.

This process is automatic. No one chooses to seek meaning after trauma or to grow a new self in its aftermath. It's a biological switch, a survival mechanism that comes online when needed. Tedeschi and Calhoun say it is important to remember that survivors of trauma don't actually see themselves as "embarking on searches for meaning or attempts to construct benefits from their experiences." Most of the time people are just trying to survive.

They point to how the American poet Reynolds Price wrote about the cancer that led to his paralysis. He said when you can't escape the upending of your identity, it forces you "to be somebody else, the next viable you—a stripped-down whole other clear-eyed person." Looking back on his diagnosis, he said he wished someone had looked him in the eyes early on and told him, "Reynolds Price is dead. Who will you be now? Who can you be, and can you get there in double-time?"

———

In neuroscience, assimilation and accommodation go by different names: conservation and active learning. When new evidence calls into question our expectations and conclusions, to solve the growing number of incongruences that the current model seems unable to address, something must give. This is the moment of doubt, that visceral sensation, the "I might be wrong" feeling that psychologists refer to as cognitive dissonance. When confronted with new information that seems inconsistent with our existing priors, cognitive dissonance draws our attention to the fact that those priors may need an update. If we couldn't experience it, we could never change our minds. This is painfully apparent in the case of Mrs. G., a patient of David Eagleman who suffered a stroke that damaged her anterior cingulate cortex, the ACC.

Mrs. G. was recovering when Eagleman first met her and her husband. During her examination, when Eagleman asked her to close both of her eyes, she could only close one. Feeling out the extent of her condition,

Eagleman asked her if both of her eyes were closed, and he was astonished to hear her say they were. Continuing the examination, he held up three fingers and asked her how many fingers she could see. She said three. Eagleman then asked how she could know that he was holding up three fingers if both of her eyes were closed.

Mrs. G. said nothing.

Eagleman then put Mrs. G. in front of a mirror and asked her if she could see her reflection. When she said she could, he asked her to close both of her eyes. When she said she had done so, Eagleman asked if she could still see herself. Mrs. G. said she could. Then he asked her how it could be possible that she could see her reflection if both of her eyes were closed.

Mrs. G. again said nothing.

Mrs. G. didn't become confused or alarmed, but she also didn't update her beliefs in light of this alarming contradictory evidence. Instead, she sat in silence for a while, like a computer rebooting.

Eagleman says this is common in patients with anosognosia, a disorder that causes sufferers to deny another disorder. He calls it a "cognitive filibuster" in which belief and perception disagree. Mrs. G. had suffered damage to the portions of the brain that settle such disputes, in particular the ACC, and so the belief that she had both eyes closed and the evidence in the mirror that contradicted that belief could not cede any ground to the other. Eagleman says that it is amazing and disconcerting to witness cases like these in which "both parties fatigue to the point of attrition," and eventually the issue is simply forgotten without a conclusion.

If the system that produces cognitive dissonance is dormant or destroyed, the alarm that usually comes with conflict is absent, and contradictory perceptions and propositions that in most people would cause discomfort flow through the mind without resistance. Since Mrs. G. couldn't experience cognitive dissonance, she also couldn't move past it. She physically, biologically, couldn't change her mind when she realized she was wrong.

When I met with Eagleman, he agreed with Piaget and Rousell. He said when things don't go as we expect, we become alert and direct all our senses and cognitive faculties to the source of our surprise. We become aware that we may need to "change our minds" when the effects we expect don't match the cause-and-effect models we use every day to pursue goals and plan actions.

When expectations are thwarted, when you don't get what you want, when your predictions fail, you enter into a state of learning in which you carefully update your model. But the brain only wants to resolve the dissonance. This means that the unfortunate truth is that experiencing the "I might be wrong" feeling doesn't guarantee people will accommodate, only that their brains will become alert to a potential conflict. Unless otherwise motivated, the brain prefers to assimilate, to incorporate new information into its prior understanding of the world. In other words, the solution to "I might be wrong" is often "but I'm probably not."

The brain walks a tightrope of adaptiveness, switching back and forth between overwriting old information and conserving what it already holds. In other words, we are forever balancing between assimilation and accommodation, because if we changed our minds when we shouldn't, we might become dangerously incorrect; at the same time, we might *remain* dangerously incorrect if we failed to change them when we should. To orient ourselves properly, we update carefully. So if novel information requires us to update our beliefs, attitudes, or values, we experience cognitive dissonance until we either change our minds or change our interpretations.

The classic example of this is a 1957 observational experiment by the psychologist Leon Festinger, who infiltrated a doomsday cult in Chicago. The leader of the cult, Sister Thedra, told her followers that a spaceship was coming to save them from a world-ending flood on December 21, 1954. Cult members gave away their possessions and their houses and said goodbye to their friends and their families. Then the day came and went. No spaceship. When their expectations didn't match their reality, they experienced an enormous rush of cognitive dissonance. To resolve it, they could have accommodated and admitted that they had all been duped. But instead, they told reporters that their positive vibes had persuaded God to prevent the flood. On the fly, they interpreted the anomalies as confirmations so that they could assimilate them into their shared reality and thus maintain it. Dissonance resolved.

———

So just how much cognitive dissonance does it take for a person to switch from assimilation to accommodation? Is there a quantifiable point at which the brain realizes its models are incorrect or incomplete and switches from conservation to active learning? Could we put a number on it?

Political scientists David Redlawsk and his colleagues set out to answer that question in 2010 by simulating a presidential election in which people progressively learned more and more terrible things about their preferred candidates. Redlawsk framed the study as if it were a US presidential primary; that way, people only learned about candidates in their party. Each subject registered as Republican or Democrat, and then they received hundreds of pieces of information about the positions of four fake politicians across twenty-seven different issues.

To simulate the constant media cycle of an election, the researchers doled out a steady stream of news items on a computer. Subjects could choose to read as much or as little information as they wanted while a timer counted down to the end of the campaign. What the subjects didn't know was that when they had filled out questionnaires in the beginning of the research, the scientists took their answers and used them to create custom-generated negative news stories about their chosen candidates. A pro-choice voter might learn her candidate was pro-life. A subject who valued civility would discover her candidate was egotistical and hostile to coworkers. Redlawsk and his team created five different groups. For each, they adjusted how much challenging information the subjects received. A control got zero negative news, and the others received a mix of 10, 20, 40, or 80 percent.

As the campaign dragged along, every few minutes the scientists interrupted the subjects with a telephone call. "If the election was today, for whom would you vote?" The scientists marked the answers and tracked them on a graph over time. Between those polls, people kept reading news stories, but it was up to the individuals how much information they read—and some read an enormous amount. A few subjects examined as many as two hundred pieces of information in twenty-five minutes.

What were the results? Like the truthers, like the people following Sister Thedra, the people in the 10 and 20 percent groups only grew more certain. In fact, they left the study feeling more positive about their candidates than did people in the control, who learned nothing negative at all. According to Redlawsk, their positive attitudes interacted with negative emotions triggered by new information, and they mounted a cognitive effort to make sense of the new information in a way that reduced their dissonance. "This process may lead to attitude strengthening," he explained.

However, this wasn't true for the 40 percent and 80 percent groups. "People became more negative, and they became more negative quite consistently throughout time," Redlawsk told me. By the end of the campaign, the 40 percent and 80 percent groups had changed their minds entirely and abandoned their candidates. "A threatening environment generates increasing anxiety, which operates to cause a person to learn more about the environment in order to prepare a response," explained Redlawsk. "Thus increasing anxiety leads to learning, which normatively should lead to more, rather than less, accurate updating of evaluations."

Assimilation, they discovered, has a natural upper limit. Redlawsk and his team call this the "affective tipping point," the moment after which people can no longer justify ignoring an onslaught of disconfirmatory evidence. Redlawsk told me no organism could survive without some failsafe for when counterevidence becomes overwhelming. Once a person reaches the affective tipping point, the brain switches from conservation mode to active learning.

At low levels of threat, what he calls "small amounts of incongruency," we become alert, but still err on the side of our priors as we evaluate incoming data. His subjects began to feel that "I might be wrong" feeling when about 14 percent of all the news they read painted their candidates in a poor light. At that level of incongruence, they still saw what they expected to see, still counterargued, and resisted updating. The result was a stronger version of their worldview than before. At higher levels, though, anxiety over potential error pushed his subjects to favor an updated point of view, to change their minds. For most, he said, the tipping point came when 30 percent of the incoming information was incongruent.

Redlawsk said that in the real world, it's likely that people are highly nuanced. Some people may need a bit more disconfirmation than others.

Also, some people may be in a situation where disconfirmation is unlikely, cut off from challenging ideas, curating an information feed that stays below the threshold. Depending on the source, a person's motivations, the issue at hand, the amount of exposure to challenging ideas, and so on, the affective tipping point may be harder to reach, so the important point isn't the specific number found in this one study, just that there *is* a number, a quantifiable level of doubt when we admit we are likely wrong and become compelled to update our beliefs, attitudes, and values. Before we reach that level, incongruences make us feel more certain, not less.

———

Kuhn and Piaget used different terms and metaphors, but their conclusions were similar. Both realized that people change their minds in much the same way that new theories in science supersede old ones.

In science, if an experiment delivers a result that doesn't match expectations, that doesn't fit the prevailing model, researchers place the anomalies aside, in a holding bucket. That way they can continue to work on problems using the tools that the current model affords and come back to the bucket of abeyance later, should the anomalies accumulate and overflow. When incongruences appear, the first assumption is that the model is fine, that there must have been some mistake in the measurements, in the tools, in the scientists themselves maybe. But over time, that bucket of abeyance begins to fill with anomalies, and at a certain point it grows too heavy to ignore. Rules of thumb are no longer useful. Exceptions cease to prove the rule. Variation and nuance reveal stereotypes for what they are.

Piaget showed us that this is similar to how minds update. Remember how in the playing card experiment the anomalies were invisible at first? In the beginning, the subjects didn't know that alternate-color cards existed. Without that mental category, they didn't expect to see that kind of card, and thus they also *couldn't* see them. Once they *did* see them, they tried to make them fit into their old model, the one where those kinds of cards didn't exist. Only when that model failed to make sense of what they were experiencing did they feel compelled to accommodate, to change their minds.

As we experience objective reality through our limited senses, we construct subjective representations inside our heads to better navigate the world outside them. When confronting novel information in moments of uncertainty, we have no choice but to favor those representations. It's dangerous to be wrong, but it's also dangerous to be ignorant, so if new information suggests our models might be incorrect or incomplete, we first attempt to fit the anomalies into our old understanding. If they do, we continue using those models until they fail us too many times to ignore.

But the research into posttraumatic growth and the affective tipping point reveals that we all have a breaking point after which we enter learning mode, eager to make sense of a relentless stream of disconfirming information.

Unless you are a hermit in a cabin or a disciple in a cult, most of us regularly confront other minds that see the world differently than our own. In the previous chapter, we saw that the research at NYU indicated we often assume, at first, that the people who reach different conclusions must be mistaken. The SURFPAD model says that in moments of substantial uncertainty, people with different priors will reach different assumptions, and thanks to naive realism, the result is substantial disagreement on what is and is not true, moral, and good.

But as Redlawsk's research revealed, there can come a moment when we realize that refusing to change is riskier than admitting we are probably wrong. To get a better understanding of how that happens, I wanted to meet some people who had done just that, and that's where we are headed next.

5

WESTBORO

It was Valentine's Day and cold in Topeka on the morning I knocked on the door of Westboro Baptist Church. The sun seemed dim, farther away somehow, its rays thinned out by the time they arrived in Kansas to warm the yellow fields on the edge of town to a few degrees above freezing.

I had imagined Westboro would be at the end of a long, snaking dirt road in a nest of decaying trees. I was shocked to turn a corner in a residential neighborhood and find it was just a house. It was maybe a bit larger than the others, with its many-angled pitched roofs, brown gables, and white walls, but it was just a house. It stood on the corner of an average suburban neighborhood two blocks away from a Starbucks, and at first glance it seemed like a quaint American cottage on which someone had played a cruel prank by pinning a giant banner to the side that read: GODHATESAMERICA.COM.

As my ears and cheeks numbed, I noticed a basketball court behind layers of gates. Above it, an upside-down American flag flapped over a changeable marquee. The signage had been elevated above the fence so it could proclaim to the busy road leading to a Sonic and the rest of America: FAG LOVE = LUST! VALENTINE IDOL IS AN EXCUSE TO SIN! GOD H8S IT! ROM I. A second, smaller marquee proclaimed that FAG MARRIAGE DOOMS NATIONS.

A young man wearing a snappy vest and colorful tie over a pink dress shirt swung open the door. He introduced himself as Isiah. As we shook hands, he asked if I had called ahead. I told him I had not. I only came over to see if I could attend today's service.

"Well, just be very quiet and don't shout," Isiah said, and led me in.

———

I had spent the previous day with Zach Phelps-Roper, a former member and one of the founder's many grandchildren. Zach, like his older sisters and brother, had recently left the church for good, and I wanted to see what he had left behind.

I would later spend time with his sister Megan because I wanted to know how she and Zach had shed their long-held beliefs and attitudes so quickly. After looking at the science behind how minds change, I now wanted to understand how that change can be encouraged by others, *how minds change other minds*, and so I wanted to learn what persuaded Zach and Megan and those like them to leave groups like Westboro. I already knew that each had spoken about how they had been summarily excommunicated immediately after leaving, or as modern religious groups often refer to it, "disfellowshipped." It seemed similar to Charlie Veitch's story; except in Zach and Megan's case, leaving the group meant leaving their mother and father and other relatives, all of whom immediately, and perhaps permanently, broke all contact.

Surely, I thought, there must be something common in these stories that I could bring to scientists for an explanation. What made them different from the people on the other side of my computer screen who refused to give up views far less controversial? In these contentious times when people seem so unable to meet eye to eye, when civil engagement seems so hopeless, what prompted Charlie and Zach and Megan to change their minds in such rapid and drastic ways?

Though Zach's and Megan's stories were different, I discovered that both shared something fundamental with Charlie's, an essential truth about what keeps the most resistant among us unable to change.

———

According to the Southern Poverty Law Center, an organization that tracks hate groups, Westboro is "arguably the most obnoxious and rabid hate group in America."

They've been the focus of several documentaries, books, news series, and other attempts to make sense of their actions. They have been parodied in a few Hollywood movies, including one that concluded with a church nearly identical to Westboro engaging in a bloody shootout with the ATF. In another, Colin Firth murdered the entire congregation in a scene NPR said was "clearly modeled" after Westboro. As those movies showed, Westboro is so well-known at this point that they can serve as a handy shorthand when you need to depict a group of radical Christian hatemongers.*

Westboro is the name of the suburb in which the church operates,

———

*Those movies are *Red State* and *Kingsmen: The Secret Service*.

and it can be off-putting to see local businesses that share the name. Not far away, a shopping center called Westboro Mart features an art gallery and florist, an interior decorator and an antique shop. For the rest of us, the word *Westboro* entered public consciousness in 1998 after the church protested the funeral of Matthew Shepard, a young gay man who was beaten, tortured, and left for dead in a remote portion of Wyoming by two men who offered him a ride home from a bar. At his funeral, the church carried signs that read NO TEARS FOR QUEERS. For more than a decade, the church's website featured an animated gif of Shepard engulfed in flames positioned next to a running count of how many days he had been in hell.

Westboro soon became famous for their outrageous, gaudy signs and their year-round picketing, but that didn't begin with the death of Matthew Shepard. It began not far from the church, in Topeka's Gage Park. In 1991, Fred Phelps and his family staged a protest they called "The Great Gage Park Decency Drive," after family members claimed they had been approached by gay men meeting in the park for casual hookups. The publicity led to local then national attention.

The church took to picketing regularly after that, stoking guaranteed publicity until they were known around the world. But as the SPLC explains, Westboro has always been a small, "family-based cult of personality built around its patriarch, Fred Phelps." Forty years before Gage Park, he was briefly featured in *Time* magazine for drawing in crowds of a hundred or more as a street preacher barking at students about lust on the campus of John Muir College in Pasadena, where he earned his associate's degree.

By their own count, with a congregation of around ninety people, mostly children and grandchildren of Fred Phelps (now deceased), Westboro has conducted almost sixty thousand pickets, more than five hundred of them at funerals. In 2006, a family in Maryland sought damages against them for picketing the funeral of their son, Matthew Snyder, a soldier who had died in a non-combat-related accident in Iraq. The case made it all the way to the United States Supreme Court. Eleven of Fred Phelps's children are lawyers, and one of them, Margie J. Phelps, defended the family at the trial by outlining how they had operated within the law, keeping their distance and picketing only where the police asked them to stand. The court ruled 8–1 in favor of Westboro. During all of this, members of the church protested outside, carrying signs that read THANK GOD FOR DEAD SOLDIERS.

———

I met Zach at a small café called The Blackbird a few blocks from the church. Despite the cold, he wore shorts paired with gigantic puffy gloves. Scruffy with a fair beard, twenty-five years old, he wore a cap that read SMILE.

As he told me his story, he often looked past my shoulder, out the windows, and took long pauses to collect his thoughts. Zach explained he didn't leave the church because he disagreed with their teachings about gay people or their picketing of soldiers' funerals; that came later. He left because he disagreed with their views on doctors, but only after he hurt his back and they refused to allow him to seek proper medical care.

On his first day working as a nurse, he was hefting a large elderly man into a wheelchair when Zach bumped it. It moved away, leaving him holding his patient suspended and limp. "It was just kind of a bad situation because he was really heavy, and his little mechanized wheelchair-thing kind of went off on its own instead of being where it was supposed to be. Either I was going to do this really aggressive move to get him back where he was safely seated, or he was going to slide down to the ground. It was one or the other."

Zach made the aggressive move, and it would take months to recover. He eventually endured injection therapy, among other procedures, but he first tried to ease the pain with home remedies. He worked night shifts at the hospital. At home, he asked his family to apply ice to his lower back several times a day because he couldn't comfortably do it himself. It seemed to help, he said, but only temporarily. As the pain intensified, he became concerned. "I wasn't sure what was going on with me."

He pored over his textbooks and other medical literature looking for some clues about how to proceed. All the while, his father told him the pain persisted because he wasn't praying hard enough. Zach was fresh out of nursing school, and it seemed nonsensical. Prayer was fine, but Zach wanted relief.

"It's not that they don't believe in any medicine," Zach explained. "Westboro isn't like that. They just view doctors as being like stewards. God gave the doctors this capacity to help you, but we don't praise the doctors. We praise God."

In their eyes, he explained, it's your faith that gives doctors the power to heal your body. Zach was pulling out textbooks and old tests, looking through the literature. To his father, it seemed like a rebuke of their beliefs, of the family.

Zach said he had started to grow frustrated with his family before he hurt his back. With Fred Phelps in poor health, the church shifted its power structure, and a group of nine elders had taken over, Zach's father among them. With that change, new rules like stricter dress codes and impermissible career options had become dogma. Zach wanted to become a doctor after dissecting a pig in his anatomy and physiology class. When he told his parents, they said he couldn't pursue that career. When he asked why, they said, "We don't have to give you an answer."

His first priority was to respect his elders and obey their wishes, they said. They told him to stop asking questions and move on. Later, when the elders told all the members of the church that everyone inside Westboro was now an equal, to Zach it seemed like the two ideas didn't fit together. When the elders told him that he could either become a nurse or a computer programmer, he chose the former, but the anger lingered.

His sister Megan had bought a book on emotional intelligence, and he read it while recuperating. He started trying to label his feelings. "I said, 'Okay, I'm feeling pretty sad right now.' My mom is on the phone chewing me out. 'Okay, this is anger.' My dad was saying, 'Zach, you don't know shit about your shoulders,' or whatever. It felt like he was making me feel ashamed of myself, so that's another emotion I labeled."

He started imagining what it would be like to save up some money and move to Hawaii. Five weeks after the injury, the pain in his back and shoulders had grown so severe that he asked his parents to take him to the emergency room. When they said no, he began to think about escape.

"The moment when I realized I needed to leave was when my dad was shouting at me, in my face, and I felt fear, and I noticed it," said Zach. "It wasn't the first time he had ever shouted at me." He pleaded for help with his back, and he said his dad told him, "You know, Zach, this is about the third time that you've told me this today, and I just want you to cut it out now."

He asked his dad if he simply didn't believe him, and his father said, "I don't."

He asked, "Since when have I ever given you a reason to not believe me?"

When his dad started shouting, Zach shouted back. He screamed, "I'm leaving tonight!"

As he packed, his father hovered nearby and tried to bring the tension down, but Zach told him, "I'm going to make this really easy for you, Dad. I don't love this religion anymore."

For Westboro, leaving for any reason is to join the damned, the wicked, the evil world of the forsaken they had been trying to save for decades. The only way to survive God's wrath was to cross the picket line and join their church, the one in Topeka and no other. Crossing that line in the other direction was tantamount to joining Satan's army, so no one is more hated than those who have abandoned the faith; they consider it a decision that demands the cutting of all ties to the congregation.

His mom rushed to grab Zach's phone and then deleted all of his contacts. Zach ran downstairs, paralyzed with fear, and sat at his computer desk for a few minutes, and then he mustered the strength to bolt out the door. He ran eight blocks in the dead of night to his cousin's house and woke them. The next morning his dad called him and told him to pick up his things. When he arrived, he found the contents of his room piled outside. After a few days, he moved in with another cousin farther away from the church.

On the day Zach left, he carried with him all the beliefs and attitudes about LGBTQ people that he had defended on the picket line since he was a boy, but that all began to change a few weeks later while sitting in an Olive Garden with his sister Grace.

Grace had left the church a few years earlier, along with Megan. They, too, had become frustrated with the elders and had tried, at first, to persuade them to change their ways, but it was Grace who received the brunt of their retributions. Grace wanted to study art, and as they had with Zach, the elders forbade it.

Grace had befriended a couple who had recently joined the church. Justin and Lindsey had traveled the world before converting, and Grace and Megan would spend hours with them listening to their stories from the outside, texting them to plan visits and ask about their lives. When Lindsey told the elders that she was uncomfortable with Grace texting her husband, as Megan put it, "punishment was swift." Grace, Megan, and Zach were all forbidden from having any further contact with the couple. The elders would later direct Justin to keep Lindsey at home and away from the rest of Westboro until she agreed to get baptized. Much of the changes the elders had made in the culture of the church were like this, directed at women who refused to demure, to obey, to step in line. As punishment for texting a married man, they made Grace take a job doing data entry at the Kansas Department of Revenue. She was forbidden to leave the building until her shifts were over, so she took her breaks on a couch in the bathroom.

But it wasn't Grace who changed Zach at the Olive Garden that day; it was their waiter. At the end of their meal, instead of leaving them the check, the waiter told Zach that he wanted to pay for their food. In fact, he already had. Zach protested, but the waiter shushed him. He explained that he knew Zach had recently left Westboro. As a gay man, he wanted to show Zach a kindness.

Zach didn't know how to interpret what was happening. It seemed preposterous. For all his life he had believed that LGBTQ people were grotesque. He had spent years picketing with signs trying to convince others of the same. Recalling that moment, he said of gay men, "I didn't know any. I just assumed that they were beasts."

After that meal, he started wondering if all of the assumptions tied to his former life were true. If his beliefs about gay men were wrong, then what else? His first thoughts were of Lady Gaga and Katy Perry and how Westboro had told him the girls who go to their concerts were "simple sluts." Simple-minded, stupid, and promiscuous. He immediately, and for the first time, questioned it. He felt overwhelmed by a torrent of information that he once considered noise. All at once, he began to feel an intense uncertainty not only about what was true, but about who he was.

He said the most alarming thing was the realization that if he had gone to Olive Garden while he was still in the church, the waiter's act of kindness might not have made any difference at all. He would have found a way to interpret it differently. Zach was still unpacking what it all meant. He was shocked to realize he was open to all sorts of change, and once he realized it, an array of alternative beliefs, attitudes, and values became newly acceptable.

"The first time I talked to a Jewish person, I thought what Westboro taught me at first, and then I was like, 'I don't want to listen to that.' I want to try to see reality for what it is. I want to think with an open mind and to make discoveries. There's a great deal of mystery in this world that I walk in, in this universe."

Today, he said, "I have gay friends. I have bisexual friends. I have pansexual friends." He was still struggling, though, still rebuilding his models, still expanding his mind. Zach said he recently began dabbling with Buddhism.

Zach reiterated that he didn't leave the church because he changed his opinions; he changed his opinions because he left the church. And he left the church because it had become intolerable for other reasons. Leaving opened him up to the possibility he could be wrong about many things, and that began a difficult period of rebirth. He had developed issues with trust and would go through a series of bad relationships while suffering intense bouts of depression. He'd check into a mental health clinic after fantasizing about harming himself. He said it was like clawing out from the bottom of a well.

"They taught me to be very judgmental at Westboro. I feel kind of torn, because part of me wants to practice unconditional love, but then you can't trust everyone out there, you know?"

———

The day after hearing Zach's story I knocked on the door of Westboro Baptist Church and was led past a room with cheap couches and wood paneling to one of three tiny guest pews at the end of a row.

I was early, and the church was empty except for the hollow hum of the lights. An old organ sat at one end of the room by an old computer. At the other end, a line of comfy chairs straddled Tupperware boxes stuffed with knick-knacks. With its cream floor and walls and columns of rich, red wood, it felt suburban and plain, like a basement renovated in the 1980s. In the silence, I tried to imagine Fred Phelps screaming from the pulpit.

I thumbed through the laminated hymnal stuffed in the pocket of the pew in front of me until the congregants, about forty people in all, arrived. Most people in the church are neighbors. Privacy fence connects the houses, making the block into a sort of compound with the church on one corner. To get here, they simply open their back doors and walk across their lawns.

As they filed in, several people stopped to welcome me. The women wore long dresses and covered their hair. The men wore blue jeans and slacks, running shoes and dress shoes, sweaters and Under Armour jackets. Then we took our seats, and we each received a printed copy of the sermon. The preacher, one of the elders, spoke it word for word as everyone read along. It was written in a conversational tone with the jokes and asides already typed out. Megan would later tell me this was another change made by the elders. Before they took over, Phelps used no notes and would leap from one citation to another from memory, sending the audience into a panic as they searched all over their Bibles to find the passage to which he was referring before he sprang to yet another.

Today, the sermon was about Armageddon and Jews. Since 9/11, Westboro had become obsessed with the end times, seeing the attack as a sign from God that they were the chosen and should prepare accordingly. Despite the banner out front suggesting that LGBTQ Valentine's Day Hallmark cards paved the path to a modern Sodom and Gomorrah, there was only the lightest mention of the ongoing "sinful secular holiday celebrating fornication and sodomy" and no mention of any other current events or political realities. They stayed on topic, and the topic was the end of the world for which they must continue to prepare.

After the sermon I sang some hymns, shook some hands, told them why I had visited, and listened in on conversations about getting more fiber and how big the kids were getting. Everyone was happy, smiling, kissing children who took no notice and remained transfixed by books offering spelling lessons through cartoon characters. I had expected fire and brimstone rants about homosexuality or joyous praise for the death of American soldiers. I expected to be singled out, asked to leave, or kept from leaving. Something awful. Instead, the more time I've had to think about it, the more I've felt something even more unsettling.

I grew up in Mississippi going to places like this every Sunday. In all, standing there singing "Gently, Lord O Lead Us," it felt like every other Baptist church I've ever been in. The good and the bad of it were not shocking, but familiar.

———

When the service ended, I walked out the front door of Westboro, crossed the street, and met with Caitlyn Cameron on the front porch of Equality House.

In 2013, a humanitarian nonprofit called Planting Peace bought the house directly across from Westboro for $81,000 and painted it the colors of the Gay Pride rainbow flag. Over the years, Equality House has held drag shows, sold lemonade, hosted a mock wedding event for Dumbledore and Gandalf, and later a real gay wedding right after the Supreme Court ruling legalized same-sex marriage.

"This is a signal that this is not what our community thinks about gay people, not what America thinks about gay people," Caitlyn explained. "Westboro's idea is one idea, but there is also another opinion out there, and we wanted to stand for that."

Caitlyn said she was passing through as an AmeriCorps Vista volunteer, one of many who stay temporarily at Equality House as they complete their community service. She told me it wasn't unusual for people at Equality House to make small talk with Westboro members over morning coffee as they walked out to their street sign to change out their weekly messages of hate. They often waved, said a few words, and then retreated back into their separate realities with separate truths.

Caitlyn said she worked with a head member of Westboro at the local jail. At work, she said he was casual, funny. He hung out and joked with her and everyone else.

"Monday through Friday I see him every day, and then on Sunday, I see him in front of my church with a picket sign, and I'm like, 'Oh. That's that guy—'" she paused for comedic timing "'—that I know from work.'"

I said maybe there was something to be said for civility. In a previous era this probably couldn't happen. One of these two houses would have to burn the other down. "They put on a show," she said. "We can see from their actions that the worst thing they do is picket. Which is rude and hurtful and disrespectful, especially going to military funerals and that sort of thing and being totally disrespectful. I can't condone that, but if that's the worst they do, well, there are a bunch of worse examples from other cultures."

Caitlyn said, to her, the fact that Westboro exists and can be tolerated, that we know they are always going to stay inside the lines of the law, that they will never firebomb a church, is a sign of progress. They know minds have changed among the outside world; they know their group's attitudes, beliefs, and values are considered wrong. Why, then, I asked her, after all their interactions with people like her and the people at Equality House, do they keep updating that sign? Every day they see you aren't monsters. Why do they persist?

"When you grow up believing certain things, and the people you love and trust tell you those things, and you're a kid, you are helpless to internalize that," she said. "I bet a lot of Westboro members don't actually want to kill anybody that's different from them, or shun them from society, or send them to a fiery death. But it's really hard when you spend all your time with a group of people who expect that from you. You have to fill that role."

Outside, sitting in my car, I glanced at the basketball court, the flag waving overhead, and recalled the familiar feeling of a Sunday sermon, the communion, the singing, the safety of the crowd, the sense of family.

My Baptist church shared the same attitudes toward LGBTQ people as Westboro. My church didn't picket, didn't control where I wanted to work. And yet there were things I knew I couldn't or shouldn't do, jobs that would have been taboo, clothes and words and ideas that would have led the others to see me as an outsider, as the other.

I left the Baptist church around age ten, after my vacation Bible school teacher told us about the story of Noah's Ark. As she thumbed through a children's book with illustrations of lions and antelopes, I asked why they didn't eat each other, and she said, "Oh, we don't ask those questions."

I felt embarrassed for asking, but when I told my father what happened, he said I didn't have to go back if I didn't want to go. He kept a gun and a Bible on the nightstand but had rejected organized religion after surviving Vietnam. He never shared his reasons other than to say he didn't trust preachers. It was my mother who wanted me to go, to fit in with her brothers and sisters. When I stopped going, she was heartbroken but added excuses for my absence to those for my father's.

Parked between Westboro and Equality House, I wondered how open-minded I really was. How many things did I believe, think, and feel right now because the people I trusted and loved shared those same convictions? Did my sense of right and wrong come from inside or out? If not for that day in vacation Bible school, would that version of me have grown up believing that saving LGBTQ people from hell was the most noble goal imaginable? Would I have seen compassion where I now see hate?

———

When we spoke, Megan Phelps-Roper was living in South Dakota. She and her husband loved the HBO series *Deadwood*, and while dating, they had binge-watched it. They later stayed in a bed-and-breakfast in the area, fell in love with the region, and soon moved to a town nearby. She said most of her time these days was taken up by her daughter, Sølvi Lynne, a source of tremendous joy and a daily reminder of the family she left behind. She said she wished her mom could spend time with Sølvi and still held out hope that maybe, one day, she would.

Megan and her sister Grace left the church together in 2012, but it was Megan who spent nearly a decade in the media spotlight, a phrase that barely captures the immense attention focused on her as she appeared in interviews around the globe, in documentaries and on talk shows, and, as an activist, for years spoke in front of audiences large and small.

In 2015, a *New Yorker* profile of Megan trended heavily on social media, prompting her to write her autobiography, *Unfollow*, which quickly became an international bestseller after its release in 2019. Her TED Talk has been viewed more than six million times, and the head of TED, Chris Anderson, said of her, "Rarely do you come across someone with the courage and clarity of Megan Phelps-Roper." She went on to consult for law enforcement agencies that monitor extremist groups, and she continues to serve on Twitter's Trust and Safety Council.

These days, "my daughter is number one. I should just start there," she told me. "She's two-and-a-half, the absolute best. I am obsessed. It's just amazing. It's like I was prepared for parenting, because it's relearning an entirely different way of thinking about children."

I asked what she meant. She said of the church, "It's very authoritarian. It's very controlling." They expected everyone to suppress unacceptable emotions, especially children. "There is this verse that says we have to 'bring into captivity every thought to the obedience of Christ.'"

I told her that children are a great way to see in action much of what the research says about how brains update, and she asked me to explain it the best I could. I ran through SURFPAD: how in moments of uncertainty we often don't feel uncertain because the brain uses our priors to disambiguate without our knowledge. I explained that when that happens, it can make the people who see the world differently seem deluded or, in the most extreme cases, insane. She laughed and said it matched up perfectly with her experiences on the inside.

Then I told her about assimilation and accommodation, how we first try to make novel and challenging information fit into our worldviews until those times when we realize we must update our worldviews to make room for them. When a child like Sølvi learns that a horse isn't a dog, she also learns that dogs and horses are part of a new category, a new level of abstraction to make sense of the world. I told her that Piaget said that when we learn to play a game like checkers, we don't just learn the rules of the game, we learn that games have rules. When we move on to chess, we've already learned how to learn how to play a game, that games exist, which makes it easier to learn than if we had first started with chess.

Megan began to tear up. "It still kind of surprises me how it was happening kind of little by little. And it's exactly that process that you were describing, like trying to take in this new information and make it fit with what I believed. It was this process. And at the time, I remember thinking that it took such a long time, and now I think, 'A year and a half. Is that really all it took?'"

Megan said her doubts, like Zach's, began with the new rules put in place by the elders. The church had always singled out "troublemakers," but their treatment of family members like her sister Grace felt unjust.

After Lindsey told the church about Grace texting her husband, Westboro held a meeting, as they often did, where she said "essentially everybody in the church" came together as if it were a court trial and laid out a case against Grace. No matter what someone said, "everything that looks bad is bad and everything that looks good is also bad. So, if the action isn't wrong, then the intent is wrong. The heart is wrong. And it was terrifying. It's terrifying to watch. Because you don't want it to happen to you."

As a child, Megan said confrontations like those felt like an extension of parenting. People older than her knew better about how to deal with other people older than her. She knew she was never going to be a leader in the group, and so said nothing. Yet, "I would think so often, like, I don't see what they're seeing. I must be missing something. I must be wrong about this."

But that was before Twitter opened her up to the possibility that it was the church that might be wrong.

———

In 2009, Megan joined Twitter and began her deconversion with a tweet about the death of Ted Kennedy: "He defied God at every turn, teaching rebellion against His laws. Ted's in hell!" She followed it with tweets about their picket of an *American Idol* concert. She quickly gained an audience thanks to relentless rejoinders fired back at comedians and other celebrities retweeting her and making fun of her posts.

The church was supportive. They felt like Megan was taking their message to social media, refusing to back down when bullied by accounts with millions of followers. Megan was met with anger, shame, hostility, and disgust, and just like the pickets, she matched that energy with contempt. But not everyone on Twitter met her with such vitriol.

"The first contradiction that came to me was from this guy, David Abitbol, who ran a blog called *Jewlicious*," Megan told me. "He said that he wasn't trying to persuade me. He said we were having these conversations in public so that people could see our ideas and to help give other people the language to argue against these kinds of ideas. And I think that's true. But I also think he recognized my humanity, that I really believed I was doing the right thing. And so, the conversation that I'm about to tell you about actually took place over DM. It wasn't in the public view."

Westboro had begun picketing in front of synagogues and Jewish celebrations. It was around this time that Abitbol began responding to Megan's tweets. An activist and web developer, years earlier Abitbol created *Net Hate*, a directory of all the white-nationalist, anti-Semitic, and hate-based websites on the internet. He had been arguing online with extremists long before social media made it fast, easy, and convenient, and so he started responding directly to Megan's tweets, challenging her reading of the scriptures. When she looked him up, she discovered the Jewish Telegraphic Agency listed him as the second most influential Jewish person on Twitter, and so she took it as an opportunity to proselytize directly to Jews around the world. Initially, they made jokes about each other. Abitbol trolled Megan incessantly, and she playfully trolled back.

Months into their debates, she learned Abitbol was heading up a Jewlicious Festival in Long Beach, California, and she encouraged Westboro to fly out to protest. News that they were coming spread across the internet, and so several groups rallied to meet them in counterprotest.

"My sister was holding a sign that said, *Your Rabbi Is A Whore*," said Megan, "and there was this huge group. These protests were insane." Hundreds of people came out to mock Westboro, and soon the cops arrived. Some counterprotesters began throwing fists, but the church refused to fight back. "People in Easter Bunny costumes and all kinds of things, they were very physically violent, pushing people. And it was just really kind of a crazy atmosphere."

That was when David Abitbol recognized Megan and pushed through the crowd. At first, he served as a human shield, and then he urged the counterprotesters to back down. Then he laughed at her sign and traded some jokes. They started debating, peppered with humor and sarcasm. "And it was very like our vibe, very similar to the way that it was on Twitter, which is kind of like cheesy and challenging, but also genuinely like, 'Hey, how are you?'"

Megan had always been keen to focus on the logic of the Bible, to stick to exactly what the scripture said, to justify her beliefs with chapter and verse. Abitbol asked Megan why Westboro didn't condemn eating shrimp, or having sex while menstruating, or live by many of the other denouncements in Leviticus. Megan recalled feeling flustered. He was making good points, and she didn't have any ready-made arguments to justify her positions. When they parted, she shared that she would be picketing the General Assembly of the Jewish Federations later that year in New Orleans, and he said he'd love to continue the conversation there. "Same thing," said Megan. "As soon as he gets in, he tells me he's bringing me this box of halvah from a market in Jerusalem where he lived. I brought him one of my favorite bars of peppermint chocolate, fancy chocolate. I hand him the bar, and he flips it over to look for a kosher symbol on the packaging." She was intrigued, and while Abitbol stood there teaching Megan about kosher foods, she held a sign that read GOD HATES JEWS.

Back home, they moved over to private messages, and Abitbol's tone changed to match their in-person conversations. She discovered he wasn't just an expert on the Old Testament, having studied it in Hebrew, he was endlessly funny and charming, patient, and empathetic, and he thought the same of her. Despite their differences, they had become friends.

"So, we're talking about these doctrines. I don't remember how it came up, but he specifically brought up my mom," Megan told me. "My mom had my oldest brother before she was married. And so, this was something that was sometimes thrown in her face as, 'Oh, look, you're a sinner, too.' And we would always say, 'Yeah, well, but the standard of God is not sinlessness, it's repentance. She repented of those sins. You can throw her sin in her face, but that doesn't contradict anything that we're saying.'"

Abitbol pointed out that Westboro carried a sign that read DEATH PENALTY FOR GAY PEOPLE. Megan said that was what the scripture said in Leviticus. "And he said, 'Yeah, but well, didn't Jesus say, "let he who is without sin cast the first stone"'?"

Megan said their canned response to that was always, "Yes, but we're not casting stones. We're standing on a public sidewalk preaching words." Abitbol responded by telling her that the sign was advocating that the government cast stones. "And I was like, 'Oh, man.' Yeah, it seems so stupid. It seems so stupid now." Megan said she felt unprepared to respond. "It's like you have these answers, and each one seems like a good response. It seems like the right answer and the truth until somebody actually articulates something like that. I'm like 'Oh my God, Oh my God. That passage was talking about the government. The death penalty.'"

Curled up on a chair, tweeting from home, Megan said she felt "set back on her heels." Then Abitbol kept going. He said by her reading of the scripture, her mom deserved the death penalty. "She wouldn't have had the opportunity to repent and be forgiven, and our family wouldn't exist." She thought of another sign that read GOD IS LOVE, HATE, MERCY

AND WRATH, and how Westboro never thought of mercy in the context of anyone but the church. "Mercy only applied to us."

She couldn't shake the contradictions. It became clear to her over the course of a few days that if gay people couldn't repent, then that went directly against their core doctrine. She thought, for the first time, "What are we doing?" It had become so important to show themselves as distinct from people outside the church, that it had become the most important thing. Any value that outsiders espoused, they would push against as a matter of principle regardless of what the Bible said about it.

"I remember being at a total loss in that moment." Megan challenged the sign among the other church members, but they didn't see things her way. They kept it in rotation, but she decided to stop carrying it; she could no longer defend it, and she was afraid what might happen if she refused to defend it in front of the others.

That one contradiction, she said, opened her up to other contradictions in their teachings, and she began to fill with doubt. Meanwhile, she was becoming more active on Twitter, having conversations with more people like Abitbol, people who would joke with her and hold space for her, people who would ask about her life outside of picketing. She began peeking into their feeds, outside of the conversations, photos from their personal lives, tweets about food and pop culture. She checked in on people when they seemed down and started talking about things other than scripture.

When Grace was brought before the elders, she realized that sort of thing had never happened to somebody in her household, to someone younger than her. "By the time that it did, I had already had these experiences on Twitter where, again, these individual doctrines felt inconsistent. For the first time in my life, I had a small sense of trust in my own judgment, more than that of the church. The idea that I could be right about something and that they might be wrong about something, before then I would never have put any faith in that idea."

———

Grace and Megan began texting back and forth, questioning the elders in secrecy. Meanwhile, Megan had a few flirtatious encounters with outsiders that awakened her desire for a romantic partner, which she kept frustratingly stifled. Relationships with people outside of the church were forbidden for women, so she hid from the others an unfurling romance with a man she met on Twitter by moving their conversations to the app Words with Friends. He kept his identity a secret, calling himself C. G., and Megan began listening to the music and reading the books he mentioned in their clandestine dalliances.

All the while, the restrictions on their daily lives grew more draconian, as she put it. Each one was supported by an excerpt of scripture, "abstain from all appearance of evil," a passage so ambiguous it could be disambiguated to justify nearly anything. Grace could no longer visit the park to climb trees. It was the appearance of evil, they said. Colorful nail polish was forbidden, and women were now required to wear shirts that covered their necks and dresses that covered their knees. If they went shopping, their clothes must be inspected by a man before they could wear them out. One of her cousins was excommunicated for rebelling.

Under these new rules, Lindsey's husband, Justin, had reached out to Grace over Twitter. Fearing what might happen if the church found out, Grace turned herself in, and the elders made it clear that one more infraction would lead to her excommunication. When the elders told the rest of the family, Megan reached her breaking point. While painting her aunt's basement alongside Grace, she felt "a moment of horrifying clarity."

Megan told me that it wasn't Twitter, nor the elder's new rules, nor the kindness of Abitbol, nor her conversations with C. G. It was all of it together, each an anomaly that alone could have been assimilated, novel information that created a mounting cognitive dissonance that at one point in her life could have been assuaged by interpreting it as confirmation of her worldview in some way, but taken together it felt like overwhelming disconfirmation.

Still, it took something incontestable and unavoidable to push her past the point of no return, and Grace's possible excommunication had served as that catalyst. In her memoir, she recalls how the next day, in her room, hanging out on her bed, she told Grace, "What if we weren't here?" Grace asked her what she meant. Megan told her, "What if we were somewhere else?"

Over the next few weeks, Megan continued to console Grace, who was terrified of what might happen. At first, Grace resisted to the point that Megan attempted to persuade the church, to bring it in line with her new values. Like a partner who tries to fix what is wrong in the relationship before submitting to their desire to escape it, they decided to present their objections to the church in hopes of changing it.

Megan started with her immediate family, pointing out to how various applications of their doctrines seemed inconsistent. She spoke with her mother, who softened a bit. She spoke with her brother, who did not. She spoke with her sister Bekah, who said it was best Megan brought her misgivings to the elders. She used Words with Friends to reach out to Justin and Lindsey, who had been completely isolated from the rest of the family since the incident with Grace. Together, they considered a formal public apology of some kind from Grace to Lindsey. When she brought the idea to her father, he exploded with rage. She gave up. It was time to leave.

Over the next few months, Megan and Grace packed up their belongings in boxes, labeled them, and moved them to a cousin's house. They reached out to Megan's English teacher, who agreed to help. The plan was working well, but then Lindsey sent an email to their father revealing Megan and Grace's intention to leave while also accusing Grace of an affair with her husband. Megan and Grace's parents called them into their bedroom. Her mother began recording a video on her phone. As their father read the email aloud, Megan realized this was it. Grace would be excommunicated for sure. Maybe her too. She turned to Grace and whispered, "We need to go."

They rushed to their bedrooms to pack what was left of their things while their father screamed. Their mother pleaded for them to appeal to their grandfather, Fred Phelps. Instead, Megan walked across their shared backyards to his home and then hugged him and her grandmother goodbye.

When the elders appeared, she walked back to her bedroom hugging and parting ways with family members along the way. A few hours later, they had loaded up the family minivan with the help of their father. He took them to a motel, paid the clerk, unloaded the van, hugged them, and drove away.

They later called Megan's English teacher, and by the end of the night they were set up in his basement. He sat with them for a few hours, and then they fell asleep on a pair of couches. The next morning, they returned with a U-Haul, filled it, and left for good.

———

"Since I left the church, my thinking about so many things has changed," Megan said. "And it's shocking to me how easy so many of those changes were. For instance, my thinking about gay people, or Jewish people, all these people that we had targeted, these groups that we had targeted when I was at the church. All these things we believed about them were just wrong."

Like Zach, Megan had left the church because she couldn't tolerate her home life. It wasn't until after she left that she changed her mind about specific beliefs and attitudes, especially concerning gay people. But, she said, "it was very easy for me to switch those gears. Part of that, of course, was because we believed that we were loving people. It's not like I hated them and then I loved them. I thought I loved them. Then I realized that's not really how you love people. This is a much better way."

I asked Megan why she and Zach weren't swayed while they were still in the church. They had confronted people who saw the world differently thousands of times as they picketed across the country, as they interacted on social media. They had seen so many counterexamples of how to treat others, how to think and feel and believe.

"Community," she said, reiterating what Caitlyn had told me on the front porch of Equality House. "I'm surrounded by all these people that I love and who love me, who show me that they love me in all of these very practical ways, all of the time. That is the air that you breathe. And so, when you grow up in an environment like that, especially like Westboro, where it is extremely doctrinaire—" She searched for the right words. "—We were thinking and talking about Bible verses and all of the evidence to support our views—all of the time. We were reading the Bible—every day. We were memorizing the verses—every day. We were standing on the streets talking to people, defending those beliefs— every day. That was the narrative, the story that you're told. You have so many reasons to believe. You have all of these experiences that show you that this is right, that this is the way. There's a lot of inertia there."

I told her that made sense, that the research supported what she was saying, but still, what about all those picket lines? Why didn't it ever foster doubts?

"From the time I was five years old, I was standing on public side-walks, being put in a position to defend these beliefs. And so, to do that, you really have to know them, and to understand them, and to be able to do all of that in a moment. Because in the protests, it could be a very chaotic environment. You know, people are coming at you and they're really angry and hostile. You have to be very prepared to answer those things. And that was also a requirement. You know, be ready to give an answer. 'Be ready always to give an answer to every man that asketh you a reason for the hope that is in you with meekness and fear.' So, your ability to defend those things is a reflection of your salvation. That's how it feels."

Megan said she was still discovering new ways of being wrong. Three years before Sølvi was born, she read every book she could find on parenting, but she attributed watching how people on the outside dealt with children as the central source of her revelations. When children would throw a tantrum in public, she said she felt a "kind of shock" that their parents weren't freaking out.

I said it reminded me of what we had spoken about earlier, an insight from Piaget: how once we learn that something is incorrect, we also learn that the source from which we learned that thing *can be* incorrect, which opens us up to the idea that maybe the sources we trust could be wrong about a lot of other things. As Pascal had told me, maybe this was the crack that let in the light.

"Yes, that was me. And I sometimes wonder how many times I've actually had a realization a year ago, a few months ago. How many of these things does it take for somebody to eventually get to the place where I got to?" Megan spoke of the abuse, spanking and worse, she and Grace and Zach had suffered.

"It was definitely over-the-top," she said, "and not infrequently. And of course, I knew that I was never going to do that. I didn't want to hit my daughter. I was never going to do that." But the deeper epiphany for Megan was in how much more effective affirming emotions could be for small children.

"It's amazing how much faster all of the negative things go away when you let them move through them. When you're there to support them through those emotions rather than trying to clamp down on it. It's amazing, having watched not just my parents but my older brother, like the way that he would deal with his children. The harder he is pushing, the more they're resisting. Just making it so much more difficult for themselves and for the kids. And it's just amazing to see the way that my daughter responds to things my family would probably have seen as like coddling. I'm doing something wrong by treating her this way. But holy hell, she is so emotionally intelligent and understanding, like when she looks at her baby, like a little baby doll, her baby is crying and she says it's OK to cry. It's OK to be upset."

———

Four of Fred Phelps's children have left Westboro, and more than twenty of his grandchildren. The people who still attend are not sequestered from the world. The adults still hold jobs in the community, and the kids still attend the local school. While inside, Zach could play *Diablo* and *Mortal Kombat* on his computer; he could go on the internet and watch movies and television shows. Megan read David Foster Wallace, watched comedians like Jake Fogelnest, listened to bands like Foster the

People. To Westboro, those things were trivial. They were fighting the real evil in the world, so it wasn't a big deal if one of the grandchildren wanted to fight a digital demon in a video game or listen to a punk band wail about capitalism. Contact with the world of the sinners was never forbidden, but the nature of their contact was tightly controlled, and much of the time that contact was hostile and antagonistic.

Despite this, Zach told me he had no friends, never held conversations with people who weren't in the family. Outside the church, he was a ghost. Zach made his way through nursing school, and though he said he liked his classmates, he never developed any bonds with them. He believed the people of the secular world were headed for hell; they weren't God's people like the people in the church, so he maintained a friendly distance as he always had. His whole life, Zach remained trapped in dogma, wearing it like a diving suit, interacting with the same world as the people shouting from across the picket line but never making actual human connection with it.

Zach has since taken off that suit. He is even taking part in the parallel universe across the street. He's spent time at Equality House and participated in pickets against the church, holding signs with messages like YOU ARE BEAUTIFUL and FORGIVE AND FORGET. At those protests, he shouts, "Let's kill them with kindness," and "Let's show them what loving your neighbor is all about."

Five months after he left the church, Zach did an "Ask Me Anything" for Reddit, a live, online question-and-answer session open to anyone on the internet. He told the people participating that he now fully supported the rights of the LGBTQ community. "They are all humans to me, and they all deserve protection under the law. Who am I to stop love or say, 'You can't get married'?"

He implored commenters to treat members of the church with love, adding that since leaving the church he had drained all the malice from his heart. For years he had prayed for people to die. Now he wanted everyone to be happy. He expressed regret for picketing the funerals of soldiers and explained that at the time he believed he was "doing the kindest thing in the world" by warning people they were going to hell unless they turned back from sin.

"You picketed my brother's funeral," said one of the commenters. "He was a soldier who died in Afghanistan. It helps me a little to know what you all were thinking at that point in time. I'm glad you got out, and for what it's worth, I forgive you and your family. I hope they can find the peace they're really seeking."

Zach still believes the church can change, but only if the people they encounter from now on refuse to reflect back their scorn. If they expect hate, receiving love instead would prove to them their beliefs were incorrect.

"Saying 'fuck you' can easily be forgotten and it doesn't change their beliefs but only makes them feel validated," he explained. "If we treat them with kindness, they will realize that their interpretations of the Bible are ass backwards, and then they will open up their minds, I strongly believe."

He told me he hopes to get back into the medical profession because he spent the first twenty-three years of his life pumping "unkindness" into the world. He said he was interested in hospice care. He hated the idea that people in their last days might be alone.

He said he became interested in the idea because his grandfather, the founder of Westboro, was alone for much of the last six months of his life. He died in 2014 at the age of eighty-four. Before then, Zach would come over once or twice a week and watch *Judge Judy* with him, a show that Fred Phelps loved. He called it "comedy art," said Zach. His grandfather also gave him haircuts every three months or so for his entire life. "I don't want to turn my heart away from someone that I feel like is in the same despairing place that he was."

Though the church denies it, Zach says Fred Phelps was alone on his deathbed because he was excommunicated. The elders of a church built on his own beliefs rejected him for what Zach calls a "change of heart."

"I was there when he was excommunicated," he said. "He stepped out of the front door of the church, and he yelled down to the rainbow house. He said, 'You are good people!'"

I asked him, what could have prompted that after a lifetime of hate?

Zach said he thinks it's because his grandmother's health had been in sharp decline. She had gone into the hospital. She had to be intubated to breathe. Margie Phelps had been married to Fred for sixty-two years. They had thirteen children, fifty-four grandchildren, and seven great-grandchildren. The thought of her dying was deeply traumatic for him.

"I don't know. I'm not exactly sure, but based on my experience, when I've felt depressed, that's when I started to really try to improve myself and change my mind and try to approach the world differently," said Zach. "What I'm trying to say is that times of great distress prompt great change."

———

Before I spent time with Zach and Megan, the most appealing answer to why they had left Westboro was that they changed their beliefs about gay people, they disagreed with the church, and then left because of those disagreements. But that is not exactly what happened. Zach's and Megan's attitudes about LGBTQ people, about Judaism, about how to raise children, about themselves even—those all changed *after* they left.

Zach's and Megan's stories were different in many ways, but what they shared was the fact that it was the loss of a sense of community that prompted them to leave. It opened them up to the potential for changing their minds, and then they started to reconsider evidence that before had seemed invisible, nonsensical, and irrelevant. Still, even when they felt their first doubts, it took others, people on the outside who listened and showed them counterarguments wrapped in kindness, to truly pull them away. For Zach, it was medical school, then people like Caitlyn Cameron. For Megan, it was Twitter, then people like David Abitbol. For both, they couldn't leave their worldviews behind until they felt like there was a community on the outside that would welcome them into theirs.

With all these concepts and the science behind them fresh in my head, I felt I was ready to return to the story of Charlie Veitch. Listening to Megan, I recalled what Charlie said about the truthers; how his peers seemed like animals to him when, after he tried to convince them that they were wrong, they ridiculed the dead and the loved ones they left behind. In those arguments, the convictions of his companions grew stronger, but his grew weaker.

I had missed it when I first heard his story, but now it seemed clear. Like Megan, he too had been spending time with people from the outside, but where Charlie's story differed was that he wasn't living in a compound at the time; he wasn't part of a family that had raised him from birth. Still, he *was* part of a community, and though it was mostly online and still very young, as you will read in the next chapter, the psychological mechanisms that motivated him are the same ones that continue to motivate the people who remain inside Westboro. And as it turns out, those that prompted him to leave are the same ones that prompted Zach and Megan and the others to do the same.

6

THE TRUTH IS TRIBAL

A block away from the combination record store and coffee shop he
was eager to show me, Charlie stopped walking and directed my
attention to a mural in the distance that he said was, in fact, a lie.

From where we stood, the spray-painted artwork looked like a beautiful, realistic bird perched on a cluster of twisted vines arching across
the masonry, but he showed me that up close you could make out the
Converse sneakers logo just below and to the right of the bird. He
laughed about it and waited for me to connect the dots. I mused, feeling pressured. I couldn't be sure of Charlie's take. For him, every pattern
held a fascination. At every turn, he seemed on the alert for hidden
meanings, for how the mundane fit into a bigger system of ideas and
agendas. I assumed the mural for him was a sort of spray-painted canary
in the coalmine. Even graffiti could be a corporate lie. It was a signal to
those with eyes to see that the world was not as it seemed. I blew a little

disillusioned air out of my nostrils to communicate as much and shook my head. Charlie smiled and turned the corner, taking us onward.

Along the way, I looked up the mural. It was the work of an artist out of Sheffield called Faunagraphic, with a list of clients who included Liquitex and IKEA. She had been hired by Converse to paint murals across the UK for an advertising project they called Wall to Wall, and sure enough, a contracted crew using two large cranes and spray paint had put up the artwork over the course of two days. Good or bad? I didn't know, but it was certainly a layer of truth I wouldn't have ever peeled back the surface to see without Charlie Veitch as my guide.

I asked Charlie how he had become a truther. He told me he had never been part of a stable community who took him seriously until the truthers welcomed him. His father was a Scottish sailor, a first officer on an oil tanker. He met Charlie's mother while working in Rio de Janeiro. Charlie spent his first seven years in Brazil before he, his brother, and his mother moved to Tanzania, and then to wherever his dad was assigned after that—West Africa, Qatar, Saudi Arabia, and so on. Every few years he left the friends he had made and started over in a new school, in a new city, in a new country, in a new culture. Always an outsider, he was constantly bullied. When he was old enough to live on his own, his parents sent him to a boarding school in the UK while they remained in Saudi Arabia. There, he daily suffered racial slurs because of his dark skin and Brazilian lilt.

Charlie said his life of constant relocation ended abruptly inside the cold comfort of a cubicle. After he graduated with a degree in philosophy, he found a job in banking. On a schedule of sleep, commute, work, TV, repeat, he said he didn't feel like a "natural human being" anymore. Philosophy began to fade into the background as he grudgingly acclimated to the routines of white-collar life. He felt like he belonged nowhere. He had no tribe.

Then in 2006, Charlie watched a video in which Alex Jones explained how 9/11 was an inside job. Intrigued, he began to spend a lot of time online watching videos that made arguments like Jones's. Soon he was part of group discussions. And eventually, part of the groups themselves.

"I was an angry young man, angry at power structures, angry at elites and how unfair the world was, so it slotted nicely into my desire to have a narrative, which is I think how most people collapse into conspiracy theory," said Charlie. "You're looking for a scapegoat; your life is meaningless; you're just a little nobody, but then suddenly you feel like you're part of an elite. You know things."

"You're in the army of the enlightened," I said.

"Yeah, you're like Neo in the car after seeing the Oracle and you are looking at all those people, like, 'Wow, look at the Matrix. Look at all these poor people; they don't know anything. I know everything; I know the truth.' It's ego. A lot of it is ego, you know, when you fall into this thing."

Charlie started making his own videos, first lampooning the Church of Scientology, then about local protests and living under surveillance in a post-9/11 London. He partnered with other conspiracy You-Tubers, and they went on giggling romps through central London with megaphones making sarcastic Orwellian public service announcements. The stunts drew crowds, and police, and hundreds of thousands of views.

The officers often asked Charlie to just move along, but when he filmed a video in front of the American Embassy, the police detained him and asked him to stop filming. He resisted, kept filming, and as more officers began to approach, some armed with assault rifles and wearing body armor, they informed him that they had the right under the UK Terrorism Act to view his videos and ensure he wasn't using his camera in connection with planned terrorism or to gather information for terrorist purposes.

Charlie posted the whole encounter on YouTube. For truthers on the lookout for Orwellian goons, the video was an electrifying confirmation of their worst fears. It immediately went viral. Within a few days he was on the phone with world-famous conspiracy theorist Alex Jones. For Charlie, it was as if a hand had been extended from out of the very videos that had originally sparked his passion. He was plucked from the audience and asked to join the conversation happening on stage.

Back in 2009, Charlie and his embassy video appeared on the Alex Jones radio and YouTube show, and Charlie directed the Jones audience to his own YouTube channel, telling them they could find dozens of similar videos there exposing the looming authority state. The more hits he got, the more content he made. Soon, he was making decent money. When he was made redundant at his bank and lost his job, he didn't look for another one.

I asked Charlie about his impressions of Alex Jones and David Icke when he first met them. Surely, he had done some googling and discovered that Jones believed that the flu vaccine was a tool of enslavement, chemtrails made frogs gay, and that the governments of the Earth were prepping a race-targeting bioweapon. Icke thought he was in psychic contact with space-faring reptiles.

He said the feeling of belonging, of acceptance, was more important to him at that point than any unusual detail. He became pliant, willing to suspend his disbelief to not feel alone.

After spending time with Megan Phelps-Roper and her brother Zach, I felt like I had seen the outlines of something they both shared with Charlie Veitch, and the first clues came when I interviewed two neuroscientists who challenged people while they lay supine in a brain scanner.

In 2016, cognitive neuroscientists Sarah Gimbel, Sam Harris, and Jonas Kaplan identified a group of subjects who held strong opinions by asking them to mark on a scale from one to seven how strongly they believed in a variety of statements, some political, some neutral. They then placed them into an MRI machine and presented five counterarguments to each subject. For instance, if subjects thought Thomas Edison invented the light bulb, they read that it had been "invented 70 years before Edison." If they thought gun control should be more restrictive, they read things like, "Ten times more people are murdered with kitchen knives each year than are killed by assault weapons." The goal wasn't to persuade the subjects to change their minds, just to measure what happened in their brains when challenged.

After reading the counterarguments, subjects again saw the original statements, and the researchers again asked them to rank their feelings on a scale from one to seven. Comparing the two reactions, researchers found that people readily softened their beliefs for neutral statements, but for topics like abortion, same-sex marriage, and the death penalty, something else happened. As the arguments mounted, subjects responded to a threat to their convictions as if it was a threat to their very flesh and blood.

When a person was challenged about political wedge issues like abortion or welfare or gun control, the scanner showed that their brains went into fight-or-flight mode, causing their bodies to pump adrenaline, stiffening the muscles and moving blood out of the nonessential organs. As Gimbel told me, "The response in the brain that we see is very similar to what would happen if, say, you were walking through the forest and came across a bear."

Why such a bodily response? Because blood had rushed into a part of the brain called the default mode network, an interconnected set of regions that become active when people think about the self in relation to others. You know how meditation and psychedelics can make you feel like you are less attached to your identity and more one with everything? That's what happens when you dampen activity within the default mode network. Increasing activity does the opposite, less one with everything and more attached to your identity. The more subjects considered their selves, the more blood rushed into the amygdala and the insular cortex, two regions of the brain involved with regulating anger, fear, and keeping a check on your heart rate and perspiration.

"Remember that the brain's first and primary job is to protect our selves," Kaplan told me. "That extends beyond our physical self, to our psychological self. Once these things [beliefs, attitudes, and values] become part of our psychological self, they are then afforded all the same protections that the brain gives to the body."

But why? I asked.

Kaplan said he didn't know, but it likely had to do with group identity, and suggested I speak with psychologists who study how group identity affects our beliefs.

———

We've been studying how groups affect the minds of their members since World War II, when psychological research into conformity and group conflict became the centerpiece of psychological experimentation.

That work led to the famous Solomon Asch experiment in which people denied the truth of their own eyes when surrounded by actors who claimed a short line and a long line printed on a large card were the same length. A third of subjects bowed to social pressure and said they agreed, though later they said they internally felt at odds with the group. It also led to the Stanley Milgram experiments into obedience in which experimenters successfully goaded two thirds of subjects, who believed they were delivering electric shocks to strangers, to crank the electricity up to lethal doses. But the study of group identity began in earnest between those experiments, in 1954, when a group of psychologists created two tribes of children who nearly killed each other.

At Robbers Cave State Park in Oklahoma, the same year *Lord of the Flies* was published, psychologist Muzafer Sherif and his colleagues, posing as camp counselors, took over a summer camp and, via separate buses, deposited twenty-two fifth-grade boys, ages eleven and twelve, into two neighboring campsites.

For a while, the neighboring camps remained unaware of each other. They began to form their own cultures, and within days arbitrary nuances shared by group members became established norms and rules of conduct. They named themselves the Eagles and the Rattlers, and each group developed differing rituals and differing taboos. When Sherif and his colleagues told the boys there was another group at the camp, each group started to describe the unseen others as "intruders" and "outsiders." They then met for some games: baseball, tug-of-war, touch football, and so on. They hurled insults, and the spectators groused about how dirty the other boys seemed. At bedtime, each group spent all night talking about the disgusting aspects of the other, of *them*.

The boys soon blamed every misfortune they suffered on the devious plots of the other group. When the swimming hole was colder than usual, they said the other group must have filled it with ice cubes. When they found garbage on the beach, they said the other group must have left it there, forgetting that it was their own garbage from a few days earlier.

The experiment eventually had to be shut down in the third week. The animosity had built between them until the Eagles stole the Rattlers' flag off the baseball field, burned it, then returned it. As payback, the Rattlers organized a raiding party and burned the Eagles' flag. The Rattlers then painted their bodies and raided the Eagles' cabins. The Eagles retaliated and did the same. At night, they talked about engaging in open combat. Eventually, when the two groups started circling and gathering rocks for an all-out war, the scientists intervened. Fearing someone might get murdered any day now, they relocated the camps some distance apart.

Fascinated by the Robbers Cave experiment, in the 1970s psychologist Henri Tajfel wanted to expand on the research. Tajfel grew up in Poland, and as a Jewish man he had become obsessed with answering the question of how one group could hate another so much that perpetrating genocide could seem reasonable. He studied prejudice throughout the 1950s, and at the time the assumption across most of psychology was that animosity between groups was based on aggressive personalities rising to power and influencing others. Tajfel was skeptical. Looking across many different examples of genocide, he noticed the differences people claimed as the source of their hatred seemed as arbitrary as the differences between the Rattlers and the Eagles—fifth-grade boys from the same town, with similar families, similar upbringings, and similar worldviews.

Tajfel wondered what would happen if, in a laboratory setting, you stripped away every single salient difference between two groups of people, even their personalities, and simply told them they were in one group and not another? He then wondered, if you started adding small differences one at a time, like one group wears glasses and the other doesn't, at what point would people start showing favoritism for their side and bias toward the other? If he could find a starting point, something he called the "minimal group paradigm," it would establish a baseline for what sort of differences led to prejudice and discrimination. What he discovered was that there is no baseline. Any difference, of any kind, would activate our innate us-versus-them psychology.

In one experiment, Tajfel gathered boys from a school in Bristol, many of them with identical backgrounds, many of them friends, and had them individually and anonymously look at a page of forty dots for half a second and then estimate how many they had seen. No matter what the subjects said, they were then randomly sorted and told that they had either underestimated or overestimated the true number.

Tajfel then told the subjects that since they were already there, it would be great if they could help his team with another experiment, a money allocation task. He told them other overestimators and underestimators, boys like them, had just performed another assignment for which they would now determine a fair split of the rewards.

He gave them a choice between a greater reward equally split, or a lesser reward split unevenly that favored one group and not the other. Tajfel expected that at this minimal level of identity, labeled only as underestimator or an overestimator, subjects would split the money evenly. Then he could add more differences to see when they began to show bias. What he found was just being labeled as an overestimator or underestimator of dots motivated the boys to favor their groups. Worse still, they vastly preferred a smaller reward if it meant their own imaginary group would be better off than the imaginary outsiders.

Tajfel's work has been replicated many times, with preferences for painters, with eye color, with hats, even with randomly assigned even and odd numbers, all with the same results: there is no salient, shared quality around which a group will not form. And then, once people become an *us*, we begin to loathe a *them*, so much so that we are willing to sacrifice the greater good if it means we can shift the balance in our group's favor.

Them. It's a powerful word, and the research, in both psychology and neuroscience, suggests that because our identities have so much to do with group loyalty, the very word itself, *identity*, is best thought of as that which identifies us as, well, *us*—but more importantly *not them*.

It's a basic human drive, like hunger or sleep. We are built by primate genes that construct primate brains that carry within them innate mental states that can be triggered by sensory inputs. Among them are empathy, sympathy, jealousy, shame, and embarrassment. These mental states, which happen *to us*, which we feel without asking to feel them, clue us into our nature. As social primates, we can't help but care a great deal about what others think about us.

Humans aren't just social animals; we are ultra-social animals. We are the kind of primate that survives by forming and maintaining groups. Much of our innate psychology is all about grouping up and then nurturing that group—working to curate cohesion. If the group survives, we survive. So a lot of our drives, our motivations, like shame, embarrassment, ostracism, and so on, have more to do with keeping the group strong than keeping any one member, including ourselves, healthy. In other words, we are willing to sacrifice ourselves and others for the group, if it comes to that.

There are a lot of terms for this in modern psychology, political science, sociology, and so on—I prefer "tribal psychology," but it's also called "extreme partisanship," "cultural cognition," et cetera. Whatever the label, the latest evidence coming out of social science is clear: humans value being good members of their groups much more than they value being right, so much so that as long as the group satisfies those needs, we will choose to be wrong if it keeps us in good standing with our peers.

When I asked sociologist Brooke Harrington her thoughts on all this, she summed it up by saying, if there was an $E = mc^2$ of social science, it would be SD > PD, "social death is more frightening than physical death."

This is why we feel deeply threatened when a new idea challenges the ones that have become part of our identity. For some ideas, the ones that identify us as members of a group, we don't reason as individuals; we reason as a member of a tribe. We want to seem trustworthy, and reputation management as a trustworthy individual often supersedes most other concerns, even our own mortality.

This is not entirely irrational. A human alone in this world faces a lot of difficulty, but being alone in the world before modern times was almost certainly a death sentence. So we carry with us an innate drive to form groups, join groups, remain in those groups, and oppose other groups. But once you can identify *them*, you start favoring *us*; so much so that given a choice between an outcome that favors both groups a lot or one that favors both much less but still favors yours more than theirs, that's the one you will pick. If you add any conflict over resources of any kind, humans will instinctively enter us-versus-them thinking, even if that's not the overall most beneficial strategy. And this is where tribal psychology gets really weird.

In times of great conflict, where groups are in close contact with each other, or communicating with each other a lot, individuals will work extra hard to identify themselves to each other as *us* and not *them*.

In such an environment, anything can become a signal of loyalty, and how you signal will paint you as a good loyal member or a traitor. What you wear, the music you like, what car you drive, all of it. If an attitude or a belief or a stated opinion on an issue that was previously neutral becomes an identifier, it becomes a badge of loyalty or a symbol of shame, a signal to others that you are or are not trustworthy.

Psychologist Dan Kahan, an expert on tribal psychology, told me this effect extends beyond politics. Any opinion, he said, can become fused with group identity.

He said the most instructive case study for him was the fact that Christian conservatives today still strongly oppose the HPV vaccine because years ago the makers sought early approval for girls before it was approved for boys, and sought to make it mandatory. Early approval meant debate in Congress. Mandatory meant debate in state legislatures. Both meant people with zero scientific knowledge raising questions about why this was a mandatory vaccine for girls instead of boys.

"The story goes, somebody comes knocking on the door, and they say, 'You know your daughter in the backyard over there on the swings? The twelve-year-old who is going to be having sex next year? She needs to get an STD shot or don't bring her to school.'" The result, Kahan said, was a left-versus-right tribal skirmish over the suggestion that the vaccine would inevitably lead to preteen promiscuity.

At the same time people were fighting about the HPV vaccine, scientists introduced the hepatitis B vaccine. On paper, it is nearly identical. It is administered to preteen girls, and it prevents a sexually transmitted disease that causes cancer. "But nobody was arguing about that one," said Kahan. It was quickly and easily approved, and today is accepted by 95 percent of parents, including Christian conservatives.

The difference was that people first learned about the hepatitis B vaccine from their doctors. They first learned about the HPV vaccine by watching reports on MSNBC and Fox News. Those programs framed the message as an us-versus-them issue, which made it a tribal issue. People then looked to their groups for guidance about how to feel, and once they felt one way or the other, motivated reasoning provided their explanations and justifications for opposing it.

In one of Kahan's studies, he showed people who identified as strongly Republican or strongly Democrat a photo of an older man. He told them he was a highly credentialed scientist named Robert Linden, a member of the National Academy of Science and a professor of meteorology at MIT with a PhD from Harvard. He then asked the subjects to indicate if they agreed or disagreed that Dr. Linden was an expert on global warming. All the subjects marked "strongly agree," the highest mark on a scale of one to six. Then subjects read about Linden's scientific opinion on the issue. Half the subjects read that Linden thought human-caused global warming wasn't real and that climate change was nothing to worry about. The other half read that he thought human-caused global warming was not only real, but climate change was a threat to the survival of the human race.

Kahan then asked subjects if they still agreed or disagreed that Linden was an expert. In the global-warming-is-not-real group, conservatives continued to say that he was an expert, but liberals flipped their ratings. In the global-warming-is-real group, it was liberals who continued to see Linden as an expert but conservatives who flipped. In each condition, for half the people, Linden instantly transformed into a crackpot. His credentials, of course, never changed.

The research into tribal psychology is clear. If a scientific, fact-based issue is considered neutral—volcanoes or quasars or fruit bats—people don't do this. They tend to trust what an expert has to say. But once tribal loyalties are introduced, the issue becomes debatable.

Despite how it may seem, Kahan emphasized that this kind of motivated reasoning is rational. The average person will never be in a position where beliefs on gun control or climate change or the death penalty will affect their daily lives. The only useful reason to hold any sort of beliefs on those issues, to argue about them, or share them with others is to "convey group allegiance," Kahan told me. If holding alternative positions might cause you to lose friends, lose advertisers, lose a job, or face public shaming, rejecting what would otherwise be neutral, empirical evidence would be a very rational decision. For issues about which your tribe has formed a consensus, others will use your agreement as a measure of how much they can trust you. If your values seem out of alignment with the group, "you could really suffer serious material and emotional harm," explained Kahan.

He spoke of Bob Inglis, who served as one the most conservative members of the US Congress for decades. When he announced in 2010 that he believed in climate change and wanted to do something about it to protect his constituents, he lost his reelection in a 71 percent to 29 percent landslide. Kahan explained that "if you are a barber in the fifth district of South Carolina where he was the representative, you know that if after you get done giving somebody a shave with a straight razor you ask them to sign your petition to save the polar bears from climate change, you'll be out of a job as quickly as Inglis was. People face that kind of pressure all the time."

———

When we sense a threat to our place within a trusted group—if we feel like *we* might be considered untrustworthy for changing our minds—we avoid it. Which for me finally explained why the other members of Charlie's group, the truthers, refused to accept the evidence before them.

What we know depends on beliefs: knowledge we assume is true. It also depends on attitudes: our positive or negative evaluations of that which we believe. And these both influence, and are influenced by, our values: our estimations of what is most important, most worth our time to pursue. But it is impossible to know or evaluate everything. The world is too vast, too complex, and ever-changing. So a hefty portion of our beliefs and attitudes are based on received wisdom from trusted peers and authorities. Whether in a video, within a textbook, behind a news desk, or standing at a pulpit, for that which we can't prove ourselves, it is in their expertise we place our faith.

These reference groups are where we get our knowledge about Saturn's moons and the nutritional value of granola, what happens after we die and how much money Argentina owes China. They also influence our attitudes about everything from jazz trombones to nuclear power and the healing power of aloe vera. We consider what they tell us to be true, the prevailing attitude among them to be reasonable, because we trust they have vetted the information. We trust them because we identify with them. They share our values and our anxieties. They seem like us, or they seem like the people we would like to be. They share our attitudes, and so we are willing to share their beliefs.

Once we consider a reference group trustworthy, questioning *any* of

their accepted beliefs or attitudes questions *all* of them, and this can
be a problem. Humans are primates, and primates are gregarious creatures. We can't help but cluster together into groups. If we identify as
Marvel fans or Christians, as loyal to QAnon or veganism, then the beliefs, attitudes, and values we share with our group become integral to
our group identity. We become the kind of people who feel a certain way,
and who believe certain things. Questioning those beliefs will threaten
our sense of self, and at the biological level we will respond with fear,
anger, and all the other emotional trappings of fight-or-flight.

When we meet as ambassadors of our reference groups, the unques-
tionable shared truths that secure our group identities have historically
led to our deepest disagreements, our most intractable arguments, our
most gridlocked politics, and our bloodiest wars.

Scientists, doctors, and academics are not immune. But lucky for
them, in their tribes, openness to change and a willingness to question
one's beliefs or to pick apart those of others also signals one's loyalty to
the group. Their belonging goals are met by pursuing accuracy goals.
For groups like truthers, the pursuit of belonging only narrowly overlaps
with the pursuit of accuracy, because anything that questions dogma
threatens excommunication.

We don't just use our previous experiences to maintain our balance
on the tightrope between being dangerously wrong and dangerously ignorant, we use the people around us; when *they* refuse to change *their*
minds, it's a greater barrier to change than whatever stubbornness our
dogmas demand. Trapped in a group hug of shared motivations, we may
find ourselves unable to change our minds when the facts suggest we
should. There's no better example of this than what happens when a
person wanders into a group of people who share their motivation to
trade information about a conspiracy theory.

Anni Sternisko, a psychologist who studies conspiratorial communities, told me that, broadly speaking, all conspiracy theorists start out by seeking out others who share their views by way of two "motivational allures." Those who are happy with their current social identity "are drawn to the content of a conspiracy theory," the details and the specific narrative. Those who are still searching for an identity, those who wish to signal their uniqueness among peers, are drawn to the qualities of a conspiracy theory, the anxieties and viewpoints it seems to confirm.

Sternisko said to think of it like picking out a movie to watch. If you are a fan of Adam Driver, you don't care what the movie is about. Horror, drama, historical fiction—as long as Adam Driver is in the movie, you're interested. On the other hand, if you are in the mood for science fiction, you don't much care who stars in it as long as there are spaceships and aliens. Both paths could lead you to watching *Star Wars*, and eventually to Star Wars conventions, and a new identity as a hardcore member of the fandom.

The same is true of conspiracy theory communities, said Sternisko. It doesn't matter which of these two motivations initially leads a person in. Once invested in ideas that seem far-fetched to their peers, people begin to feel the threat of ostracism, and the embrace of those who share your reality becomes increasingly inviting, until you eventually identify more with the conspiratorial community than any other. At some point, the motivation to belong supersedes all other motivations.

Conspiratorial thinking becomes most resistant to change once a person becomes bound to a group identity as a conspiracy theorist. After that, a threat to the beliefs becomes a threat to the self, and the psychological mechanisms that bind us together as groups take over; those are what prevent the metacognition necessary to escape.

———

Steven Novella, a neurologist and conspiracy theory expert, told me that at the cognitive level, we likely have some evolved sensitivity for people conspiring against our interests. There's research backing this, suggesting our brains possess ancient psychological mechanisms that evolved to help us detect "dangerous coalitions."

Couple that with the internet and our incredible powers of pattern recognition, and when that same mental wiring is used to make sense of a complicated, threatening event like 9/11, we begin to suspect evil-doers could be anywhere. Novella said that when we are fearful, we are constantly attempting to reduce the chaos and complexity of an uncertain world into something manageable and tangible, something we can fight, like the work of a small group of malevolent puppet masters. At our most anxious, we give the side eye to governments and institutions and political parties—to the groups that we feel are not our own—not just a few nearby individuals.

This kind of thinking can lead to the "conspiratorial loop," a logic prison that makes escaping the conspiracy theory very difficult. If conspiracy theorists discover any disconfirmatory evidence, then they may conclude it was planted by the conspirators to throw them off the trail. It suggests the conspiracy is even bigger and more complicated than they first imagined, and more research needs to be conducted. If the theory has gaps, then they may conclude the missing evidence indicates a cover-up, and the conspiracy becomes grander in scope to account for the missing pieces.

People become trapped. If the evidence disconfirms their theory, it's evidence the theory is true. If there is no evidence, then the conspirators are more powerful than they imagined.

Like most people, the people who would eventually identify as truthers experienced a host of fears and anxieties after the events of 9/11. For people who already distrusted authority and state control, everything after the attacks seemed like an excuse to tighten it. Over time, they found one another online and formed a community that produced an endless amount of investigative material for anyone else who was similarly motivated to seek out the truth. Once inside, they narrowed their circle of trust.

As social animals with the power to persuade and be persuaded, there is a way out. When we feel it's not *them*, but our own peers who have become untrustworthy, we will unconsciously attempt to change the group through argumentation. If that fails, we reach for empathy, for connection, outside our group if we must. If we find it, we become open to the challenging ideas of those who show us kindness: first about *them*, then about *us*. The beliefs, attitudes, and values we share with the group then become safer to question. If we change our minds about *them*, we then change our minds about *us*.

So how did Charlie escape? I would learn it wasn't the facts, not by themselves. He had become open to the facts because, like Megan, he had found others in communities more in line with his values than the one to which he was bound; and, like Megan, he had met a romantic partner there. When they couldn't express their shared values among the truthers, those bindings began to corrode, and with them, his resistance to change.

———

Months before traveling to New York, Charlie met his partner, Stacey Bluer, at a festival called the Truth Juice Gathering.

Truth Juice groups meet across the UK to listen to New Age,

transhumanist, occult, spirituality, and conspiracy theorist speakers deliver lectures to small audiences about a wide range of topics: from geopolitics to telepathy to hallucinogens to King Arthur to the BP oil spill to evidence for aliens and a flat Earth. Sometimes they use microphones and slides; sometimes they seem more freestyle, like beat poets. Truth Juice gatherings bring all those groups together for an outdoor event with tents, music, and campfires. They aren't looking for a particular truth, but *the* truth.

It was at this sort of gathering that Charlie began to move away from the truther tribe and into another, less-paranoid group of like-minded people who shared his core values.

At the 2011 Truth Juice Gathering, his followers, who he called the Love Police, merged with the festivalgoers and lay on the ground in a square in the town of Wrexham, Wales, to form the word *LOVE* with their bodies. As host of the first open-mic night at the first Truth Juice Gathering in 2010, Charlie talked about escaping society's "glass and metal cages" and how unnatural it was to have a "photocopier chat" instead of riding across the plains chasing buffalo. He asked the audience to tap into their inner divinity and to go "infinitely into yourself, forever . . . we all have the secrets of the universe deep inside us," because consciousness is "infinite, fractal," and "holographic."

At Truth Juice, Charlie said he was a bigger phenomenon than he had ever been as a truther; but more importantly, he felt like his authentic self. When Charlie was riding this swell of acceptance, Stacey was one of the many people constituting the wave. She said at the time it felt something like "a new Summer of Love."

Falling deeper into this separate subculture, the mission of the Love Police became less about exposing the absurdity of the coming police state and more about raising awareness for humanist causes. Charlie partnered with another YouTube-heavy activist group called the Kindness Offensive, whose mission was to hack the "slave-work-money-gift" paradigm. He became what people in the New Age community call a "light worker."

Charlie said that for the first time in a long time, he felt fantastic. His health improved, along with his haircut. People clamored to take photos with him, praised his light work, and pleaded for a chance to hang out. His day-to-day interactions shifted in tone. His comment sections and emails overflowed with approval, along with invitations to more New Age, spiritual, and enlightenment events.

Charlie had left his megaphone behind to ascend the ranks of the UK's neo–New Age community when the BBC came calling. He was planning to attend a neo-hippie, environmentally conscious, anti-GMO music festival called Sunrise when he received their first email. The producers who would later take him to New York met him at the festival.

The truth was that when Charlie met with the other truthers a few weeks later, he was already part of another tribe, and it was through that new group identity he filtered the evidence. One can hear it in his video from Times Square. "We're not gullible. We're truth seekers in a 9/11 Truth movement just trying to find out the truth about what happened." And it's in the title on YouTube: "No Emotional Attachment to 9/11 Theories—The Truth is Most Important." And it is in his signoff at the end: "Honour the truth—Charlie."

In New York, the evidence that seemed like confirmation of a conspiracy to the others seemed like disconfirmation to Charlie, and what was once evidence of a hidden truth became evidence of deeper one. He was free to question his beliefs because he was free of the fear of ostracism for doing so. Changing his mind as a truther labeled him a heretic, but in Truth Juice it was further proof that he had seen the light.

Throughout the 2000s, research into what psychologists call identity maintenance found that reputation management is the glue that binds us to our peer groups. When we feel as though accepting certain facts could damage our reputation, could get us ostracized or excommunicated, we become highly resistant to updating our priors. But the threat to our reputation can be lessened either by affirming a separate group identity or reminding ourselves of our deepest values.

In one study, in the aftermath of 9/11, scientists brought subjects into the lab who strongly supported the war in Iraq. Half then completed a self-affirmation activity that emphasized the importance of their patriotic values. Scientists asked subjects to recall times when they had lived up to those values. The other half completed a control task that emphasized their sense of humor and creativity. Then participants either met experimenters who wore flag pins or experimenters who wore lab coats. Each person then read a report critical of the foreign policy of the United States, suggesting the country bore some responsibility for the conditions that had led to the attack. Most people rejected the evidence and the arguments, but not those whose core values had been reaffirmed *and* who felt they were in the midst of fellow patriots. When those conditions were met, the subjects reviewed the evidence thoughtfully and without bias.

In a follow-up study, scientists divided pro-choice subjects into two groups. One group wrote an essay about how they had made someone feel good, and the other wrote an essay about how they had once hurt someone's feelings. Subjects in both groups were then asked to pretend they were a Democrat legislator who was about to negotiate a new abortion rights bill with a legislator from the opposing party. Subjects who got a chance to affirm they were good people were much more likely to compromise and reach an agreement with their ideological opponent than people who felt their reputations were at stake.

Charlie joined a conspiratorial community thanks to what psychologists call an oppositional identity: he saw himself as a subversive, an underdog who opposed the status quo and, as Charlie might say, the power structures of elites. Once inside, he fell into tribal psychology, and the beliefs of the truthers became signals of trustworthiness to his peers. But he eventually learned that the values that led him into 9/11 conspiracy theories didn't make him such an extreme outlier in the world at large once he could express them as a member of Truth Juice. Unlike the other truthers, it freed him to feel empathy for widows and widowers, to accept the expertise of demolitions experts; it made his fellow truthers seem callous and close-minded.

If we feel we are falling short of our values, if we are not good people by whatever standards we consider important, we become motivated to signal otherwise by publicly endorsing beliefs that will re-ingratiate us to our peers. But if we feel affirmed, accepting challenging evidence or considering new perspectives poses less of a threat. And that affirmation grows stronger if we're reminded that we belong to several tribes and can rush to the safety of more amenable groups when the ones that judge us the harshest begin to feel less welcoming. If people recall that they already live by their core values in some way across groups, self-affirmation puts the onus on our peers to live up to them as well. If we realize our groups fall short of those values, like Megan and Charlie had, we can feel justified in leaving. We can feel safe to change our minds.

———

Charlie's story reveals that it is rational to resist facts when one has no social safety net. When he admitted that he was wrong, when he changed his mind in a way that signaled he disagreed with the dogma of his truther tribe, they did what we most fear: they shunned him, then ostracized him.

But as Megan's, Zach's, and Charlie's stories reveal, when the conditions are just right, even people trapped inside tribal psychology can be persuaded to change their minds. Even the boys in the Robbers Cave experiment, where they more or less created *Lord of the Flies* at a summer camp, changed their minds. When the experimenters presented those two tribes with common goals, like fixing the engine of the bus that would take them home, they were able to rise above their tribal psychology and work together. After, they merged into one community and even sat together on the ride back.

I asked Tom Stafford, a psychologist and cognitive scientist who studies decision-making and learning at the University of Sheffield, why he thought fact-allergic subcultures like cults, truthers, and anti-vaxxers proliferate in the modern world.

Stafford said, "Truth is social." The problem with conspiracy theorists, he said, is that they thrive in social groups that are not social. A true tribe would live in a buzzing community brimming with contact. "When you see someone cry, you want to cry with them," said Stafford. "You are eating together and hunting together and building together, whereas cults have this weird insularity and hierarchical structure." If you are interacting mostly through text, you don't see people crying. "The social truth is still there, but in an abnormal social structure."

Conspiracy theorists and fringe groups may hold individually coherent theories, but there is no true consensus, just the assumption of consensus. If they hung out together, they might catch on to that, but since they rarely do, they can each keep their individual theories and still assume they have the backing of a tribe. They never get a chance to argue face-to-face, so there is no evolution of ideas, no central theory strengthened by constant challenge and defense. Everyone can believe a different aspect of the 9/11 story or see vaccines as harmful in their own way and not realize how many people in the community disagree with them. Despite a fragmentation of beliefs, individuals aren't motivated to argue with one another. Everyone is advancing everyone's ideas, even if they don't agree.

Stafford contrasted it to how an institution like medicine operates. "You get a real doctor, and they won't try and defend everything about medicine," said Stafford. "They'll say, 'Oh some of this must be wrong, but we don't know which bits,' or 'We don't know why this works, but it seems to work. These could be the reasons we are doing this now, but we know we didn't do it ten years ago.' Whereas a conspiracy theorist has to defend all of it."

Stafford suggested I look at the psychological research into arguing, because when isolated at a computer adding one's ideas to a pool of propositions, people trapped in tribal psychology may feel as though they are debating, deliberating, and reasoning together, but they are often part of an antisocial social group in which everyone is reasoning alone.

———

Though we change our minds constantly, we also change them carefully. For all learning machines, biological or artificial, updating one's priors is a risk-versus-reward proposition. If the brain assumes the risks of being wrong outweigh any potential rewards for changing its mind, we favor assimilation over accommodation, and most of the time that serves us well.

If your roommate tells you that drinking bleach is completely safe, in fact it's good for you, you'll probably change your mind about your roommate, not bleach. But you *will* change your mind about *something*.

A mind before an argument is not the same mind after, and that's uniquely human. Every creature that can learn can change its mind through experiences, but humans can use their experiences to change the minds of others, even others they will never meet. After talking with Stafford, I felt compelled to learn more, and in the next chapter we will explore how we gained that ability, and why.

———

"The truth is tribal," Charlie told me. "From 2009 through to 2011, I'd only hang out with very out-there conspiracy-minded people, so I was in that subculture, separate from the mainstream."

The film crew that shot *Conspiracy Road Trip* helped, he said, because they were "alternative, fun types," like he saw himself, like he saw Stacey, like the people he hung out with at Truth Juice, "yet they didn't have these conspiracy beliefs." It added to the self-affirmation that opened him up to the possibility he was wrong. The fact that he was traveling with those people in proximity for ten days and felt closer to them than to the truthers inflamed a dissonance he couldn't shake. He said it primed him to listen to what the experts had to say.

"I've always been looking for my tribe, and something started happening in my brain on that 9/11 trip," Charlie said. "Meeting all these people. I started to see that perhaps the tribe that welcomed me so much were not mentally healthy people."

I asked him what hope there was to change people's minds if most of them can't do what he did. You can't take a climate change denier and send them to Antarctica to meet a scientist working with core samples. Even if you could, not everyone can betray their tribes. Not everyone has a social safety net like he did.

He suggested that wouldn't be necessary. For issues like climate change, he said to do as psychologists suggest: appeal to their deeper values. Ask them why they joined the groups to which they identify. Discover their motivations. If they value family, show deniers the effects of the ongoing drought in South Africa, the worst drought in a hundred years. "Show them families whose children have maybe died or are malnourished because the crops have failed. That's the only way into their brain. Through the heart. Otherwise, if you try to keep it abstract, they will say, 'You are a fucking liar. Where are your facts coming from?' You can't argue with a screaming baby. A screaming baby is what it is."

Before we parted, Charlie paraphrased David Hume, the Scottish philosopher, saying, "'Reason is a slave of the emotions.' And it's true. If you're going to change someone's mind you've got to hit them in the balls—which is the heart. The heartballs."*

---

*Hume's actual quote, from Book II, Part III, Section III: *Of the Influencing of Motives the Will* in *A Treatise of Human Nature*, is: "Reason is and ought only be the slave of the passions, and can never pretend to any other office than to serve and obey them."

7

ARGUING

Back in 2011, I wrote a book titled *You Are Not So Smart*, and then a follow-up titled *You Are Now Less Dumb*. Together they ran through the science of the day concerning human reasoning, decision-making, and judgment.

The general thesis of those books was that we are unaware of how unaware we are; we are the unreliable narrators in the stories of our own lives. In psychology, this is called the introspection illusion.

Decades of research had shown that though we often feel very confident that we know the antecedents of our own thoughts, feelings, and behaviors, along with the sources of our motivations and goals, we are rarely privy to such information. Instead, we observe our own behavior and contemplate our own thoughts the way an observer would another person, and then we create rationalizations and justifications for what we think, feel, and believe. Guesses, basically. Sometimes right, often wrong. Yet we rarely admit to that fact, preferring instead to live within a fictional biography that continuously portrays us as reasonable, rational people carefully contemplating the evidence before us, soberly reaching conclusions that anyone else would reach if they were as smart as we believe ourselves to be.

In the books, and later in lectures, I liked to demonstrate this with three different examples. In one, I give people a chance to play a game created by the psychologist Peter Wason. The premise is this: I am going to pick three numbers out of all the numbers in the universe using a secret rule, and your task is to figure the rule I'm using. Here we go.

2–4–6

Think you already have it figured out? Here are three more:

10–12–14

By now it should be clear. But just in case, here are three more:

24–26–28

In large groups, I ask everyone to raise their hand before we begin, and then to lower their hand if they feel sure they have figured out the rule. By the third set, typically everyone's hand is down. Next, I ask if anyone would like to prove they know what it is by picking out three more numbers using my rule.

Imagine I've asked you to do it. What would you pick? Most people go with three even numbers like:

32–34–36

If you had chosen these three—or any three even numbers in order—I would say, "Yes! Those three numbers correspond to my rule."

And if we stopped here and moved on, you might live the rest of your life pretty sure you had confirmed your hunch was right. But here are some more numbers that I can pick out using my rule:

1–2–3
55–56–67
33–3,333–99,999

That's because the rule is any three numbers in a row, one bigger than the last. But since three even numbers in a row corresponds to that rule, when you guess that's the answer you stop looking for more information. Once it seems like you've received confirmation that you are correct, you don't go looking for disconfirmation just to make sure. And that's the essence of confirmation bias, our most fundamental cognitive predisposition. When motivated to find a reason for a hunch, we tend to search for evidence to confirm it, and when we believe we've found that confirmation, we stop looking.

My second example came from a study by Mark Snyder and Nancy Cantor in which a group of subjects read about a week in the life of a woman named Jane. The scientists made sure that throughout the story Jane sometimes seemed extroverted and at other times introverted. After two weeks, the subjects returned to the lab, this time divided into two groups. In one, the researchers said Jane was considering a job as a real-estate agent. They then asked the subjects if they thought she would be well suited to the role. Most of them said yes, remembering all the times that Jane seemed outgoing. They then told them Jane was also considering a job as a librarian and wondered if they thought she should go for it. This time, most of the subjects said no. Leaning on stereotypes, they said Jane was too extroverted for a job like that. In the other group, they asked the questions in the reverse order. Would she be a good librarian? Yes, they said, remembering the times she had enjoyed keeping to herself. She was also thinking of becoming a real-estate agent. No, they said, she's too introverted. She'd hate it.

The subjects in the Jane study started with the same evidence, but when differently motivated by different questions, they generated different arguments for different conclusions. When those conclusions were challenged, they pointed to the evidence that had confirmed their hunches. Thanks to confirmation bias, just by reversing the order, and thus reversing the initial positions, a once unified group became divided on how it saw the truth.

For years I had used these examples to demonstrate the power of motivated reasoning. Further still, and the research on this is clear, the more intelligent you are, and the more educated, the more data at your disposal, the better you become at rationalizing and justifying your existing beliefs and attitudes, regardless of their accuracy or harmfulness. Basically, when motivated to find supporting evidence, that's all we look for. When we desire to find a reason for A over B, we find it.

For me, there is no better example of that phenomenon than the third study I have most often referenced. Peter Ditto and his colleagues asked people to place yellow strips of construction paper in their mouths and told them they would turn green within twenty seconds if they did not have a terrible disease. Since it was only construction paper, it never changed colors. People waited for minutes to watch it turn. They often rechecked dozens of times. Some even asked to take strips home. But when he told another group the paper would change if they *did* have the disease, they waited the twenty seconds, took one look, handed the paper back to the experimenters, and left the room. As psychologist Dan Gilbert once said of the study, when the bathroom scale gives us bad news, we reweigh ourselves a few times to make sure. When it gives us good news, we step off and go about our day.

Thanks to confirmation bias, when motivated to find a reason for a hunch, we don't always employ our reasoning in pursuit of the truth. When otherwise motivated, we reason toward conclusions that meet a need or ensure a desired outcome. For instance, in studies where scientists present a series of numbers and letters, people paid to identify all the letters are more likely to mistake the number 13 as an uppercase B. But if offered cash to find numbers instead, people are more likely to mistake an uppercase B as the number 13.

When there are few downsides for making mistakes, we prefer to search for evidence that confirms our assumptions. Even inside our own memories, when we find that evidence, we produce biased arguments to defend what feels like confirmation. A lifetime of doing this leads to worldviews that feel like they are based on careful, meticulous research and pure, unadulterated reason.

I used to think examples like these demonstrated just how flawed and irrational our reasoning is. But after spending time with scientists who study how reasoning evolved, and how we employ reason during disagreements, which is where we are headed next, I now see things a bit differently.

To understand, we need to go back to when our ancestors spent most of their time in trees.

———

The anthropological evidence suggests our ancestors spent most of their time up in the branches, eating leaves. Since many mature leaves are toxic, primates like us who didn't develop the digestive power to deal with toxic leaves developed a behavioral solution instead: they stuck to the trees with the youngest leaves.

The problem with mostly eating young leaves is that it requires a large territory. A group foraging for leaves will quickly strip a single tree, and so our lineage evolved territoriality on top of our existing leaf-eating behavior. Territories can't be shared with other groups—not enough leaves to go around. They need to be defended, and so we developed tribal behavior on top of our territoriality. That gave our special mix of genes an advantage, first over all the other animals, and then over the other groups of our own kind, and then over our family versus all the others. Stronger together, we became leaf-munching, territorial, social animals bound by trust that was hard to earn and easy to lose.

Defending against your own kind requires kinship, and that requires identification. We evolved the ability to tell our own group members from other members of our species through signals—smells and hoots and barks. That signaling had side benefits as well. When any member can signal danger to all the others, the whole group benefits. So the thinking goes that hominids like yourself first evolved the ability to read one another's emotions, then to communicate with intent and, over time, the ability to communicate with a goal in mind.

Imagine three proto-humans on a hill, each looking in a different direction. The power to pool each individual's perspective into a shared worldview without turning to see what the others were seeing was an enormous evolutionary advantage. Scale it up, add abstractions, and you've got yourself the vital intellectual gumbo we call culture. Under the pressure to survive, with the availability of peer-to-peer communication, proto-humans developed an array of tools and capacities, including language, facial expressions, empathy, shame, embarrassment, mirror neurons, and emotional contagion. The human brain became incredibly adept at using and manipulating signals to get ideas out of one's head and into another.

As all these complex data got traded back and forth, a shared model of the environment, a communal worldview, came into focus. Without the influence of other groups to get in the way, each member's world-view was broadly similar to that of other members trying to make sense of rocks and rivers and goats and clouds; depending on the unique problems any one group faced, in many ways the worldview of that group was unique to the members who shared it. Each worldview evolved over time, much the way genes do. Norms and ideologies, rituals and prac-tices, values and beliefs were imperfectly copied from brain to brain and updated between them as those brains regularly met up and traded news, taught skills, and explained the mysterious.

This system worked extraordinarily well, but as it developed it also introduced a new dilemma. All those individual sources of information weren't passive observers objectively recording and reporting on reality. And in such a rich information pool, with so many individuals with their own personal goals, even a trusted peer might want to deceive or mis-lead so they might gain at another's expense. Genes are selfish that way. Even when the intentions of a peer were good, each brain could only add to the pool what it could observe. Confounding the process further, brains are prone to making errors and may misinterpret what they at-tempt to pass along. Communication, no matter how useful, was bound to be imperfect.

Despite this imperfection, since no one person can see the little pic-ture clearly, nor see the big picture by themself, receiving a constant flow of information from as many other people as possible would have been too valuable to give up. Information from our peers and our kin was, for most of our evolutionary history, vital to our very survival; so we developed a tool that comes online when we are on the receiving end of a data transfer. It's called epistemic vigilance.

———

In an information exchange, epistemic vigilance helps protect individuals from updating too hastily. Without the order afforded by rough consensus, social situations would become unnavigable, and the behaviors that usually put food in your belly and keep your blood in your body might fail in both regards. By avoiding bad information, even from people you typically trust, brains and groups maintain their vital cohesion.

In their book *The Enigma of Reason*, cognitive psychologists Hugo Mercier and Dan Sperber compare this balance of trust with vigilance to a busy sidewalk. When a person leaves a subway station, climbs the stairs, and enters the flow of foot traffic, they can focus on their own space because they know that others are focusing on theirs. Even though each person is tending to their own path, the fact that *every* individual is doing the same means that *each* individual can move forward assured that bumping into a stranger is unlikely. In the busy sidewalk metaphor, problematic, untrustworthy people become much less of a problem because the entire crowd can go on autopilot with the assurance that if any one person notices someone intentionally trying to run into others or carelessly disrupting the flow, they will move out of the way, helping signal to the people nearby to do the same.

In a biased but trusting environment, individuals can enjoy a communal, constant, forward flow in several directions. Biased motivations and imperfect senses paired with collective vigilance and trust ease the cognitive load on all the individual brains, thus reducing the overall cognitive load of the collective.

If your friend tells you that rubbing poisonous berries on a bee sting will make the pain go away, it would be good to apply a measure of skepticism, to seek out more information, to see if others agreed. If that same friend misled you or others in the past, their reputation would precede them. According to Mercier and Sperber, the biological tools humans use to send and receive information would never have evolved to their modern level of complexity without such a system. We needed a way to guard against misinformation, deception, and the abandonment of our hard-earned order. With it, even bad information became useful, because the receiver now had the tools to analyze and filter it for errors or deceit. If there were no such cognitive tool, communication between brains would hold too much risk. We developed a processing hierarchy that is trustworthy of our peers by default but that remains constantly vigilant for bad information.

Yet our dependence on that vigilance led to a second dilemma. Sometimes it produces false negatives. Some completely accurate and extremely useful new ideas, discoveries, and innovations seem too good to be true—or sometimes too challenging or socially costly. Berries that look poisonous but aren't could be overlooked. A taboo new way to make fire could remain the innovation of a single individual. If a promising change to belief, behavior, or attitude was too much of an outlier, epistemic vigilance might incorrectly tag it as suspicious. Should too many people tag it that way, good information that could benefit the group would fail to spread.

This is what Mercier and Sperber call a "trust bottleneck." The normal flow of information gets jammed up as people begin to question a new idea that runs counter to the shared worldview. To avoid this, the brains of our most human-like ancestors evolved a new trick—arguing.

This is where group selection comes into play. Natural selection favored groups that could outperform other groups, and groups that could bypass trust bottlenecks would, over time, outperform those that did not. That selective pressure, at the group level, evolved a mechanism for when epistemic vigilance led to trust bottlenecks: argumentation.

"For me to be able to anticipate why you might disagree with me, I would have to do a lot of cognitive work," Mercier told me. "Because you've got a lot of beliefs I don't have, and it would be very hard for me to anticipate why you might think as you do."

Mercier said to imagine we want to persuade a friend to go to a Japanese restaurant. We know there is a chance she might object, but we can't anticipate all the reasons why. There are many potential arguments she could produce to counter our proposal. She might not like Japanese food. She might think it's too expensive. She might have gone recently. She might have an ex who works there. It might have made her sick in the past. It's far too much work to sit down and brainstorm all the potential reasons she might object and then prepare a perfect argument that would address each one. Mercier said it's easier to just open with the weakest argument we have: "Let's go to that Japanese restaurant near the park, because I like the food there."

If our friend objects, we can then ask them why. When we learn her specific justification, we can escalate from there. If she tells us she hates sushi, we can refine our argumentation by telling her the restaurant also serves Thai food and see what she says in return.

"Rather than looking for flaws in our own arguments, it's easier to let the other person find them," explained Mercier, "then adjust our arguments if necessary."

By producing arguments in a biased and lazy fashion, individuals can quickly off-load their unique perspectives and save their mental energy for the evaluation process. It could be as simple as figuring out what movie to watch, or it could be of monumental consequence, like whether to keep a loved one on life support or enter a world war. Deliberation through argumentation reveals all the varied points of view in a group. Generating increasingly better reasons for one decision or another, the group can, together, zero in on the most reasonable justification.

Because we are biased and lazy, when we argue with ourselves, we usually win. We draw self-serving conclusions based on our unique experiences and motivations, and then we employ reasoning to create justifications and rationalizations for our own thoughts, feelings, behaviors, plans, and goals.

To paraphrase Mercier, this is why, psychologically speaking, reasoning ain't logic. Reasoning is often confused with *reason*, the philosophical concept of human intellect and rationality. Logic is an amazing tool, a formal language for trading and evaluating propositions, and humans possess an array of cognitive talents we can categorize as *reason*, but *reason-ing* is something else. In short, reasoning is coming up with arguments—plausible justifications for what you think, feel, and believe—and plausible means that which you intuit your trusted peers will accept as *reason-able*.

Two experiments demonstrate this well. In one, Chris Hsee and his colleagues gave subjects the choice between two chocolates as a parting gift for a separate study. One chocolate was an obviously cheap, low-quality, small Valentine's Day heart. The other was a big, expensive, obviously high-quality, realistic, chocolate cockroach. When researchers asked people to predict which they would enjoy the most as their reward, most people said they would rather have the heart.

But when they finally came to the end of the study, most people chose the roach. Unsure which was the better option, they employed their reasoning, which is to say they began creating justifications for each conclusion—"I should get the heart" or "I should get the roach." The list of reasons they could bring to mind for the roach that seemed justifiable to others—bigger, more expensive, better quality—simply outweighed those for the heart. They picked something they knew they would not enjoy because they couldn't justify doing otherwise.

In another experiment by Amos Tversky and Edward Shafir, an experimenter asked subjects to imagine they had flipped a coin, and then asked them to call it. Then the experimenter presented a randomized sheet of paper revealing the imaginary outcome. If it came up in their favor, the subjects were to imagine they had won $200. If it didn't come up in their favor, the subjects imagined they lost $100. No matter the outcome, win or lose, the experimenter then asked, "You are now offered a second identical gamble. Do you take it?"

In the first run of the experiment, when people won, they tended to say, "Yeah, I'd like to play again." (*I'm ahead, so I can risk it.*) If they didn't win, they tended to say, "Yeah, I would like to play again." (*I need to win back what I just lost.*) Win or lose, they found a reason to take the second gamble. But here is the crazy part of this study: in a second run of this experiment, they didn't tell people the outcome of their coin toss. And even though most would take the bet after either outcome, if they did not tell people the outcome, most people did not flip again. Why? Because without that information, they couldn't find a reason to justify their decision. They could have said, "Well, no matter what comes up, I'm going to say yes." But they didn't, because they couldn't.

———

Research shows people are incredibly good at picking apart other people's reasons. We are just terrible at picking apart our own in the same way.

In a 2014 study that Mercier helped design, a team of Swiss cognitive scientists led by Emmanuel Trouche tricked people into evaluating their own justifications more thoughtfully by making it seem as if they came from the mind of someone else.

To do this, subjects read a series of questions, reached a series of conclusions, and then wrote arguments defending those conclusions. For instance, subjects read about a grocery store that sold many kinds of fruits and vegetables. Some of its apples were not organic. The scientists then asked, what can you say for sure about whether this store carries organic fruits? The correct conclusion is that you can only say for sure that the store carries *some* fruits that are not organic. In the study, though, many people inferred that *none* of the fruit was organic, and then said there was really nothing conclusive you could say one way or the other.

After subjects reached their conclusions, the scientists then asked them to write out their justifications. If at any point they found their own reasoning lacking, they could reach a different conclusion, but the vast majority of people didn't do that. Right or wrong, most people stuck with their original conclusions and came up with reasons they felt justified them. In the next stage of the experiment, subjects got a chance to see all of the questions a second time along with the reasoning of subjects who disagreed. If it seemed like the others had stronger arguments, they could change their answers. What the experimenters didn't reveal was that they had actually hidden in those answers some switcheroos.

For one of the questions, the supposed justifications from another person were actually the subject's own. Just as Mercier and Sperber had predicted, when subjects thought the justifications weren't theirs, 69 percent of people rejected their own bad arguments and then switched to the correct answer. When their poor arguments were presented back to them as those of other people, the flaws suddenly became obvious.

"People have been thinking about reasoning in the wrong way," Mercier told me. "They've been thinking about it as a tool for individual cognition. And if that was the function of reasoning, it would be terrible. It would be the least adapted mechanism that ever showed its face. It would be doing the exact opposite of what you'd like it to do." When reasoning alone, it only looks for reasons for why you're right, "and it doesn't really care whether the reasons are good or not. It's very superficial. It's very shallow."

With no one to tell you that there are other points of view to consider, no one to poke holes in your theories, reveal the weakness in your reasoning, produce counterarguments, reveal potential harm, or threaten sanction for violating a norm, you will spin in an epistemic hamster wheel. In short, when you argue with yourself, you win.

Mercier and Sperber call all of this "the interactionist model," which posits that the function of reasoning is to argue your case in a group setting. In this model, reasoning is an innate behavior that grows more complex as we mature, like crawling before walking upright. We are social animals first and individual reasoners second, a system built on top of another system, biologically via evolution, and individual reasoning is a psychological mechanism that evolved under selective pressures to facilitate communication between peers in an environment where misinformation is unavoidable. In an environment like that, confirmation bias turns out to be very useful. In fact, bias itself becomes very useful.

As part of a group that can communicate, every perspective has value, even if it is wrong; so it's best that you produce arguments that don't run counter to your point of view. And since the effort is best saved for group evaluation, you become free to make snap judgments and quick decisions based on good-enough justifications. If others produce counterarguments, you can then refine your thinking and update your priors.

"If you think of it as something that serves individual purposes, it looks like a really flawed mechanism. If you think of it as something built for argumentation, it all makes sense," said Mercier. "It becomes something that is extremely well-tailored to the task in a way that I find quite inspiring, and sort of beautiful in a way."

———

Reasoning is biased in favor of the reasoner, and that's important, because each person needs to contribute a strongly biased perspective to the pool. And it is lazy, because we expect to off-load the cognitive effort to a group process. Everyone can be cognitive misers and save their calories for punching bears, because when it comes time to disagree, the group will be smarter than any one person thanks to the division of cognitive labor.

This is why so many of the best things we have produced have come from collaboration, people working together to solve a problem or create a work of art. Math, logic, science, art—the people who see the correct path from moment to moment are able to guide the others and vice versa. With a shared goal, in an atmosphere of trust, arguing eventually leads to the truth. Basically, all culture is *12 Angry Men* at scale.

Cognitive psychologist Tom Stafford calls this the "truth wins scenario," and in his book *For Argument's Sake*, he details dozens of studies in which group reasoning arrives at the correct answer in situations where individual reasoning fails.

In studies in which people work on puzzles from the Cognitive Reflection Test, a tool for measuring people's tendency to favor intuitive reasoning over active processing, people almost always get the wrong answers when reasoning alone. In groups, however, they tend to settle on the correct answers in seconds.

Here are some example questions from the exam:

> *If it takes 5 machines 5 minutes to make 5 widgets, how long would it take 100 machines to make 100 widgets?*

> *In a lake, there is a patch of lily pads. Every day, the patch doubles in size. If it takes 48 days for the patch to cover the entire lake, how long would it take for the patch to cover half of the lake?*

In the widget problem, the answer is five minutes. Each machine makes one widget every five minutes, so a hundred machines working together will make a hundred widgets in five minutes. In the lily pad problem, the answer is forty-seven. The pads double from covering half to covering the entire pond the day before the last day.

Reasoning alone, 83 percent of people who have taken this test under laboratory conditions answer at least one of these sorts of questions incorrectly, and a third get *all* of them wrong. But in groups of three or more, no one gets *any* wrong. At least one member always sees the correct answer, and the resulting debate leads those who are wrong to change their minds—lazy reasoning, disagreement, evaluation, argumentation, truth.

"If people couldn't change their minds there would be no point in bringing arguments forward," said Mercier, adding that if a disease were to run rampant across humanity causing everyone afterward to be born deaf, then spoken language would soon fade out of the human brain, because there would be no one to hear it—like deep-ocean shrimp that no longer have eyes because no light has reached them for thousands of years. If people just endlessly exchanged arguments with no side ever gaining any ground, no one admitting they were wrong or accepting the propositions of others, then argumentation would have long ago been tossed into the evolutionary dustbin.

———

If all of this is true, then why does social media feel like soul poison? Mercier and Stafford both told me that the main reason is that it is much more important to reason in the proper context than it is to be a good reasoner. Arguing online can seem like deliberation, but if people are insulated from essential group dynamics, from outside perspectives, then individuals will essentially argue with themselves.

If we do debate, we tend to fall prey to what legal scholar Cass Sunstein calls the "law of group polarization," which says that groups who form because of shared attitudes tend to become more adamant and polarized over time. This is because when we wish to see ourselves as centrists but learn that others in our group take a much more extreme position, we realize that to take the middle position, we must shift our attitude in the direction of the extreme. In response, people who wish to take extreme positions must shift further in that direction to distance themselves from the center. This comparison-to-others feedback loop causes the group as a whole to become more polarized over time, and as consensus builds, individuals become less likely to contradict it.

In the case of moral and political issues, we are often deferring to experts and elites. "Deferring to experts is rational," Mercier and Sperber write. "If we didn't, we would be clueless about a wide variety of important issues about which we have no personal experience and no competent reflection. Once we defer to some experts, it makes sense to put relatively little weight on challenging arguments from third parties."

Despite these psychological traps and rhetorical echo chambers, Mercier and Sperber say that deliberative democracy is not in peril. It's only when we leave the context in which arguing evolved that problems emerge. They point not only to the abolition of slavery, the result of extensive legislative argumentation, but also to the research of political scientists like Robert Luskin and James Fishkin, who studied the town hall meetings of Catholics and Protestants following bombings by the Irish Republican Army in Northern Ireland. They found that people there readily updated their views and corrected their misconceptions about the most polarized topics in their community during a time of high anxiety and intense outrage.

———

Mercier and Sperber are adamant that our reasoning isn't flawed or irrational, just biased and lazy, which is both adaptive and rational in the context in which it evolved, a language-based information ecosystem where the selective pressures favored the production of justifications for individual perspectives during group deliberation to reach consensus on inferences and shared goals. "In other words," as Stafford explains, "Their big idea, briefly, is that human reason evolved to convince others (and be skeptical of other's attempts to convince you)."

Mercier, Sperber, and Stafford are certain that this means the filter bubble is a temporary nuisance, and quite permeable. Sure, the internet makes it easier to form groups around our biased and lazy reasoning; but it also exposes us to the arguments of those outside of our groups. Spend enough time in places like Reddit or Twitter or Facebook, with all the arguing and all the bad ideas fighting one another, and even if you remain silent, someone will voice something that resembles your private opinion, and someone will argue with them. Even as spectators, we can realize when the weaknesses of our justifications have been exposed.

For Stafford, this means if we can create better online environments, ones designed to increase the odds of productive arguments instead of helping us avoid arguing altogether, we may look back on this period of epistemic chaos as a challenge we overcame with science. He's optimistic about such a future and told me, "like germs, the misinformation was always there, and the truth has always been hard to come by. Cities created a crisis around sanitation . . . and we will have to generationally learn the information equivalent of washing our hands."

I wondered, if all of this is true, when an argument generates that "I might be wrong" feeling, what aspects make it different from the arguments we find less persuasive? As I mentioned in the introduction, Mercier and Sperber's work reveals how thousands of years of information exchange led to our ability to both persuade and be persuaded, especially when we feel our groups are misguided, misled, or mistaken. But what increases the odds that a persuasive message will change minds? In the next chapter, we will take a closer look at how we evaluate the arguments of those who wish to persuade us, and from there we will dive into the psychology of persuasion itself.

8

❋

PERSUASION

By the 1980s, the state of persuasion research was, to put it lightly, a mess.

The psychological study of influence had always been a major focus of the social sciences, but after World War II, the whole world was asking how the Nazis rose to power, what tricks had they used to persuade people to participate in genocide?

The focus of scientists who study the mind, many of them employed by the US government, turned to understanding the power of advertising, marketing, and propaganda. It would take another forty years to create a unified theory, but its outlines began to emerge once psychology realized that beliefs and attitudes were vastly different mental constructs.

Science discovered the power of attitudes during World War II, when the United States Army enlisted the help of famed Hollywood director Frank Capra to create a series of films to fight back against German propaganda. Like thousands of others, Capra, who had directed *It Happened One Night* and *Mr. Smith Goes to Washington*, re-enlisted right after Pearl Harbor. A veteran of World War I, at the age of forty-four he was commissioned as a major. They army gave him his own department to produce films that they hoped would change the minds of new recruits on several matters of public opinion that, according to the United States government, might cause problems with the war effort down the line. Early estimates said that combined with the draft, more than 12 million Americans would enlist—most of them teenagers who had never held a gun. They feared they would arrive still pining about Jell-O and drive-ins and making out in hotrods, and that morale would plummet once homesickness set in and blood began to spill.

Thanks to massive funding and a staff of conscribed social scientists, Capra created a series of inspirational films for the army called *Why We Fight*. With animation created by Disney, the first film ran through the history of civilization. Quotes about freedom from Moses, Muhammad, Confucius, and the Constitution swept past as the narrator explained that these ideas were like lighthouses in the darkness, and the Nazis were working to put out all the fires of freedom around the world. Then scenes of Nazi propaganda appeared. Massive rallies. Hitler barking at the crowds. Endless rows of goose-stepping soldiers. Pearl Harbor isn't why you enlisted, the narrator said. *This*, he proclaimed, is why we fight.

The films also included messages designed to dispel the widespread misconceptions the army feared could derail their efforts. The majority opinion in the United States at the time was that the war would be over within a year, because most believed the German military was tiny and weak. Most people also believed that the British weren't doing their fair share of the fighting, and so public opinion held that America was headed across the ocean to pick up the slack. The films painstakingly attempted to correct misinformation with facts. For instance, during the scenes depicting The Battle of Britain, they showed how mighty the German air force had been before the fight commenced and Britain's many disadvantages on the way to repelling the attempted invasion. Capra emphasized the grit and determination of British civilians and showcased the courage of the RAF.

The top brass of the United States Army thought what everyone thinks at first. Give people the facts, and they will change their minds. But when the military brought in psychologists to test the impact of the films, their research showed the same thing that later psychologists would discover when using fact-based approaches to change opinions. The films did a fantastic job of teaching facts—correcting the recruits' misconceptions and filling in the gaps in their knowledge—but when it came to their opinions, the answers they gave after watching the films remained nearly identical to those they gave before. Most opinions barely changed a percentage point.

Though the army officials behind the Morale Unit were crestfallen, the social scientists who told them so were overjoyed. Beliefs, they realized, were separate from attitudes.

Today, psychology defines beliefs as propositions we consider to be true. The more confidence you feel, the more you intuit that a piece of information corresponds with the truth. The less confidence, the more you consider a piece of information to be a myth.

Attitudes, however, are a spectrum of evaluations, feelings going from positive to negative that arise when we think about, well, anything really. We estimate the value or worth of anything we can categorize, and we do so based on the positive or negative emotions that arise when that attitude object is salient. Those emotions then cause us to feel attracted or repulsed by those attitude objects, and thus influence our motivations. Most importantly, attitudes are multivalent. We express them as likes or dislikes, approval or disapproval, or ambivalence when we feel both.

Taken together, beliefs and attitudes form our values, the hierarchy of ideas, problems, and goals we consider most important.

But during World War II, the very word, *attitudes*, was a relatively new scientific term, and one that had rarely been used in hard-core scientific research. Most books before then used terms like *beliefs, attitudes, opinions,* and *values* interchangeably. The realization that opinions were more influenced by attitudes than beliefs revealed an unexplored territory. It demanded a new taxonomy of mental constructs, and it led to the creation of the Yale Communications and Attitude Change Program, a lab where the psychologists who studied *Why We Fight* joined other scientists to determine what sort of messages *would* change people's minds.

The research that followed changed the entire field of psychology, and soon every university was producing research into attitude change. Yet as the decades went by, the results of that research failed to coalesce into a grand theory. So many scientists were producing papers that their collective output produced an enormous amount of evidence, but it didn't seem to fit together in any meaningful way. A message that worked in one setting wouldn't work in another. A setting that magnified the power of some messages seemed to dampen the power of others. A speaker whose rhetoric was compelling in front of one audience would in front of a different audience fall on deaf ears. By 1980, attitude-change research was about to collapse under the weight of an enormous amount of seemingly contradictory evidence.

But starting in 1984, a model sorted out the disarray. Two psychology grad students, Richard Petty and John Cacioppo, developed what many consider the best model of how humans make sense of, and are persuaded by, messages that intend to change their minds. But they developed the elaboration likelihood model (or ELM) not so much to change the course of psychology but to make sense of their own textbooks so they could pass their college courses.

———

Petty and Cacioppo had become frustrated in graduate school because passing a test meant more or less memorizing the outcomes of every individual study of attitude change.

"There wasn't any conceptual coherence to help you try and pull it all together," Petty told me. "When you read the textbooks at the time, they really were confusing. We had studies that said we found this effect, but this study didn't find any effect, and 'Oh my gosh!,' this study found the opposite effect. And people would throw up their hands, because you'd get this stuff like, 'Well, a credible source causes more persuasion, but in this study it caused less persuasion, and in this study it interacted with this other variable. It was just a series of findings without a theory."

So to help make sense of it all, Petty and Cacioppo painted an entire room in the house they were renting in blackboard paint. They then began organizing the psychological literature. As they worked their way through the literature, they chalked up summaries on the walls around them, and to pass their tests they began grouping them together to create study guides. To their surprise, they noticed a pattern.

Much of the research had been based on an idea put forward by a sociologist and political scientist named Harold Lasswell. He said that all communications between humans could be broken down to: "Who says what to whom in which channel and with what effect?" *Who* re-ferred to the communicator. *What* referred to the message. *To whom* referred to the audience. *In which channel* referred to the medium or the context. *With what effect* referred to the impact the message had on the audience.

That impact had been the focus of psychological research for de-cades, with the rest considered independent variables. Psychologists were sure that the *impact* depended on *understanding* the *content* of the mes-sage; it seemed mysterious that a message increasing persuasion in one situation almost certainly reduced it in others, in the same way a tuxedo will improve your looks at a snazzy nightclub, but not so much at a base-ball game.

Petty and Cacioppo realized the reason it didn't make sense was because there were two higher-level variables at play. If you grouped messages by how likely a person was to pause and reflect on its content, all the findings sorted neatly into two categories, one of two kinds of thinking. Both kinds of thinking could lead to attitude change, and dif-ferent qualities of the message and its delivery affected which was more likely to become active from one context to the next.

Petty and Cacioppo used the terms "high elaboration" and "low elab-oration" to describe these two kinds of thinking. They consciously avoided the word *learning*, which was part of the process, but separate.

Since the 1920s, psychologists had thought that if we wanted to change people's attitudes about something like cigarettes, we needed to figure out how best to teach people how bad they were. If we wanted people to wear seatbelts, we needed to teach them about the dangers of not wearing them. Give people the facts, and they will change.

This is why most early studies measured what sorts of messages were easier to learn. Petty and Cacioppo's blackboard indicated that a person could learn every detail of a message and still not be persuaded, or a person could not learn the message at all and be totally persuaded. So the first idea in the elaboration likelihood model is that persuasion isn't only about learning the information. Elaboration is contextualizing the message after it gets inside your head, something more akin to how people arrive at different interpretations of inkblots in a Rorschach test.

Petty explained with the example of laundry soap. If an advertisement says, "Use this laundry soap because it will make your clothes smell good," then learning that information alone won't be sufficient to persuade some people. Individuals vary in how they assimilate such concepts into their existing models. One person may hear that message and think, "If my clothes smell good, then people will hang out with me." Since another person might think, "It would be embarrassing if I smelled like flowers all the time," the same message that persuaded one person would discourage another. Petty and Cacioppo's insight was that if elaboration leads to a positive evaluation of the reasoning behind an argument, persuasion will succeed. If it leads to neutral or negative evaluation, the persuasion will fail.

The second big insight was that the likelihood a person will elaborate can be influenced by a variety of conditions. Not every individual will feel motivated or able to elaborate on a persuasive message. Motivation is the willingness and desire to process information carefully, and ability is the cognitive wherewithal to do so.

Motivating factors that increase likelihood include not only relevance but incentives to reach accurate conclusions, a feeling of responsibility to make sense of the message's claims, and a personality trait called "high need for cognition." Ability factors include a lack of distraction, experience or expertise with the topic, and how clearly communicated or well-articulated the message is. Anything that enhances both motivation and ability will increase the likelihood of elaboration, and the nature of that elaboration will then lead to acceptance or rejection.

When elaboration likelihood is high, people tend to take what Petty and Cacioppo called the "central route"; but as likelihood drops off, people tend to move onto what they called the "peripheral route."

Think of the central route as a busy street straight through the heart of Argument City. On the central route, we feel the need to go slow, pay attention, and navigate carefully. What are the speaker's main points? Are they logical? Are they cohesive? Are they strong? Do they cite evidence? Is the evidence well vetted, and are its sources trustworthy? The peripheral route is the equivalent of taking a highway bypass around Argument City. We feel like we can go fast, and though we can still see the city from afar, we do so at the expense of learning all its details. The message becomes hazy, and only the most salient and simple cues have any impact. On the central route, you get to see Argument City for what it really is, the good and the bad, the grimy streets and charming shops, the unique characters and the mundane office workers. On the peripheral route, you only see Argument City in the abstract, the skyline and the billboards, the famous landmarks and the neon lights. Is the speaker attractive? Does this message contain lots of big words? Do they speak eloquently? Do they have a prestigious degree? Are they famous? Is there pizza at the end of this lecture?

As likelihood increases or decreases, variables that mattered on the central route become meaningless on the peripheral, and vice versa. This, they realized, was why some variables worked in some situations and not in others. On the central route, the merits of the message matter. On the peripheral route, the merits are ignored and people focus on simple, emotional cues.

In one experiment, Petty and Cacioppo told university students they wanted to hear how they felt about a policy that would now require seniors to pass a comprehensive exam to graduate. They told some students ahead of watching a video presentation that the policy would go into effect that year. They told others it would go into effect many years later. Right away, some students felt motivated to pay attention while others were less inclined. They further divided the motivated and unmotivated students into two groups each. One saw either nine or three strong arguments, and the other saw either nine or three weak arguments. The strong arguments included the fact that the most prestigious universities require such exams to ensure their degrees communicate excellence. Students from such universities were more likely to get hired at higher-paying jobs. The weak arguments said the comprehensive exams harkened back to the traditions of the ancient Greeks, and the fear it produced would probably encourage people to study more.

Petty and Cacioppo found that the more motivated the students, the more they took the central route. On that route, they paid more attention, and so the stronger arguments were more persuasive. The more of them they saw, the better. But on the central route, the weak arguments were ineffective; students saw the flaws in the emotional, opinion-based messages and ripped them to pieces. In fact, if a motivated person listened to nine poor arguments, they were less likely to support the policy than if they heard only three.

Unmotivated students took the peripheral route. For them, the strong and weak arguments were equally persuasive. So when they heard more arguments, of any kind, even bad ones, they were *more* likely to support the policy than if presented with fewer. Instead of paying attention to the content of the arguments, they paid attention to their number.

Uninterested in the reasoning behind them, they just thought: more arguments, better policy.

In another experiment, Petty and Cacioppo had subjects watch ads for two different brands of disposable razors. They told one group they'd get to take home a box of them but had to pick one brand or the other to do so. The other group received no such offer. For some subjects, the ads were delivered using strong arguments—scientifically designed, ribbed handle to prevent slippage, comparison tests show it shaves three times closer than the competitors. For others, they featured weak arguments—floats in water, a memorable experience, comes in several colors. For some, those arguments were delivered by a famous tennis player, and for others by an unknown actor. They found, just as the ELM predicts, that the people who expected to take home some free razors felt more motivated, and the strong arguments persuaded them more than the weak ones. But for those who weren't promised any razors and therefore weren't motivated to make the best decision, the strength didn't matter at all. The most persuasive element was whether a celebrity endorsed the product.

Research has found that successful attitude change via the central route may take more effort, but it also creates more enduring attitudes. Messages that persuade via the peripheral route tend to do so quickly and easily, which is great for making a sale or getting people to go vote, but the changes they produce are weak. They fade with time and can be reverted with minimal effort.

So which route should we encourage people to take? That depends. Vodka, for instance, is colorless, odorless, and mostly tasteless. There's no great distinction between brands (until the next morning). With something like that, we would be correct to encourage people to take the peripheral route. It would be better for a vodka company to focus on interesting packaging, celebrity endorsements, and ad campaigns that play up the luxury, prestige, or playfulness of the brand. To make up for the fact that the peripheral route doesn't lead to long-lasting change, they would need to continually deliver emotional appeals and routinely change out the presentation of the messages. Advertising can accomplish this with a constant stream of rotating celebrities, slogans, logos, and so on.

However, if we are trying to change attitudes about complex fact-based issues like immigration or health care or nuclear power, we need to know our audience. What motivates them? Are they knowledgeable? Are they distracted in some way? For facts to work, we need to move them onto the central route and keep them there. If we know they are already motivated and knowledgeable about the topic, most of the work is done for us. If not, facts must be delivered by a trusted source in a setting where people are amenable to learning new information.

Petty said that the biggest change in how people process messages since he and Cacioppo first developed the elaboration likelihood model thirty years ago is that many more issues are now tied to people's self-concepts and group identities.

"You know climate change is a hoax because that's what my group thinks," he said, adding that in the old days a scientist's credibility alone was a simple cue for people who weren't familiar with a topic. Today, he said, the scientist would need to seem trustworthy by the standards of their in-group or, if possible, completely politically neutral. Either way, the message can't seem threatening to a person's group identity, or the central route will remain barricaded.

———

Soon after Petty and Cacioppo introduced the elaboration likelihood model, a second framework appeared that attempted to organize the persuasion research of the day into something similarly cohesive. Though it was developed in parallel, today it is considered complementary to the ELM.

In the late 1980s, Shelly Chaiken and Alice H. Eagly introduced the heuristic-systematic model (HSM). It posits that when lazily thinking about alternative ways of feeling about the world, we use heuristics or simple rules of thumb that mostly show we are right. When thinking effortfully, we systematically process information considering all the ways we might be wrong.

The HSM's major contribution to psychology was to show that people are motivated to hold correct attitudes; and by "correct," the HSM means self-serving or group-serving. In other words, it's about reputation management. When a person feels like their justifications aren't yet strong enough to be considered reasonable by their peers, they seek more information until they cross the "confidence gap."

Like the ELM, the HSM agrees that we process messages differently depending on our ability and motivation to do so, but where it differs slightly is that it postulates heuristic processes (meaning rules of thumb and mental shortcuts) and systematic processes (meaning careful and deliberate) can happen simultaneously. Most of the time when there's a handy heuristic available, the HSM says we will fall back on it. Brains are cognitive misers, as psychologists like to say. Most of our calories are spent thinking; and rather than spend even more calories thinking about thinking itself, we prefer to use simple cues to get the gist of the world around us based on our expectations and experiences with it, including persuasive messages.

"The ELM has this lofty premise, which is that people want to have correct information about the world, therefore they will process it to the extent they can achieve that goal," psychologist Andy Luttrell told me. Once a student of Petty's, he continues to research both the ELM and the HSM. "The HSM says, yes, people want to be correct. It's just that they think they already are. Certainty gives an air of objectivity to the subjective. When a person says, 'This is the best movie of 2019.' They mean it. That feels like a fact to them."

Luttrell said that it might seem like we would want to put in the work required to hold the most accurate beliefs possible, to make sure the rustling in the leaves is the wind and not a tiger, "but it is costly to re-evaluate everything all the time. If my only goal in life was to be perfectly correct, then I would constantly subject all incoming information to scrutiny." It takes fewer calories to assume if everyone around me says something is true, it is. If I read it three times, it's likely. If it feels good, keep doing it.

"You receive a billion messages a day from advertisements, politics, social media, and so on," said Luttrell. "You can't engage with all of them, but some will affect you, and how they affect you is different when you are invested or can dig through the evidence. Both models have the insight that, at the end of the day, it depends on how deeply the audience is engaging with the message. And that hadn't been considered until these models."

Luttrell said this was why it was so important to sort out a person's values and motivations. If you asked someone to support a petition for Walmart to stop selling baseball caps, they likely won't be persuaded.

But if you ask them what matters to them, and they tell you they are highly concerned about the environment, telling them baseball caps are the number one contributor to climate change would engage their active processing of the message.

———

Both the ELM and the HSM were built on Yale law professor Howard Lasswell's 1948 model of communication mentioned earlier, which said all persuasion had to take into account "who says what to whom in which channel and with what effect."

With the elaboration likelihood model, psychologists could finally make sense of the seemingly conflicting findings that testing Lasswell's model produced. Within the giant corpus of evidence collected since then, there are several qualities that consistently make a persuasive message more likely to succeed.

Who: The communicator must seem trustworthy, credible, and reliable.

The most important factor in evaluating trustworthiness is something called source credibility, and the research suggests we evaluate it in three ways. We ask ourselves if the speaker is an expert. We look to see if the speaker is trying to trick us in some way. And we look to see if the speaker agrees with the groups with which we identify.

But even when people discredit a message from an untrustworthy source, if the argument is compelling, it will linger in their minds. If we hear the same information presented in other formats or from other speakers, the association with the untrustworthy source weakens. As our reasons for discounting the ideas wash away, the persuasiveness of the message remains. In psychology, this is called the sleeper effect: an initial rejection is often followed by a ghostly increase in agreement over time. When people's reasons for rejecting a message are more about the communicator than the message itself, presenting it from multiple sources can sometimes turn a failure into a success.

What: A message becomes more impactful when paired with popular counterarguments, what psychologists call a two-sided communication.

If people are initially skeptical of a persuasive message, sharing counterarguments alongside the message works best. In studies of courtroom trials, if the defense brings up damaging evidence first, then the defense seems more credible to the jury. Be it a rap battle or a political debate, by presenting your opponent's arguments before they do, you not only demonstrate confidence in your ideas by revealing you've considered the other side, you also demonstrate trustworthiness by revealing you respect the audience's intelligence.

Given that it is better to provide both sides of an argument, which side should come first? The research suggests that presenting the argument most in line with the audience's current attitude is the most effective. That way, a person feels confident and positive about their own attitudes and will be far more tolerant of counter-attitudinal appeals. Saying "I know you don't want to go to sleep, but you have to go to school in the morning" is far more effective than "You have to go to school in the morning, so you better go to sleep."

To Whom: A message must match the processing abilities and motivations of its audience.

It was here that the exceptions to the rules grew so numerous that a need for overarching models became necessary. Making messages clear and simple improves ability, and making it seem impactful to people's lives increases relevancy. But the simplest trick is to frame messages as rhetorical questions. "Wouldn't it be nice if marijuana was legal?" encourages people to produce explanations and justifications for their attitudes. "Do you think marijuana legalization should be legal?" merely primes people to express them as conclusions.

In Which Channel: The message should fit the medium through which it is conveyed.

A message that works well in a book must be revised to work well in a film, and vice versa. A YouTube video based on an essay must use the language of YouTube, not the essay, to maximize its impact.

No matter the message, face-to-face messaging is far and away the most effective channel. We are biologically hardwired to respond to the human face. Newborns show a preference for human faces and recognize them above all other patterns from the moment they arrive in the world. This is because an area of the brain along the temporal lobe functions primarily to do just that one thing. Facial recognition is a biological imperative, because face-to-face communication establishes the essential rapport that aids in the receptivity of any person-to-person message.

As Susan Pinker explains in her book *The Village Effect*, we evolved as group-living primates who depended on our ability to read gestures and facial cues, mostly to determine intent. When paired with voice intonation and body language, and as long as things seem to be going smoothly, face-to-face communication causes the brain to produce oxytocin on both sides of the exchange. Take that same message and deliver it via any other channel, even Zoom, and the oxytocin will not flow as well. The more oxytocin is flowing, the less guarded we become.

Not all media campaigns can go door-to-door, nor can they hold seminars and face-to-face meetings, but the research is clear that if you can produce content that encourages the people who hear your messages to interact with one another and have conversations among themselves about your product, message, or candidate, then you can increase the odds of your persuasive message changing their minds almost as if you *had* engaged them face-to-face.

———

With these truths established, we are now prepared to move into the final section of this book. In the next chapter, we will explore how to take everything we've learned so far, going all the way back to SURF-PAD and deep canvassing, to change minds at the level of a single conversation. You are about to gain a superpower, a step-by-step script of how to change people's minds on any topic, without coercion, by simply asking the right kind of questions in the right order.

9

STREET EPISTEMOLOGY

I t was August in Texas, so Anthony Magnabosco waved from within
the edge of the immense shadow cast across the cobblestone square
by the Convocation Center at the University of San Antonio.

Over the drone of summertime cicadas, a young woman yelled,
"Morning!" They exchanged pleasantries, then he asked, "Do you have
time for an interview today?" She said sure, and the people listening in
through his AirPods settled in for another demonstration.

The foot traffic an hour or so before lunch guarantees Anthony a
few opportunities to practice a persuasion technique so effective that
over the years he has gained an audience of thousands, some of whom
log into Discord to listen live. At least once a week, he opens the channel. He stands between the buildings at the heart of the University of
San Antonio holding a dry erase board, kitchen timer, Tic Tacs, and a
ring of colored puzzle pieces. As people walk by, he asks if they would
be open to challenging their deeply held beliefs.

"Street epistemology is where you ask questions to explore a claim someone makes because they think it is true," Anthony explained as the young woman joined him in the shade. "Wow, that's interesting," she said. "Cool."

He told her the last woman he spoke to said she thought aliens existed, and then together they explored her confidence and her reasons for saying it was true and her reasons for arriving at them. "Oh, that's fun," she said. It could be anything, he continued, but opinions are usually trickier. Fact claims are better. "So maybe you believe there's a higher power, perhaps you think karma is real, or the Earth is flat, or vaccines cause autism or don't cause autism. The idea here is to pick a claim that motivates you to behave, and then ask you questions in a respectful way."

She said she was willing to have the conversation, and Anthony asked about her major. She said biology, but she wanted to minor in music and was having a hard time transferring. Anthony asked if he could start a timer for four minutes, and she said sure, introducing herself as Delia.

Anthony pointed to the GoPro on his chest, and then to the other mounted on a light post nearby, and said he'd be recording the conversation if she was okay with that. Delia said she was, and then he wrote her name on his whiteboard. Next, he opened by asking for a claim.

Delia said she was iffy on the "spirit thing," and Anthony asked why.

She said it was hard to determine what was a hoax and what wasn't, but it was comforting to believe in spirits like guardian angels. Anthony shared a story about a woman he had interviewed on a hiking trail whose husband had died a week before a hummingbird landed on her shoulder. She had been sure it was her husband, reincarnated. He asked Delia if she held any beliefs like that because they gave her comfort. She said yes; in fact, she was thinking a lot about her faith as a Catholic, having been exposed to so many other religions in the last few years.

Anthony asked if she had any specific claim, something she believed in within the Catholic faith that gave her comfort. She said why not go with the belief in God. "That would be like a rock I could confide in," she said. Something she could pray to at night. That phrase, "rock-solid," she said, meant a lot to her. If she were to continue wondering about it while praying, it would no longer be a comfort.

Anthony then moved on the next step in street epistemology. He told Delia he wanted to understand her reasons for believing, and then see if she could verify if those were good reasons. Delia was willing. Anthony said that, if he'd heard her correctly, questioning if God was real could steal her well-being. She said yes, the idea of starting back at square one was an unsettling proposition.

Anthony said he understood, repeating back to Delia what she had told him and expanding on it some. "It could be devastating to think something that was a rock of comfort was an illusion." Delia agreed.

Then Anthony asked, if it turned out the rock wasn't real, would she want to know?

"Of course not," she said. "I wouldn't be comfortable knowing that for sure." Again, Anthony repeated and expanded, and again he said he understood exactly where she was coming from. She said the mystery of it all—that was what keeps religions alive. It's like a meditation. You must condition yourself to believe, to feel better, to function in life. "That's what religion boils down to."

Anthony asked if it could be possible to feel comfortable and to function, to live a fulfilling life and find meaning without a religion. As she answered, they crossed the four-minute mark, and then the fourteen-minute mark.

Then Anthony asked if there were any downsides to thinking something is true if you don't have good reasons.

Delia said maybe. "I question myself daily, and I'd like to not do that." He dug deeper, asking what it felt like.

She said when she began to question, maybe while singing at church, she looked around and wondered how other people did it. "Wow, these people are living their entire lives, and they're not questioning anything." How did they do it? She felt isolated, questioning something that was so "firmly in everybody else's mind." It was at those times "that sense of community no longer exists, just in those moments, just within me. It's like all the sudden I'm alone in a large crowd. Have you ever been, like, lost? Like you are in another country, and you have no familiar faces?"

"I have," said Anthony. "It's like I'm surrounded by people, but they don't understand me."

"Yes," she said, "it's like that."

Anthony asked if maybe in church, in moments like that, there could be other people around her feeling the same thing.

"Oh sure, totally," said Delia. She often wished people had thought balloons so she would know.

Anthony shared that he was once like her. He sat in the pews and felt like he didn't have good reasons for believing the same things the others around him believed. Maybe they, too, didn't have good reasons and were satisfied with that, but for him, he needed more.

Anthony felt satisfied that together they had helped Delia discover her true reasons for continuing to believe, and that he had helped her consider whether they justified her confidence. His job as a street epistemologist was done for now, and he wished her well.

Packing up, Anthony looked over his notes from the conversation.

Rock of comfort. Mystery might be a big component for her. Very open, very honest. Mentioned angels. "Then she turned around and said the very same thing she just got done besmirching was foundational," he said aloud to the people listening on Discord who offered some notes. One suggested he could have asked: Would a person question if they didn't want to know the truth? He said that was great feedback.

I scuttled out of the bushes and joined him. I had been watching from just behind some decorative shrubbery, logged into Discord along with the others so I could hear Anthony work. I was happy I had been sharing his other AirPod, because two men wearing tubas kept circling as a growing crowd of students nearby set up for a performance of the marching band.

"She gave this wonderful visual. Gosh, how many of us can relate to that? Sitting in a church, a Mosque, or a Temple, wondering if the people around us are questioning this?" Anthony grabbed his cooler and cameras, packed up his whiteboard, and we headed to the car.

What about the Tic Tacs, I asked? Anthony said he had experimented with several ways to assess his interlocutor's view of truth during the rapport-building stage, and a box of Tic Tacs was easily the best.

He asks if they agree that the total number of candy pieces in the box must be either odd or even. They usually do, though sometimes they say it can be both. Either way, he asks how they would go about determining that. Whatever they say, he then asks what if someone else said there was an even number after you had counted them out and found they were odd? What if they told you that was *their* truth?

———

At his home in San Antonio, Anthony showed me his YouTube page where he had uploaded hundreds of conversations like the one with

Delia, going back more than six years. He had walked people through their beliefs in the law of attraction, conspiracy theories, ghosts, intelligent design, justice, *The Secret*, and a host of established ideas in history, science, and medicine. The idea was to keep getting better, to offer up the conversations online for others to pick apart and comment on so the community could improve together.

"One of the fun discoveries is that we can probably explore pretty much any claim using this method," he told me from his couch. "The template of how you approach the claim by clearing up exactly what you're talking about, then figure out the reasons that they're giving, and then exploring the reliability of the method that they're using to get to their conclusion—that template can be overlaid to anything."

Anthony said he had started out asking people about religion, but "street epistemology expanded naturally, because there were often people who said they didn't believe in any deities or didn't want to talk about that." Rather than just end it, he continued the conversations. "There was also some pushback from people in the religious community who thought this tool had been specifically built to destroy their structure."

Anthony admits that, yes, that was his original idea; frustrated with how often religious beliefs made their way into schools and laws, he had once been an angry atheist. He had joined several atheist activist organizations both locally and globally, and after reading a book by philosopher Peter Boghossian about how to question people using the Socratic method, he visited the Alamo Drafthouse on the weekends to use it on the street preachers who stand in front yelling at people.

Low-hanging fruit, I said, for both of you.

He laughed. Not at all.

"It was like running a hundred miles an hour to a brick wall, because the venue was inappropriate. I was still falling back into my counter-apologetic ways." Anthony said he wasn't listening. He wasn't trying to understand. But as he uploaded his videos, people started giving feedback.

"'Try this.' 'Do that.' 'Why did you ask that?' I was open to their suggestions instead of being like, 'How dare you tell me how to do this.' It really hurt to read what they said, but I thought, 'How can I take that and improve?'"

Debriefing became an essential part of his practice, first in comment sections, then live as he spoke over Discord. A five-minute conversation would become a week's worth of discussion about how it could have gone better. "Did you notice at the start they went down this path, then you said this, and they went down another," said Anthony. "We threw everything against the wall to see if it would stick."

Other people started trying it out, and they did the same with their videos. A community began to form, and soon they created a website with resources and diagrams, then came podcasts and workshops and social media and an app called Atheos. Psychologists and biologists and philosophy professors joined, offering tips, trying it themselves. Thousands of conversations using street epistemology entered the collective vetting process, everyone looking to improve and trade insights, in countries around the world, and on topics as far-ranging as racism and politics, scams and internet hoaxes. Today they sell T-shirts and stickers with an official Street Epistemology logo, and Anthony speaks at conferences around the world.

After six years and hundreds of conversations, Anthony said his anger had subsided. Like many militant atheists who met online in the 2000s, he and others in the street epistemology community had distanced themselves from controversial figures like Richard Dawkins and even Peter Boghossian, who had taken to social media to complain about "social justice warriors."

Anthony and others like him are part of a humanist schism, enthusiastic about trans rights and racial justice, down to drop acid and eat pot brownies and talk about the mysteries of the universe as long as others are willing to fall back on street epistemology to dig as deep as one can go discussing quantum mechanics or ancient beings seeding the Earth with mushrooms to accelerate our evolution. Nothing is taboo, and people who believe strange things aren't seen as rubes or maniacs anymore.

Anthony said street epistemology was freeing in that regard. The community sees it as a tool for arriving at a better way of thinking in general, and the goal is to share it as far and as wide as possible. The aim is no longer to attempt to change people's minds. The goal is to help people arrive at a more rigorous way of thinking, a better way of reaching certainty or doubt. What a person believes is no longer the point of the conversation, but why and how they believe those things and not others. But it seemed to me that encouraging a person to change their epistemology *was* changing their minds. It's changing something in their brains deeper than beliefs, attitudes, and values.

He'd later clarify, as so often is the case, that the phrase "change your mind" can mean many things. What he meant was that he doesn't set out in a conversation to change people's conclusions about what is and is not true, or moral, or important. Regardless, that's usually what happens if someone takes the time to go through all the steps with him.

———

I had learned about Street Epistemology after a teacher of the deaf and hard of hearing in Victoria, British Columbia, emailed me. I had been tweeting about my interest in persuasion, detailing some of the people I had met while writing the early portions of the book. The teacher wrote me that a lot of what I was talking about seemed like things they had incorporated in their program from street epistemology. He shared a link to one of Anthony's videos and wrote that I should check it out.

A few weeks later, I was on the phone with Anthony, and the next month, in his living room, I asked Anthony to teach me the method.

HERE ARE THE STEPS:

1. Establish rapport. Assure the other person you aren't out to shame them, and then ask for consent to explore their reasoning.

2. Ask for a claim.

3. Confirm the claim by repeating it back in your own words. Ask if you've done a good job summarizing. Repeat until they are satisfied.

4. Clarify their definitions. Use those definitions, not yours.

5. Ask for a numerical measure of confidence in their claim.

6. Ask what reasons they have to hold that level of confidence.

7. Ask what method they've used to judge the quality of their reasons. Focus on that method for the rest of the conversation.

8. Listen, summarize, repeat.

9. Wrap up and wish them well.

He explained the idea is guided metacognition: to encourage a person to think about their own thinking, but only after they've already used their own reasoning to produce a claim and presented its justification. With help, they can assess their own methods, question their reasons, and evaluate the merits of their own arguments.

STEP ONE: ESTABLISH RAPPORT

It's important to remember that the other person must be open to all of this. You must ask for consent. You must be transparent. Ask them about themselves, about their lives, about what is taking up most of their time, what they are doing that day. "Listen to their story. Listen to the emotion of the story," Anthony said. It can be frustrating when you want to get into a topic, "but it really is important, because people want to feel heard. People want to feel like you are going to listen to them."

He compared it with bedside manner. You trust a doctor or a nurse who gets to know you, "who listens to what you are saying." And it avoids the threat of shame, he said. The quickest way to end a conversation before it begins is to communicate hostility. Anything that can be misconstrued as "you should be embarrassed for thinking that way" will be met with anger. "There's so much disrespect that when you actually find somebody who wants to listen and ask you a few probing questions about your story, people feel safe, and when you feel safe you open up more."

STEP TWO: ASK FOR A CLAIM

Even if you already know, ask outright. Street epistemology works best on empirical, fact-based claims like "the Earth is flat" or "the government is listening to our Alexas," but it can also be used to explore attitude-based claims like "Joe Biden is a bad president" or "strawberry ice cream is better than vanilla," or values-based claims like "tax dollars should go to forgiving student loans, not aircraft carriers." Either way, the point of street epistemology is to investigate the reasoning that supports a claim, and you can't do that until both parties agree on what they will be discussing.

STEP THREE: CONFIRM THE CLAIM

Repeat back to the other person in your own words: "If I understand you correctly, you are claiming that . . ." But there's no need to be formal about it. Once you've done it a few times, you'll find ways to reflect and paraphrase that feel natural.

STEP FOUR: CLARIFY DEFINITIONS

The problem with most arguments is that we often aren't actually arguing, because our definitions of the terms aren't the same as theirs. Take "the government," for example. *You* might see it as a collection of civil servants trying to appease their constituents. *They* might see it as a smoke-filled room where a ring of wicked billionaires share plans to divvy up the country. If you assume that you are both talking about your concept of "the government," then you end up arguing with yourself rather than focusing on the other person's ideas.

"We start talking past each other," said Anthony. "It's critical when somebody mentions a suitcase word like 'psychic' or 'true' or 'faith.' You must unpack it. But that's just a small piece of it. Identifying what you mean by the words, identifying what you are actually stating is only like 10 percent of it."

STEP FIVE: IDENTIFY A CONFIDENCE LEVEL

The conversation truly begins after step five. Ask them to put a number on their feeling of confidence, from zero to one hundred, so they can begin to step backward into their processing and ask themselves how sure they are about that feeling. Anthony said you often can see something happen in that moment; you can tell when someone's never really done it.

If you've established trust and you've been very open and honest, the other person should feel exhilarated for a chance to explain themselves. It also creates opportunities to move forward naturally. If a person says they are an eighty out of one hundred, you can ask: "Why not one hundred?" Which then opens up the conversation to the next phase, exploring a person's reasoning.

STEP SIX: IDENTIFY HOW THEY ARRIVED AT THEIR CONFIDENCE LEVEL

Basically, ask them what reasons they have to hold that level of confidence. If they offer several, try to settle on one by noticing what is common among them. What contributes most to their feeling of confidence?

"Sometimes the reasons that they give are post-hoc, because they're just now struggling to think, 'What are the reasons for me thinking that this is true?'" said Anthony. "The reason they give might be just the thing that came to their brain. But it may not actually be the real reason. There's something else propping up their view. So, one of the most important questions we ask a person is, 'If you discovered that was not a good reason for holding a high degree of confidence in what you think is true . . . is true, if you discovered that on your own or through this dialogue, would it lower your confidence?' And if they say, 'My confidence wouldn't change even if I discovered that reason wasn't good', you've now basically eliminated that reason as being part of the mix, and you can just sort of rinse and repeat that as many times as necessary until you hit the real reason."

STEP SEVEN: ASK WHAT METHOD THEY'VE USED TO JUDGE THE QUALITY OF THEIR REASONS

Step seven is the most important step, but you don't have to ask this outright. The goal in this step, as Anthony put it, is to encourage people to test the reliability of the method they typically use to "judge the quality of their reasons," and then ask if, using that method, those reasons still support their current level of confidence.

On the street epistemology website, in their fifty-page PDF, in their seminars, this step gets the most attention because there are endless variations of questions one could ask. The best reveal contradictions and weaknesses in a person's epistemology, Socratic method style. Anthony offered a few, noting that each should be reworded to address what the other person has shared so far: "Could your method also be used to arrive at completely different and competing conclusions?" and if so, "What does that say about the quality of the method you're using to arrive at your belief?"

He added that one technique many street epistemologists use is to ask people to imagine someone has looked at the same evidence and reached a different conclusion, and now a third person is looking at both their arguments—how would that third person determine which conclusion was true?

I told Anthony that I planned to spend time with Mark Sargent, one of the most prominent flat-Earthers. I was wondering how it should play out using the steps he had explained so far. He said to ask, "What would you say is the biggest reason why you think the Earth is flat today? The reason that would influence your confidence the most? The reason that would lower your confidence the most if you discovered that it wasn't true? If you were to teach a class to a roomful of kindergartners about why the Earth is flat, what would be your go-to argument?"

I said he'd likely mention how they track aircraft across the globe using radio telemetry, and that they never cross the Southern Hemisphere because there is no Southern Hemisphere. That was a common, though easily debunked, argument among flat-Earthers.

Anthony said that would be a great opportunity to get to the real reason. He said to ask a flat-Earther to go back to a time before they believed. "What was the definitive event that caused you to be as certain as you are today that the Earth is flat? Was it the aircraft, or did you have more confidence that the Earth was flat after you learned that?" If they say they had always felt suspicious of the government or something similar, the real reasons are likely a distrust of science or authority, but you can't reveal you suspect that. They need to discover that for themselves.

With the flat Earth example, he said to ask if it could be demonstrated to your satisfaction that the planes weren't traveling over the Southern Hemisphere not because the Earth is flat but for some other reason, would it affect your confidence? He imagined himself asking, "I'm not an expert in this but if we had people from aviation, experts that we both trusted, and they could spend ten hours with us to explain the intricacies of flight travel and how this can actually work in a global model, would it influence your confidence in any way?"

You need to know how important evidence really is, he said. Ask how they would react to someone who saw the same information and reached a different conclusion. Do you use the same standards for counter-evidence? How did you conclude this was the best explanation of your observation? The point here is to move away from the claim itself and help them see how they are evaluating it. Are they willing to disconfirm, to falsify? It's the most difficult part of the process, and so this is where the Tic Tacs come in handy.

"It's uncomfortable for me to see you uncomfortable. There's an urge to move on. Don't move on though, because that's where the seeds get planted. Somebody commented on one of my videos once, 'You're so good at making people comfortably uncomfortable.' And that's exactly what it is. I want you to be just uncomfortable enough so you are thinking about your thoughts, but comfortable enough where you're not ready to just storm out of here in a huff. This isn't like getting them in a gotcha moment. This is to figure out how they're getting to their conclusions and helping them see it."

STEP EIGHT: LISTEN, SUMMARIZE, REPEAT

In a way, step eight is moving back through all the steps again, reflecting and paraphrasing. If the other person stops to look away, wait it out. In philosophy, these are called aporias, moments of consternation and reflection, and it's important not to step into a pause to interrupt a person's thinking. It's also your cue to wrap up, which is step nine.

If you like, you can return to the numbers and ask for their confidence level a second time, from zero to one hundred, but Anthony said that's not necessary. What's more important is to thank them for their time and encourage them to keep thinking about what you've discussed, to keep thinking about their own thinking. If it hasn't already occurred, feel free to share your own beliefs on the matter, and if the other person wants to explore them the way you explored theirs, agree to do so. Otherwise, finish with step nine.

STEP NINE: PART COMPANY BY SUGGESTING YOU CONTINUE THE CONVERSATION LATER

Anthony emphasized that street epistemology is about improving people's methods for arriving at confidence, not about persuading someone to believe one thing more than another. Maybe in the beginning it was, but today there's no belief they are pushing, no agenda, no policy on which they want people to vote yes or no. After all, if they've learned anything from the method, it's that he or anyone else in the community could be wrong.

He reiterated to stay honest. Ask outright, "With your consent, I would like to investigate together the reasoning behind your claims, and perhaps challenge it so that it either gets stronger or weaker—because the goal here is for both of us to walk away with better understandings of ourselves," or something like that. And if that isn't your goal, it won't work. You can't fake it.

Let them know, "I have no desire to misrepresent you, so please correct me. I have no desire to straw-man you, so if I get your arguments incorrect, correct me." Don't cut them off. Move at their speed. Allow for pauses. Use their meanings and their reasoning. Stay in their head and out of yours. "I want to know if your confidence is justified. This is not about being factually correct. I'm not an expert, and we don't have enough time for that anyway. So instead of debating whether these claims are true or false, I just want to explore, together, whether your confidence in these conclusions is justified."

You are trying to eject them from a loop, to get them into a state of metacognition. You can't copy/paste your reasoning into another person. That's what this is all about, he said. You're guiding them through their reasoning so that they can understand it. "That's it. It's surprising how that is really it."

———

Watching Anthony work and then listening to him explain the method, I couldn't help but notice that street epistemology and deep canvassing seemed incredibly similar in many ways.

Deep canvassing was goal-oriented; the Leadership LAB wanted to change minds to agree with theirs, and it was less about beliefs than it was about attitudes, though beliefs were important. Still, it was also about getting people to think about their own thinking, why they felt confident, that had proved more successful than focusing on claims and facts.

Street epistemology was also similar to four steps Megan Phelps had shared with me as a guide for reaching out to people in groups like Westboro—don't assume bad intent, stay calm, ask questions, make an argument. I also saw bits of the ELM and HSM—trustworthiness through rapport, engage people face-to-face, reduce cognitive load and limit distractions, make the message relevant to the person on the other side, patiently listen. Most of all: encourage active processing and send people down the central route to ensure that when they change, they do so in a way that sticks and can endure.

When Anthony showed me a pyramid that he used in training, with *WHAT* at the small part at the top, *WHY* in the middle, and *HOW* at the bottom, indicating the relative importance of the claim, their reasons, and then their method as topics of discussion, I was reminded of the deep canvassing layer cake. It became clear to me that all these people had independently discovered the principles that work best when it comes to persuasion.

For different reasons, and for different purposes, they had iterated on their methods for years, through thousands of conversations, throwing out what didn't work, keeping what did, until they hit on something reliable. Like inventors on separate continents attempting to build the first airplane, the science was waiting to be discovered and applied. The inventions that took flight would naturally appear similar because the underlying physics was the same. Likewise, persuasion is the same wherever it is perfected, because brains are the same wherever people converse.

That became even more apparent a few weeks after meeting with Anthony Magnabosco, when I met with Karin Tamerius of Smart Politics.

She had emailed me after I shared on Twitter that I was researching techniques like deep canvassing and street epistemology. She wanted to know if I could connect her to someone in each organization, because she had hit on something similar as well. As a psychiatrist, she believed the same tenets that work in therapy would work when discussing politics, and she had started having conversations just as the Leadership Lab and Anthony Magnabosco had, with similar results. She created Smart Politics to help teach progressives how to have conversations with conservative family members and had recently written an article about her startup in *The New York Times*. She even created an unclebot, a simple AI to stand in for an argumentative relative.

I asked if we could meet so we could compare notes.

"It's an illusion that you are talking about facts," she told me. "You both think that you are talking about the issue, but what's more important is the person."

Tamerius said her experience as a psychiatrist told her that in any persuasion attempt, your priority should be to curate the conversation in a way that strengthens the relationship between you and the other person, and every second work to demonstrate to the other person that you are not an other, that you are not a member of what they consider *them*. At the same time, do the same thing within yourself. Try your best not to see them as an other and not to frame them within the category of *them*.

I asked her about her method, if it had steps, and she said it did.

First, ask a nonthreatening question that's open-ended. Something like, "I've been reading a lot about vaccines lately, have you seen any of that?" Next, just listen for a while. Then communicate your curiosity and establish rapport by asking a nonjudgmental follow-up question.

Next, reflect and paraphrase. Summarize what you've heard so far to make the other person feel heard and respected. Then look for common ground in the person's values. You might not agree with their argument, but you can communicate that you too have values like theirs, fears and anxieties, concerns and goals like they do. You just think the best way to deal with those issues is slightly different. Then share a personal narrative about your values to further connect. Finally, if your views have changed over time, share how.

Tamerius said the key to her method was to learn what motivates others. She too had a diagram. She called it the Change Conversation Pyramid, modeled as a hierarchy in which each motivation must be met before moving on to the next, with change at the top. At the bottom is comfort. Next is connection. Then comprehension, compassion, and finally change. Writing about the pyramid on her website, she said, "The mistake we make in political dialogues is going straight for the top of the pyramid without attending to all of the other needs that people must fulfill for change to be possible."

I told Tamerius that Smart Politics was very similar to deep canvassing and street epistemology; and the tenets created by Megan Phelps, shared in her TED talk. Tamerius said she thought it might be, and that it seemed to her that everyone was pulling from the same kinds of lessons that therapists had learned over the last fifty years dealing with people resistant to change. In particular, she said, techniques that aim to change minds in therapeutic settings often use bits and pieces from the motivational interviewing literature.

I asked her to give me an example—maybe vaccination, because at the time we spoke many people were frustrated with vaccine-hesitant loved ones.

HERE ARE THE STEPS:

1. Build rapport. Assure the other person you aren't out to shame them, and then ask for consent to explore their reasoning.

2. Ask: On a scale of one to ten, how likely are they to vaccinate? If one, ask: Why would other people, who aren't hesitant, be higher on that scale?

3. If above one, ask: Why not lower?

4. Once they've offered their reasons, repeat them back in your own words. Ask if you've done a good job summarizing. Repeat until they are satisfied.

STEP ONE: BUILD RAPPORT

As you open the dialogue, assure the other party you aren't out to shame them or put them in a position to be ostracized by their peers. Demonstrate your openness and respect, and continuously ask for consent. Don't attack. Tolerate their views, even if you disagree. Listen without interrupting. Attempt to understand their position without replying. And most of all, try to find common ground. An engaged, curious, and compassionate listener is far more persuasive than any fact or figure.

STEP TWO: ASK: ON A SCALE OF ONE TO TEN, HOW LIKELY ARE THEY TO VACCINATE? IF ONE, ASK: WHY WOULD OTHER PEOPLE, WHO AREN'T HESITANT, BE HIGHER ON THAT SCALE?

If they answer one, then that person is in what psychologists call the precontemplation stage. As Tamerius explained, people only change their minds within a learning mindset. If a person doesn't feel safe, they won't feel motivated to learn. This means you can't move on to the persuasion attempt. First, you must move them into a state of active learning, out of the precontemplation stage and into contemplation.

According to motivational interviewing, the four most common reasons a person is not yet ready to enter the contemplation stage are: one, they haven't been confronted with information that challenges their motivations; two, they currently feel their agency is being threatened; three, previous experiences have made them feel hopeless to change; and four, they may be stuck in a rationalization loop. All of this, by the way, we know from decades of work helping people escape alcoholism and addictive substances.

In motivational interviewing, some people need exposure to new and challenging ideas. Others need assuring their agency isn't under threat. Others require new experiences that challenge their preconceived notions. In therapy, one can encourage all this, but in the sessions it's the loop that gets the most attention through exploring their reasoning, exposing it to them so they can escape rationalization.

Tamerius said that once a person is out of the precontemplation stage, when you ask them where they are on a scale of one to ten, they will answer at two or higher because the feelings they carry about the issue are now ambivalent.

STEP THREE: ASK: IF ABOVE ONE, WHY NOT LOWER?

Once a person is ambivalent, you should open by asking why they aren't lower on the scale. If a five, ask why not a four. The idea is to help the other person articulate their ambivalence.

STEP FOUR: ONCE THEY'VE OFFERED THEIR REASONS, REPEAT THEM BACK IN YOUR OWN WORDS

Tamerius warned that you shouldn't focus your time drawing out the other person's justifications for avoiding change, because the goal here should be to help them see how reliable their reasoning is; and in the process, as they produce their own counterarguments, put more emphasis on the other side of their ambivalence. Focus on why they aren't lower on the scale. It isn't easy. It takes time. And it often takes several conversations.

As with street epistemology and deep canvassing, step one, building rapport, is the most important. No one will enter into active processing or become amenable to learning if us-versus-them feelings abound. And building rapport may take several conversations. If the relationship has some negative history to it, resolving that must come first.

It's also easy to ruin rapport once you've built it. Therapists have learned that it's natural to want to tell a client in crisis what they should think or how they should behave—what therapists call the righting reflex—but it should always be avoided, because it puts that person on the defensive. Clients will produce reasons to reach for the bottle even if they would otherwise agree with your reasons to avoid it. They begin arguing for the reasons to drink, or whatever they came to therapy to tackle, and they resolve their ambivalence away from change.

———

After we spoke, I copied Tamerius in an introductory email to Dave Fleischer and Anthony Magnabosco, explaining that I thought perhaps they had all hit on the same thing and should meet, maybe even put together a conference of some kind. In the meantime, I dug deeper and was surprised to learn that deep canvassing, street epistemology, Smart Politics, motivational interviewing, and other persuasion techniques had already been grouped together under the label "technique rebuttal" just a few months earlier.

I reached out to the psychologists who grouped them, Philipp Schmid and Cornelia Betsch. They had gathered all the research into different persuasive techniques and published a paper in which they found each could be neatly organized into one of two different strategies, the other being "topic rebuttal."

They explained that persuasion that depends on topic rebuttal responds to claims with facts alone. It's the preferred method of people in good-faith environments like science, medicine, and academia, because in those environments there's an established sense of trust and accountability that comes from a commitment to favor the conclusions with the most supporting evidence (by the standards agreed upon within that profession and its particular specialty). In those environments, the more facts the better. On the other hand, persuasion that uses a form of technique rebuttal focuses on how a person processes information and what drives their confidence in one conclusion over another. It makes the opposition to an idea the focus of discussion more than the idea itself and points out the flaws in the methods used to oppose it. Technique rebuttal asks people to step backward through their processing to understand how they arrived at a conclusion and whether their reasoning is sound.

Schmid told me that people are often hesitant to use technique rebuttal, especially in front of an audience, because it seems like "the dark arts" to go digging into the motivations and reasoning that leads another person to their conclusions. It feels like handing people the facts and walking away is taking the high ground. When your opponent seems emotional, we want to seem rational, so there's a sense that emotions should never enter a debate, especially over the facts. But experts on reasoning like Schmid told me this was impossible, because certainty itself is an emotion.

———

When the Space Shuttle *Challenger* exploded in 1986, psychologist Ulric Neisser had his class of 106 people write down how they heard, where they were, what they were doing, and what they felt. Two and a half years later, he asked them these questions again, and only 10 percent got them all right. But the interesting thing is not that their memories were faulty; it's that they refused to accept that their memories *could* be faulty. Even after looking at their own journals and seeing the truth, one student told Neisser, "That's my handwriting, but that's not what happened."

When neurologist Robert Burton read about that study, he became fascinated with the very idea of certainty itself. "What struck me was that there was no reason to get that psychologically invested. You can just say, 'Oh, I guess I made a mistake.' But he was dead certain that what he was looking at wasn't right. The feeling of the new memory was so strongly correct that it made it impossible to see that he might be making an error. And I thought, 'Well, you know, if that's not psychological, maybe it's on a more basic cognitive neurologic basis.' And that's what got me prompted to think about whether the sense that he was certain was beyond his control, which led me to think about it as a feeling state that was a sensation as opposed to a thought."

He wrote a book on the topic titled *On Being Certain* in which he explored the neuroscience of certainty itself. Using the *Challenger* example, he explained that when challenged with evidence we are wrong, if the brain continues to produce the mental state of certainty, we have no choice but to believe we are correct, even when our own handwriting is the source of that challenge. Depending on its strength, that feeling of "knowing we are right" that we can't help but feel when faced with the fact we might be wrong—factually, morally, or otherwise—will encourage us to argue with our own past selves as if trapped in a neurological prison of our own convictions.

Burton said he looked all throughout the psychological and neurological literature but couldn't find a term that satisfied him. So he created one: "the feeling of knowing." It lumps together a lot of ideas: certainty and conviction and correctness and rightness. We know when we feel it, and we know when we don't.

Burton uses this example to illustrate the feeling of knowing; see if you make sense of it.

A newspaper is better than a magazine. A seashore is a better place than the street. At first it is better to run than to walk.

You may have to try several times. It takes some skill, but it is easy to learn. Even young children can enjoy it. Once successful, complications are minimal. Birds seldom get too close. Rain, however, soaks in very fast. Too many people doing the same thing can also cause problems. One needs lots of room. If there are no complications it can be very peaceful. A rock will serve as an anchor. If things break loose from it, however, you will not get a second chance.

When you read this, you can feel your lack of certainty about what is being described. But if I tell you that the text describes a kite, you feel a completely different emotion when you read it again, and you have no choice in the matter. It happens *to* you. We don't decide or choose to be certain or uncertain; we just feel it. But Burton says that's not a conclusion, it's an emotion that feels like a conclusion.

He told me the vast majority of what the brain does happens "beneath thought, and then it's projected into consciousness." He says that the brain is constantly calculating things, like how to best go about reaching for a cup of coffee, or keep our car on the road while we carry on a conversation. It's the same with thirst. "When there is high osmolarity in the body, we sense it, we experience thirst, and then, perhaps, consciously articulate it in language as 'I am thirsty.'"

Burton said the same thing happens when we feel certain or uncertain. "When you are thinking two plus two is four, and you feel this is correct, do you feel it is correct because you have some innate mathematics module, or do you feel it is correct because you've laid down a groove from experience and received wisdom, from childhood, from being taught that this is the correct answer? Either way, there is something in the brain delivering a sensation of certainty at the subliminal level, the way you experience thirst, that you can't help but feel, even if you don't articulate it."

Burton said to imagine you see a face in a crowd that shouldn't be there. On vacation in Belize you see your grandfather, despite the fact that he is dead. "You will feel the probability that this person is, indeed, your grandfather at the bodily level, a visceral sense of certainty that could be articulated as a percentage." You could say you were 10 percent certain that was your grandfather. But if you saw a face of an old acquaintance, the machinations of your inner certainty would produce something higher. It would be worth approaching that person to see if you were correct—to see if, with more information, you could adjust the number.

"That whole feeling is really a brain calculation at a subliminal level. Then for a lot of evolutionary reasons, that comes into consciousness as a combination of both the calculation and the feeling, absent of any thought at all. It's a sensation that feels like a conclusion. It is an enormous, marvelous trick of evolution."

As Burton explained, beliefs and doubts are better thought of as processes, not possessions. They aren't like marbles in a jar, books on a shelf, or files in a computer. Belief and doubt are the result of neurons in associative networks delivering an emergent sensation of confidence or the lack thereof. When those networks weight that feeling in one direction or another, we sense a proposition is either true or false.

"It seems, I mean, maybe it's because I spent so much time on this. It seems so intuitively obvious that unfortunately I can't believe anything else."

After spending time with Anthony Magnabosco learning the steps behind street epistemology, the ones that increase or decrease a person's emotional state of certainty, that feeling of knowing or not knowing, I emailed Josh Kalla and David Broockman to see if they had any updates into their investigation into the science behind deep canvassing.

We met over Zoom, and I shared with them some of the things I had learned. They said it all lined up with what they had found in the literature, and perhaps they'd move on to street epistemology one day; they were currently still conducting research into deep canvassing, producing several new studies focused on its application in other domains. The good news from their studies was that it still works. No matter where applied, it has been incredibly effective at everything from changing the candidate for whom people intended to vote to shifting attitudes on immigration.

Kalla said when I first visited, there were so many things going on, so many steps, that "within that broad kitchen-sink approach" it wasn't clear exactly what was the active ingredient and what was filler.

TO SUMMARIZE DEEP CANVASSING, HERE ARE THE STEPS AGAIN, FRAMED LIKE THE OTHERS:

1. Establish rapport. Assure the other person you aren't out to shame them, and then ask for consent to explore their reasoning.

2. Ask how strongly they feel about an issue on a scale of one to ten.

3. Share a story about someone affected by the issue.

4. Ask a second time how strongly they feel. If the number moved, ask why.

5. Once they've settled, ask, "Why does that number feel right to you?"

6. Once they've offered their reasons, repeat them back in your own words. Ask if you've done a good job summarizing. Repeat until they are satisfied.

7. Ask if there was a time in their life before they felt that way, and if so, what led to their current attitude?

8. Listen, summarize, repeat.

9. Briefly share your personal story of how you reached your position, but do not argue.

10. Ask for their rating a final time, then wrap up and wish them well.

"We wanted to know what parts were important and what parts were not as important," Kalla said, both for practical reasons and scientific ones. All of these technique rebuttal steps are difficult to train on, he said, "so if you could say fifteen minutes is as effective as seven minutes, you could have twice as many conversations." That's the practical part. But when it comes to science, "What do we know that maps on to this?"

Since we had last met, Broockman and Kalla had conducted three experiments with 230 canvassers who used deep canvassing to discuss immigration policies and transphobia with nearly 7,000 voters in 7 different locations in the United States. To find the active ingredient, they kept the persuasive arguments in but removed the nonjudgmental exchange of stories for some conversations and not others. They found that when they employed deep canvassing without sharing their personal narratives, it no longer had any impact, while identical conversations that included storytelling still worked incredibly well.

"Remove the non-judgmental listening and story-sharing, no effect. Put them back in, the effect returns," said Kalla. He defined the nonjudgmental exchange of narratives as a strategy where one attempts to persuade another by listening to their personal experiences while respectfully listening, then sharing stories of one's own while the other party listens.

The most interesting finding, he said, was that it didn't matter if the stories you share about the topic are your own or someone else's, only that it involves someone affected by the issue at hand. Even sharing a video of someone else telling a story was effective. But removing this exchange from deep canvassing also removed all of its persuasive power.

"The cleaner, simpler approach seems best," he said. "I show up at your door. Tell you a sympathetic story. Listen to yours. Through that you begin to humanize and empathize and demystify one another. That seems to be doing most of the work." Even the question about where you stand on a scale seems to help, because the person on the other side realizes they will not be shamed or judged after you don't react negatively to the number they share.

"No matter [what] they say on the scale, you respectfully listen. Why do you feel that way? What led to it? Be a genuine, curious listener, that's what makes them feel open to considering new viewpoints. That's really what the first three or four minutes are about," he said. "If I just show up at your door and launch into my story about transgender people, it feels unnatural. But by starting out with non-judgmental listening, we develop rapport and trust. You are able to feel comfortable and be honest about what we are talking about."

The second active ingredient, which only works once rapport is established and resistance is set aside, is the power of narrative transport. This is where the social science maps on to deep canvassing extremely well, said Kalla. Narrative transport is that feeling when you become so fully immersed in a story that you forget yourself for a moment, be it a book, play, podcast, TV show, movie, or a story told around a campfire or at someone's front door. A long line of research shows that for narrative transport to take place, a story must contain three features: a component that keeps your attention from wandering, a component that consistently evokes strong emotional reactions, and a component that evokes mental imagery.

Why does transport persuade us so? Because it can eliminate counterarguing. When we're engaged with a story, we don't prepare a rebuttal, because we feel swept up. A story isn't trying to change your mind. It isn't threatening your autonomy or your identity.

I asked Kalla if I was hearing him correctly. The first step was to say I'm a social primate, you're a social primate, but we are good here. Then share information in a way that they will not feel compelled to counterargue against it.

"Yes, that reflects my current thinking."

———

Among the persuasive techniques that depend on technique rebuttal, street epistemology seems best suited for beliefs in empirical matters like whether ghosts are real or airplanes are spreading mind control agents in their chemtrails. Deep canvassing is best suited for attitudes, emotional evaluations that guide our pursuit of confirmatory evidence, like a CEO is a bad person or a particular policy will ruin the country. Smart Politics is best suited for values, the hierarchy of goals we consider most important, like gun control or immigration reform. And motivational interviewing is best suited for motivating people to change behaviors, like getting vaccinated to help end a pandemic or recycling your garbage to help stave off climate change.

Across all these techniques, one-eighties sometimes happen, but not always. Usually the change takes several conversations. Just building rapport can take more than one. For each, once our guard is down, we enter into a state of active processing. If the person on the other side encourages us to think about our own thinking without judging or shaming us, it's almost impossible for our certainty not to go up or down a smidge, or our attitudes to move a bit in one direction more than another, or our values to feel worth reconsidering somewhat, or our intentions and plans to adjust.

Crossing the middle line from true to false or positive to negative is often the same amount of change as moving from certain to doubtful or very positive to slightly positive. Because of this, Karin Tamerius told me not to get discouraged by seeking total conversions. They happen, but any change of any kind counts as changing that person's mind.

All these techniques are still iterating on their methods, street epistemology perhaps more than the others, because the community is so new, so connected, and so enthusiastic to share their conversations with one another for feedback.

"There's a better version of it now than there was two years ago," Anthony told me. "In ten years, we will laugh at the videos that are uploaded today and think, 'How primitive was that?'"

When I asked Anthony what kept him going, what drove his passion, he said, "I want to live in a world where people believe true things. But I've realized that ridicule, being angry and telling people that they're mistaken, is not going to help them. We're all sort of in the same boat. We're just grasping for reasons to justify the views that we've already built. Once you know that, you begin to feel empathy, you really do. You begin to have epistemic humility about what you yourself believe."

———

After leaving Texas, I got a chance to use street epistemology at a retreat in Canada where I was invited to give a lecture about conspiratorial thinking and confirmation bias.

I traveled deep into the countryside by train, then by bus north of Montreal where about forty of us spent a weekend giving talks and hanging out around campfires, sleeping in bunks at an enormous lodge on the site of an astronomical observatory. In that summer-camp-for-adults atmosphere, without internet, we all became fast friends, laughing and drinking, eating together in the cafeteria and trading stories about our presentations and obsessions.

Most of my stories were about persuasion techniques. I mentioned street epistemology in the lecture but didn't go into detail. Afterward, one of the people I had spent the most time with around the campfire, startup entrepreneur Nathan Fischer, said he'd like to see the technique in action. I said, sure, let's sit down and do it tonight at dinner.

Word got around, and so when we sat down across from each other, a small crowd watched on, most of them Silicon Valley types, but also some activists and journalists. I told Nathan our topic could be anything, but for the best display of this technique it needed to be something that was sort of fundamental—something that guides your thinking in other domains. Did he have a belief he would like me to challenge?

Nathan boldly presented his belief in God. I cautioned him that it was risky to put something like that on the line, but he was willing.

Rapport was already built because we had spent so much time together, so I moved to the next step and asked him, on a scale of zero to one hundred, how much confidence he had in the existence of God. He said he was a fifty, sometimes more, sometimes less. I asked why not zero, why not one hundred, what reasons justified his confidence? Nathan said he would have to tell me a story, one he only tells once a year, but this felt like the right time to do it. I sat back and listened.

"I was living in the town that I grew up in, working at a video store because I hadn't brought myself to go to university. And this guy came in who loved old movies," Nathan told me. "We ended up having lots of conversations, and he eventually invited me over to his house, and it turned out he had been an American soldier doing some deployments overseas. And then, after he was discharged, he went to Afghanistan."

Nathan said his friend started working with the Northern Alliance to fight the Taliban. However, when his mother got cancer, his friend returned home, and Nathan ran into him again about three weeks later. After Nathan moved away to go to college, he grew listless, started reading a lot of Hemingway, and wrote his friend a letter around October saying that he wanted to try to become a photojournalist. Nathan said he wanted to go to the Middle East and asked for his friend's take on "whether or not you think that this is something I'd be capable of and whether or not this is a good idea?" His friend called the day before Christmas Eve: "I think it's a great idea, and I'm going with you."

Nathan flew to Israel with his mercenary fighter friend, who had verses from the Koran tattooed across his chest. Over several weeks they had what Nathan described as "this, like, super fucked-up experience. But, that's really the prelude to the story."

In Jerusalem, Nathan met many people who knew way more about his Lutheran faith than he did. They stayed with a family in a settlement and attended a wedding in which the father of the bride was a Talmudic scholar. Nathan spent the night going through the texts with him, discussing all the different ways one could interpret the Hebrew characters and the history.

"He was more knowledgeable at that point than I knew I would ever be about this thing that I sort of claimed to believe in." Nathan started spending most of his time attempting to systematically disentangle the religion he grew up in. His goal, he said, was to become an atheist.

When he felt the situation was growing more dangerous where he was staying, Nathan returned to Jerusalem. He set up in a hostel called the Palestine Hotel, close to the Church of the Holy Sepulchre.

"I don't know if you are familiar, but that's one of the holiest sites in Christendom. It is supposed to be close to the site of Jesus's crucifixion; like, it is the holiest site, depending on your denomination."

Walking around the church, Nathan had what he called a crisis of faith. "Basically, if God wanted me to keep on believing, he should provide me with someone that would, you know, give me some answers to fill in these logical questions I had about the history of the Bible and how all these things were interconnected, and why it was interpreted in this way and not another."

As he wandered around, a member of the church invited him inside. He pulled him into the center of the church, where Nathan broke down and told him about his doubts; all these things that had happened, how broken he was as he tried to give up his faith.

Instead of providing comfort, the man told him he had access to secret documents from the Vatican that proved without a doubt that Jesus had been who he said that he was. He told him he would show him if Nathan gave him one hundred dollars.

"I told the guy to go fuck himself."

Nathan stood up and decided to take one more walk around this church and that that would be that. "I would walk out, and I would be walking out on everything that I had believed in up to that point." Walking around the church, stepping in and out of its niches, admiring its fourth-century windows illuminated by flickering candles as the sun set, he heard the faint sounds of a girl crying in the alcove nearby.

Nathan paused his story to take a ragged breath. By now all forty of the speakers had joined us, some standing, some in chairs relocated to the table. Nathan rubbed his beard and looked down for a moment, then looked up and continued.

"I went up just to see if she was OK. All of these monks from inside of this church were coming out, and they were doing their end-of-the-day prayers. They have to go to all of these different sacred artifacts and pray to them before they can close out the church. And so, I went up to her to ask if things were fine, and she was very close to losing consciousness."

Nathan saw a suicide note, which he said he still had. He asked her what she had done, and she told him she had taken some pills and wanted to die. He found out later, after reading the note, that she had wanted to marry a Muslim boy, but "she was this beautiful, Christian-Arab girl, nineteen years old, and her family had forbidden it. And so I picked her up and carried her through these stone streets until I found a taxi and got inside and took her to the hospital. And they pumped her stomach. And she lived."

Nathan said he waited by her side in the hospital. She had a book with phone numbers inside, and he called them one at a time until he reached her family. When they arrived, he stayed with them until the doctor said she was going to make a full recovery. A week later, he visited their home and they cooked dinner for him. "Now she's a nurse, she's got a family."

Nathan pulled up a photo on his phone of the note, still stained with her tears.

"It all clicks together, you know? Like, there's so much adrenaline, just trying to get this body down these streets and into a cab and making sure that she was OK. So, yeah, that's the story that I've carried with me since that night. I went looking for this one thing and found this other thing. I thought, well, if nothing else, we see it through a glass darkly. I got to the deepest point. I put my toe over the edge. With respect to that experience, I feel like I owe it allegiance." He went there to question his religion, but he felt like, in doing so, he had regained faith in something that he was still trying to understand, and if there is a God, that's what it is. If there *is* something more, he became a manifestation of it in that moment, the true version of it.

When Nathan finished, I ran through the method in my head. I knew the next step but wasn't sure if I should proceed. I asked, what was he before that experience, on the scale of zero to one hundred? He said he was a zero, and then repeated that now he was a fifty, some days higher, some days lower.

Improvising, I asked him, "If I could produce a device right now, something like a button under a glass case, and I told you that if you flipped open the glass and pressed the button, your faith would return to zero, would you press it?"

The crowd waited for an answer—we all felt his immense hesitation—and then he looked at me in the eyes and said, "No. I would not."

I took a moment to consider all the lessons I had learned, and I looked over my cheat sheet, the same one I would later use in Sweden. I could think of so many ways to move through his fundamental claim. Whatever else it may mean for someone else, he felt he had come close to the divine, and I had no desire to pick that apart. I had spent years learning how to change minds, but in that moment I didn't think there was any good in doing so. I told Nathan that if I proceeded, I was confident it could be like having him press that button, and there was no way I would do that.

He thanked me, and I thanked him for his story, and he said that it had never been so clear to him how much of a choice his faith was until then. And I said that was enough, really. Knowing that, and knowing there was a button he could press to lose it, and that he was not going to press it that day, was enough. And then we stood up and embraced across the table. I remember looking over at journalist David Boyle, who had absentmindedly leaned all the way in, and he leaned far back, clutched his stomach and sighed, "Wow."

Then he joined the embrace, and the rest of the crowd collapsed on us, and we wept.

———

When I told my friend Misha Glouberman, a communication expert, about my experience with Nathan, he told me that it sounded like I had stumbled onto one of the most important principles of conflict resolution: always start by asking yourself why you want to change the other person's mind.

Ask yourself, "Why is this important to you?" Whatever your answer, ask again, and again. Then share your answers with the other person.

This is crucial, he said, because people tend to clash at the level of positions instead of interests. Our positions are what we say we want, and our interests are why we want them. Often, our positions are antagonistic, but our interests align.

Misha said that on the surface, debate seems like a civil way to manage disagreements, because instead of attacking each other with clubs, we attack each other with words. But this is a dangerous concept, because the only way to win a debate is to avoid changing one's own mind. Only the "loser" of a debate learns anything new, and no one wants to be a loser. The more civil approach, he said, is to avoid asking ourselves which one of us is right, and instead ask ourselves why we see things differently. This creates a collaboration, both sides working together to figure out where their differences come from.

Transparency leads to trust, he said, and trust assures us that we are being heard, that our agency is not at risk, and that it is ok to show vulnerability. Once that kind of trust is established, or reestablished, disagreements become far more effective at opening both sides to considering challenging ideas.

Misha added that in any conversation, we ache for the freedom to safely disagree, that way, if we discover differing perspectives, we may both benefit from the discovery. This is why in his conflict resolution workshops he encourages three pillars of open communication—transparency, curiosity, and compassion.

I decided there was another step that should be added to persuasion techniques like the ELM and motivational interviewing and deep canvassing and street epistemology: a step zero.

Ask yourself, *Why do I want to do this?*

Why do you want to change a person's mind? What are you doing here? Ask yourself, *If I want to leverage the power of one hundred years of psychological research into persuasion in a way that is very effective, why? What are my goals? What are the thoughts, feelings, and values I'm exerting in this dynamic?*

I wouldn't want to give anyone these tools without challenging them to first ask those questions.

10

SOCIAL CHANGE

Around 2.5 million years ago, our ancestors had created a few implements and artifacts, but after those promising advances, the fossil record indicates that nothing really happened for a very long time.

Though brains kept getting bigger, likely to accommodate language, the latest in Stone Age technology remained mostly unchanged for more than 100,000 generations. We know from the fossil record that our ancestors were copying some behaviors of their kin, preserving them as memories, and passing them from one generation to the next. But a thousand years later, we still had the same stony gadgets, just different users—the same flinty practices, just different practitioners. True culture, the accumulation of cross-pollinating ideas and practices, had yet to take off. All our propensities for cultural accumulation were there, but it hadn't happened yet.

And then the world changed.

After a long period of environmental stability, the land grew cold

and hostile. You are likely familiar with this period, called the Pleistocene, through its more common name: the Ice Age. We've come to
think of it as an era populated by now-extinct wooly mammoths and
saber-toothed cats, but not everything died off in that cycle of great
winters. Deer and rabbits and bears all survived, as did our ancestors.
But our ancestors didn't just *survive*. They *thrived*. They advanced, surg-
ing forward technologically, breaking free of the cultural stasis of the previous era in an unbroken cycle of change that led to this very sentence.

The climate before the Ice Age was much like that of the twentieth
century, and it had been for a good long while. But the last half of the
Pleistocene brought with it great impermanence. Alternating bouts
of harsh and cold weather yielded little rain. Ice trapped much of the
groundwater for long stretches, causing sea levels to dramatically rise and
fall. Animals that thrived for a while in one extreme perished in the next
as food and space routinely became scarce.

It was, as zoologist Peter J. Richerson told me, like a "fruit-cart upset
world with lots of high-frequency environmental change." That high
frequency of change remained constant, and many animals that depended on slow-moving genetic evolution didn't make it. The ability to
hunt prey, build nests, dig dens, howl to locate kin, or flock to mating
grounds without having to be taught only keeps you alive when your
generation is likely to face the same environment as the last twenty. As
a result, the mammoths and the tigers, the giant sloths and dire wolves,
didn't survive, but our ancestors did.

As glaciers continually advanced and receded, environmental changes
began to occur on the scale of centuries, far too fast for genes to compen-
sate. Our ancestors couldn't build new bodies in the time it would take
to match them to the new conditions, nor could they quickly evolve new

brain structures with new built-in behavioral solutions to fit the novel environments. But their existing brains *had* developed a suite of tools for creating new behaviors on the fly and copying them from brain to brain—plasticity, abstraction, metacognition, language, social learning, perfect imitation, theory of mind, argumentation, and reasoning. These abilities provided an extreme adaptive advantage that set humans apart. We also had big brains to store large cultural repertoires. And most of all, we lived in groups that had adapted all the social mechanisms required to manage the political life of primates.

With the pressure on, a small number of skilled or lucky innovators could produce variations to the behavioral status quo. Since each individual had the ability to imitate the best innovations with great fidelity, the new ways rapidly and reliably spread from brain to brain and replaced the old behaviors across the group. Engaged in this process, unlike their ancestors who lived in less-chaotic environments, the proto-humans of the Pleistocene soon developed hammers, fire, cooking, and other technologies. A status quo lasting a million years shattered in a few generations.

The hominids of the Pleistocene, with bodies ill-suited for a changing world, began to change their own minds faster than genes could do it for them. It was still genetic evolution at play, but the genes provided the ability to make, change, and accumulate ideas, beliefs, and practices. We evolved the ability to produce culture, and then culture became the environment in which we began to evolve anew.

Culture shaped genes, and genes shaped culture. Though these two processes run in parallel, around 1.5 million years ago they clasped hands and have been spinning on the evolutionary dance floor ever since.

Pressured by an unpredictable existence, we adapted to overcome the slowness of genetic evolution at a time when that slowness would have wiped us out. The chaos of the Ice Age led to the adaptation of culture, a tool that freed us from waiting on genetic change to save us when things go sideways, and now when the environment changes quickly, we change quickly.

Imagine a group of early hominids who lived in the savanna for decades, but conditions forced them to migrate into the forests. At first, since no one knew what to do in that new land, they each kept the old skills and ideas, the old beliefs, norms, and customs. People starved, injured themselves, and became food for predators because the old savanna practices and technology didn't work well in the new forest setting—but as innovators happened upon behaviors and tools and skills more suited to woodland life, early adopters began to replicate them, followed by holdouts, and together groups tossed out the old ways as their new culture complexified. Within a generation, the group shifted to the new traditions and folkways. When a new batch of savanna stragglers arrived and made contact with this band of first-generation forest dwellers, they too would have had no idea what to do. But if they changed quickly—conformed to better ways—they could change even faster than did the first settlers and avoid death, disease, and starvation.

Now imagine a group of iguanas migrating onto tundra, pushed out by dwindling food sources. Their survival would depend on a slow-motion genetic lottery, and if the tundra melted a century or two later, the lottery winners would be thrown right back into a new game of chance. The grind would eventually end them, whereas we grew stronger thanks to that grind.

Pressured by environmental chaos, we gained the ability to do the right thing when what used to be the right thing changed without warning. Back then, the right thing was that which kept you alive in the unforgiving wilderness. Today, the right thing is difficult to determine, and there are so many cultural variations to choose from that people clump and cluster around a host of popular alternatives. But when we need to reach a majority consensus and change quickly, as a group we have the capacity to do so thanks to the adaptations of our ancestors.

Through an accumulation of gradual improvements to our tools, both mental and physical, we have spread across the planet into regions ill-suited for our slowly evolving bodies, and where we have settled, we have survived and thrived. Along the way, what used to be the right way of doing things routinely became the wrong way. Social change gave us the ability to recognize that and rapidly adapt as individuals. With that adaptation, we gained culture and the ability to change our collective minds in a rapid, society-wide cascade when we realized our norms were harmful, misguided, dangerous, or incorrect. Changing our minds became our greatest strength as a species.

"Cultural change occurs because environments change," explained psychologist Lesley Newson, who years ago teamed up with zoologist Peter Richerson on a paper that predicted the rapid changes in attitudes toward same-sex marriage and how they could be explained through the lens of cultural evolution. I caught them grilling on a houseboat one afternoon in London, and they patiently ran through the science with me.

According to Newson and Richerson, the environmental change that led to widespread acceptance of same-sex marriage and continues to drive its spread was the relative wealth and stability of national institutions. The more people who grow up within, or eventually obtain, physical and economic security will always develop values of individuality, autonomy, and self-expression.

But since members of the same community comparison shop from the same pool of ideas about how to respond to their shared environment, in the immediate period after an environmental change the most popular ideas remain the most influential. So a total, culture-wide response to an environmental change is often delayed. First comes the environmental change, then the cultural change; but the cultural change lags behind, sometimes for a long while. That change is inevitable, but it can take generations. In some instances, though, it happens within a lifetime.

When economic development following the industrial revolution upended the social structures and institutions that had been stable for hundreds of years, Westerners transitioned from self-sustaining homesteads to factory work, and people began to commute or relocate to the factories. Cities grew large and complex, and people began to spend more time interacting with friends, coworkers, and fellow city dwellers— and less time with their kin. The balance of influence shifted. The mix of socially transmitted information tilted more in favor of peers than parents. People became members of multiple tribes, and with that came the freedom to change their minds without paying social costs. Before then, people lived in communities that featured a host of cultural norms that promoted the perpetuation of large families, and most of those norms were transmitted via older family members. Having a large family was vital to survival. It was a cultural solution to the shared challenges of homestead life.

"These norms encourage individuals to believe that it is morally correct to perceive the interests of their family to be identical to, or more important than, their own interests and preferences," explained Newson.

Over the next 150 years, norms surrounding marriage and child-rearing dramatically changed. Separated from homesteads, Westerners in the nineteenth century began to abandon the belief that large families were a moral imperative. Westerners in the twentieth century worried less about marriage as a reproductive enterprise and started to see it more as an incubator for love and happiness. Once marriage was about love, Newson said that ideas about what made for a suitable spouse underwent a sudden, rapid, culture-wide shift.

Research at the University of Wisconsin in 1939 found that men ranked "mutual attraction and love" as the fourth most desirable trait in a wife, and women ranked it fifth in a husband. The most important trait? Women said they wanted "dependable character" in their partners, and men said they wanted "emotional stability" in theirs. When that same research was repeated in 1977, "mutual attraction and love" had risen to number one for both men and women: a major change in marriage norms that took about thirty-eight years. This led to another shift in attitudes and beliefs, and thus norms. Once attraction and love were the most important reasons to stay married, people began to see the loss of those feelings as a reasonable justification for divorce. In the latter half of the twentieth century, divorce rates for first marriages skyrocketed in the United States, but that rate tapered off and dropped by 2016, because people began to marry for love from the beginning instead of realizing they wished they had in the middle. Sometimes, when a norm changes rapidly, it breaks an institution before it remakes it.

Once choosing to not have a big family was normal, and choosing to marry for love was normal, and choosing to divorce for lack of love was normal, the idea of choosing to not have children, have children

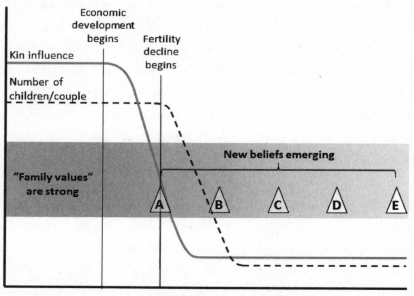

Time

From *Moral Beliefs about Homosexuality: Testing a Cultural Evolutionary Hypothesis* by Lesley Newson and Peter J. Richerson, Department of Environmental Science and Policy, University of California, Davis, 2016.

A. It is acceptable for couples to limit the number of children they have if they want to.

B. People should marry someone they are in love with and who makes them happy.

C. Even if they have children, couples can divorce if one or both of them is unhappy.

D. Divorced and single people and unmarried couples can make perfectly good parents.

E. If homosexual couples are in love and want to marry, they should have the right to do so.

without marrying, or just cohabitate and do neither all became normal as well, and at an even faster pace than the changes to the previous norms that paved the way. By that time, the idea that same-sex couples should be able to marry if they so choose seemed obviously true, and this set the stage for norms, attitudes, and beliefs surrounding same-sex marriage to flip in a little more than a decade.

On May 9, 2012, ABC interrupted its regular programming for a special report. Barack Obama, they announced, the president of the United States, had changed his mind about same-sex marriage.

"I've been going through an evolution on this issue," Obama explained on national television. He had thought it over quite a bit. He had conversations with friends, family, and neighbors, with people who saw things differently. He realized he had been wrong when he told the world four years earlier that marriage was, and should be, strictly between a man and a woman.

Some of his children's friends had LGBTQ parents, he explained. He knew people on his staff who were LGBTQ, and they had children. He had constantly thought of members of the military who, even after his administration rolled back "Don't Ask Don't Tell," were unable to marry, even after risking their lives for the country. It all added up, a death by a thousand cuts, he told ABC's Robin Roberts. His old justifications—respecting tradition and the religious beliefs of others, not wanting to divide the country by taking a controversial stance— simply couldn't stand up to the new arguments swirling in his head.

The fact that Obama, running for reelection, wanted to make his change of mind public reflected that the country as a whole had shifted on same-sex marriage. Whatever political alchemy was taking place be- hind the scenes in his campaign had determined it was not only safe to admit his support, but it would help his odds of winning. Republicans said they were still mostly opposed, but among Democrats attitudes concerning same-sex marriage had crossed the halfway mark. Polls showed 51 percent were now in favor.

The shift in public opinion was incredibly swift. Twenty years ago, 81 percent of Republicans opposed the idea; today it's 56 percent. Among Democrats, 43 percent shared in that opposition, but today 75 percent of Democrats are in support. For all Americans, in 1997, 73 per- cent were opposed, but now 70 percent are in favor. When polled in 2016, more than half the nation said they weren't just supportive, but that it had become an issue that would affect their votes.

That wasn't the first time Americans said same-sex marriage would affect their support for a candidate. Twelve years earlier more than half the nation said they preferred the opposite stance and would only vote for politicians who wanted it to remain illegal. Many pundits agreed that his resistance to same-sex marriage won George W. Bush his second term.

When Massachusetts became the first state to pass a law grant- ing marriage rights to same-sex couples in 2004, Bush publicly en- dorsed a constitutional amendment to ban same-sex marriage across the country.

Nine years later, the *Boston Globe* reported that George W. Bush would not only serve as a witness at the marriage of two women in Kennebunkport, Maine, but that he offered to perform the ceremony.

———

In 1969, when police raided the Stonewall Inn, one of the only bars for LGTBQ people in New York where dancing was allowed, the patrons rebelled. They sang "We Shall Overcome," and a crowd of around 150 gathered to see what was happening. When an officer shoved a patron, she shoved back. The crowd booed, and a scuffle broke out. When she was struck by the police, she pleaded to the crowd, "Why don't you guys do something?"

The crowd became incensed, and the altercation quickly grew into a riot with people throwing bottles at police. Before it was over, between five hundred and six hundred people had entered the fray. The police barricaded themselves inside the Inn as the crowd moved on to hurling garbage cans, rocks, and bricks, and then they lit fires and smashed windows.

After several nights of rioting, the demonstrations shifted from violence to protest. In defiance of norms and laws, LGBTQ people openly displayed affection and made no attempt to hide their sexuality. Some of the people involved organized their efforts, and that organization led to the formation of the Gay Liberation Front and other early LGBTQ rights groups. That unification, organization, and publicity would directly lead to more protests, more defiance, and a push by leaders in many communities to live openly.

Most of America was oblivious to these efforts, but when those protests led to the 1973 removal of homosexuality from the *Diagnostic and*

Statistical Manual of Mental Disorders, they reached a much wider swath of minds. The *DSM* is the guide published by the American Psychiatric Association for diagnosing mental problems, a text used by psychiatrists and psychologists across the country, and after that change, people interacting with the profession in every state were confronted with a new scientific and professional understanding of the LGBTQ community.

The movement was both stalled and catalyzed when the 1980s brought the AIDS epidemic to national attention. Originally called "gay cancer," opponents of gay rights used AIDS as a way to paint LGBTQ people as disease-carrying deviants. But that opposition also fueled activists to further organize into a series of marches on Washington—the largest in 1993, in which more than a million people came to the nation's capital to raise awareness for the LGBTQ community. The planning before the march, and the workshops, speakers, and vigils during, all led to the establishment of a vast network of LGBTQ activists and allies across the country who could now ramp up efforts using their new lines of communication.

Thanks to those efforts in the 1990s, AIDS was depicted more sympathetically in the media. Academy award–winning movies featured characters struggling with the disease. The word *homophobia* entered common usage. And during that time, many same-sex couples applied for marriage licenses, boldly and publicly challenging state laws. In response, the US Congress passed the Defense of Marriage Act. The backlash extended to the states, and thirty eventually established provisions preventing similar cases from reaching their courts.

But attitudes were changing. High-profile cultural moments like the march on Washington, Tom Hanks in *Philadelphia*, Pedro Zamora on

The Real World, Ellen DeGeneres coming out on the cover of *Time* magazine, and *Will and Grace* dominating the ratings both reflected and contributed to these changes. People coming out in communities around the country put constant pressure on the old model of reality to accommodate in more and more brains. And then the internet began to seep into our lives, multiplying contact with these ideas. Where it was safe to do so, more people came out. In small towns, in companies, in living rooms—contact with LGBTQ friends, family, and coworkers became unavoidable.

Contact changes minds. It's the fundamental argument of one of psychology's most robust theories, the contact hypothesis. Psychologist Gordon Allport outlined its principles in his landmark 1954 book *The Nature of Prejudice*. Psychology had been studying prejudice for a long time, first in interracial combat units and then most intensely following World War II during the civil rights struggle in the United States.

Allport spent years researching prejudice, and in his book said that before minds can change concerning members of a minority or an out-group, they must make true contact. First, members must meet, especially at work, under conditions of equal status. Second, they must share common goals. Third, they should routinely cooperate to meet those goals. Fourth, they must engage in informal interactions, meeting one another outside of mandated or official contexts, like at one another's homes or at public events. And finally, for prejudice to truly die out, the concerns of the oppressed must be recognized and addressed by an authority, ideally the one that writes laws.

Allport's research also showed that mere contact was not enough. He noted that in the 1950s racially segregated communities, housing, schools, and churches meant that most of the contact that occurred between black and white Americans was at the borders of separate worlds, and so that contact was rife with conflict. White Americans could avoid almost all contact with black America, and if they did work together, that contact was imbalanced since people often didn't share equal status. Poor contact like that, he said, leads people who are already prejudiced to reinforce their opinions, especially those who live and work far from such sociological borderlands.

The change in attitudes in America toward LGBTQ people and same-sex marriage was incredibly swift by comparison to attitudes about race, because black Americans had to fight to make contact, to gain equal status, and to enter schools and workplaces. When LGBTQ people began to come out and live openly, people across America discovered over the course of a few years that their bosses, coworkers, and employees were already part of their communities. Family and friends, people in positions of authority, people at public gatherings and in the public eye—they all came out seemingly within the same short period of time. The buildup was long and difficult, but once it happened the anomalies had accumulated until they were too great to ignore. The bucket of abeyance overfilled. The old models couldn't bear the incongruences. Soon, in many states, legislation lagged behind public opinion.

As with all mind change, at first people resisted and tried to apply their current model of reality to the new evidence, to resolve the dissonance by assimilation. Anti-LGBTQ sentiments sprang from many sources, but their justifications all grew weak in the face of unavoidable and compelling evidence: twenty years of activism, increasingly positive and realistic portrayals in the media, and then most importantly, widespread personal contact with members of the LGBTQ community or their allies. The categories most of the country used to make sense of LGBTQ issues had to be updated to accommodate.

———

The creation of new conceptual categories is the greatest sign that accommodation is occurring on a large scale, and thus social change is imminent. For instance, the term *designated driver* was invented by the Harvard Alcohol Project as a public health initiative and then seeded into popular television shows like *Cheers* and *L.A. Law*. Seeing characters put a name to a particular behavior created a new conceptual category in the viewer. If you accepted the term and used it, then it created dissonance with the urge to drink and drive. Why would there be a word for a person who drives his friends around while they drink if it's perfectly okay to drink and drive? To resolve the dissonance, the existing model had to be updated—people who drink do not drive. According to the Project, after introducing the term to the public in 1988, alcohol-related fatalities dropped by 24 percent in four years, an extremely rapid shift in attitudes. Today most Americans say they've served as the designated driver at least once in their lives.

In Kwame Anthony Appiah's book *The Honor Code*, he argues that the widening definition of dignity led directly to the abolition of slavery in the UK. Dignity in the 1500s was considered hierarchical. Philosophers like Thomas Hobbes said that it was plainly obvious that some people had more dignity than others, so the idea that the world was arranged in hierarchies was already a widely accepted paradigm. There was a linear order to everything from plants to people; in fact, the two were connected. Peasants ate dirty plants that grew underground, and nobles ate beautiful fruits that budded high above. To the people of that era, it was unthinkable that a person who made candles out of animal fat had as much dignity as a king.

Appiah defines honor and dignity as the state one inhabits when deserving the respect of others. The concept that all humans, just by virtue of being human, deserved such dignity was not an idea that the honor codes of the time could support. But when technology led to factories, and factories led to political clout and wealth among laborers, the concept of a working class emerged. It was a new category, and people within it demanded representation in the government and respect from society.

The fact that the definition of respect could accommodate this concept made it possible to widen it further. Through a progression of accumulating ideas, it became illogical to treat people with greater levels of dignity only because they were born into a certain economic stratum. Dignity was redefined. It soon encompassed class, then gender, then race, and then all of humanity. Appiah says that once enough people shared a schema that asserted all human beings deserved dignity, the consensual model of reality could not support the anomalies generated by the institution of slavery.

The practice of dueling disappeared in a similar fashion. To a person living in the late 1700s, honor was of utmost importance. To have honor was to be seen as deserving your status among your peers. That kind of honor couldn't be earned, nor did it exist in degrees. Either you had it or you didn't. People who believed in this way lived in what Appiah calls "honor worlds," his term for a sort of moral paradigm. People within an honor world feel shame for not meeting its standards. To not feel shame revealed you were without honor, and the lowest a person could be was shameless. If someone disrespected you, called you a liar, or in some way hinted to others that you had no honor, first you had to ask for an apology, but if the slight was severe, you challenged them to a duel. You must be seen as though you would rather risk your life than be considered dishonest and therefore dishonorable.

Dueling was long-reviled, and by the 1800s most academics and

pundits had said it was abhorrent to civil society. Still, hundreds of people died every year shooting each other over insults. So how did it go
away? Newspapers. The innovation of the printing press and its widespread adoption led to a surge of literacy and new media. When the
newspapers published articles about prominent members of society who
were getting away with murder, they ridiculed the practice. They made
fun of it in cartoons. At the same time, wanting to emulate the upper
class, some wealthy tradesmen and merchants began to engage in copy-
cat dueling.

For a century, the duel was a way for nobles to communicate their
superior honor to the common people. When it became laughable and
commonplace, the aristocracy abandoned it in less than a generation.
Appiah quotes Oscar Wilde to sum up its demise as a social norm: "As
long as war is regarded as wicked, it will always have its fascination.
When it is looked upon as vulgar, it will cease to be popular." As another historian put it, "Solemn gentlemen went to the field of honor
only to be laughed at by the younger generation. That was more than
any custom, no matter how sanctified by tradition, could endure."

One of the curious aspects of moving from one paradigm to another
is that the moment a better explanation comes along that can accommodate the anomalies that the previous paradigm couldn't assimilate,
the anomalies simply become facts. We rearrange our categories, create
new ones, and fill them with refined definitions.

Kuhn called it "picking up the other end of the stick." The same information is there that was there before, but we handle it differently. With
slavery, dueling, drinking and driving, and LGBTQ people, the essential
qualities didn't change. The categories and definitions changed. Invok-
ing Thomas Kuhn, Derek Penwell, a Christian minister in Kentucky, said
of the shift in attitudes in America, "Proportionally, there aren't more

gay people today than there were in 2004, but our relationship to gay people has shifted."

President Obama would say of the sweeping change of beliefs, attitudes, and opinions concerning same-sex marriage, "Compared to so many issues, America's shift has been so quick." Indeed, the social scientists I've interviewed have all agreed this was the fastest flip of a long-held, nationwide public opinion in recorded history. But that was before COVID.

About 86 percent of people in the UK who when polled in December 2019 said they refused to get vaccinated against COVID-19, said in April 2021 that they had changed their minds. So what happened here, and how can we make use of what we've learned?

Researchers say, in short, it was about trust—we don't live in a post-truth world, but a post-*trust* world. A general distrust of media, science, medicine, and government makes a person very unlikely to get vaccinated no matter how much information you throw at them, especially when the people they *do* trust share their attitudes.

Just like in the United States, the people who were most hesitant in the UK were the people who had existing negative attitudes about authority. As NPR reported, "The flood of disinformation found fertile ground among some Black Britons and South Asians whose ancestors grew up under the British Empire and who were more likely to distrust the system. . . . The history of using minorities for drug trials added to people's skepticism."

So how did they assuage this distrust? Instead of depending on messaging, on facts, they started distributing the vaccine at mosques.

For the least hesitant among the most hesitant, the approval of a leader in their faith was enough to encourage them to get vaccinated. More than fifteen thousand doses went out in the first few days. Then that group became influential to the next most hesitant. After that, the hesitant saw that not only were their religious elites in favor of vaccinating, but so were many of their peers. A cascade began in which each new cohort of less-hesitant people influenced the next most hesitant until the attitude change had swept through the population.

Each group that changes adds to the total population of the changed, and thus the strength of the influence of your peers. This network effect, sometimes called diffusion and sometimes called percolation, is the force behind all major public opinion shifts. Large groups of people change their minds in a sequence that goes from innovator to early adopter to mainstream to holdouts, and it always happens in that order. The trick is getting enough early adopters who are deeply connected to the community as a whole to flip and adopt the attitude, which then creates an influential social unit that can kick off the cascade.

So the research suggests that to shift hesitant attitudes about vaccines or anything else, we must identify who is hesitant, what institutions they most trust, and then distribute the vaccine from the manifestations of those institutions that will appeal to the most socially connected groups within that population.

———

In complex human social environments, a variety of factors influence cascades of change, but the factors most crucial are the individual conformity thresholds among people who regularly interact.

Earlier in the book, we looked at the research behind the affective tipping point, the moment after which a brain can no longer assimilate anomalies and becomes motivated to accommodate instead. That threshold varies in individuals. Sociologist Mark Granovetter calls these "thresholds of resistance." In any group of people, some will be early adopters and others will be stubborn holdouts, and many will be in between.

Imagine a group of people trying to get into a college classroom. The classroom is empty, but the first person who shows up makes a conscious decision not to attempt to open the door and check. The reason he doesn't check has something to do with his disposition, what sociologists call an internal signal.

Let's say he opened a door his first week on campus. The class was still going, and they all turned around and laughed at him. It was extremely embarrassing, and since then he is overly cautious. Today, he has decided to stand by the door and play on his phone because he assumes the class will let out shortly. The next person who shows up has never experienced the same sort of embarrassment, but he doesn't want to make small talk with a stranger or make a fool of himself, so he just avoids eye contact and starts playing with his phone over in the corner. Now a third person shows up. Normally, if she were the first person on the scene, she'd have no problem checking to see if the classroom was empty, but since there are two people already waiting, she assumes they know something she doesn't, and bases her behavior on their behavior. She ignores her internal signal thanks to the strength of the external one.

Already we have a cascade beginning to unfold. Each person decides to adopt the behavior of the others depending on their personal threshold for conformity. Person One based his behavior on past experience with similar situations in the natural world. Person Two based his behavior on social anxiety, which is based on his past experience with social worlds. But Person Three based her behavior on the number of people ahead of her in the current situation. Now the cascade is already self-propagating. The power of the behavioral cascade comes from how, with each additional person, the gumption required to break the cascade increases.

The fourth, fifth, and sixth people to arrive at the door will base their behavior on the crowd's behavior ahead of them, and as the crowd grows, it becomes more and more unlikely that a newcomer will be the sort of person who doesn't care what so many people might think of them if they embarrass themselves publicly. It is safer to assume that everyone waiting to get inside the classroom has good reasons to do so—even though they don't.

The network, not the environment, is now determining the behavior of the minds within it. Person Fifteen might have a very high threshold, but the cascade is too powerful to resist. In the past, even if ten people were waiting, she would have checked to see if the class was truly empty. If she discovered it was, she would have shattered the cascade. Behind her, everyone else would have adopted *her* behavior, not the group's. But since her upper conformity threshold is ten, fourteen others is just too large of a consensus for her to question. Her threshold for rebellion has been met. When she joins, the crowd grows to fifteen people, and the bar is raised even higher for the next person who comes along. To break the cascade, someone who is more brave and willing to look silly by checking the door than anyone else in the crowd so far must arrive, and at a certain size of group, for that sample of people, there might not be any such person.

The only way the cascade will break is if new information is added to the system, like if the professor opens the door from inside to see what's wrong with everyone, or if enough time passes that the anguish of waiting outweighs the predicted pain of embarrassment should that person be incorrect.

You may have seen how quickly cascades like this can spread at a house party. Social gatherings like parties often empty out without any group coordination. When one person who is tired or bored leaves, if there are no other like-minded people with low thresholds for conformity left behind, the revelry continues unabated. But if there are other tired people with low thresholds left behind, an early leaver can encourage them to do the same. Now the number of people who have left is large enough to encourage people with higher thresholds to check out, and a cascade ends the party as if everyone agreed at the same time to go home.

Now imagine the psychology behind classrooms and house parties taking place within clusters of people throughout a culture, persuading groups of friends and coworkers to quit smoking, for example, and you can begin to see how a cascade of change can spread culture-wide, and a status quo stable for decades will seem to, all at once, shatter as a global cascade changes the minds of millions.

Innovation researcher Greg Satell, in his book *Cascades*, asks us to imagine three groups of people—A, B, C—and in each group, people are paying attention to what the others are thinking, feeling, and doing. But in each tightly connected group there are some people with regular contact with individuals in other groups. Because of this, in each group, not only is there a mix of people with different thresholds for conformity—some very low, some very high, many in the middle—there is also a mix of people whose resistance can be overwhelmed through the influence of people outside their immediate groups.

This complexity of connections and thresholds—which itself is constantly changing as people form and break bonds, join and leave groups, and so on—makes the entire network quite stable most of the time. But if everything lines up in just the right way so that people with low thresholds of conformity are in regular contact with people among a few interconnected groups, it leaves the surrounding network vulnerable to a global, or network-wide, cascade.

Satell asks us to imagine that in three groups:

- One person in group A with a threshold of 30 percent (they need a third of their peers to adopt an idea before they will do the same) is connected to one person in group C with a threshold of 0 percent (they conform very easily).

- A second person in group A with a threshold of 70 percent (a hold-out), is connected to one person in group B who has a threshold of 0 percent (they conform very easily).

- Meanwhile, groups B and C are connected to each other via two people: one in group B with a threshold of 20 percent is connected to another in group C with a threshold of 70 percent.

With just these three conditions, if people begin changing their minds in group A, and it leads to a cascade, it will spread from group A to both groups B and C. And since each group is connected to the other two, the larger the cascade grows, the faster it will spread.

Here is how it could play out:

If a cascade begins in group A and grows strong enough to reach the person with a 30 percent threshold, their influence will meet the threshold of that one early adopter they know in group C. When that person flips, it sets off a separate cascade. Later, when the cascade in group A reaches the point where it flips its 70 percent threshold holdout, it will spread from that person to another early adopter, the person they influence in group B, setting off yet another cascade in that group. By the time the cascade in group C reaches its holdout, the person connected to them in group B has already flipped, so the holdout in group C will feel influence from both inside their group and outside, making it more likely they flip *and* flipping them faster than the holdout in group A did.

Sociologists call a cluster of groups connected in this way a percolating vulnerable cluster, a clump of strongly connected groups with weak connections to other groups. Taken together, they share a perfect mix of thresholds at the point where they connect, allowing for a chain reaction. A shock, as they call it, that begins in such a cluster, or any cascade that spreads far enough to reach it, stands a chance of flipping all the people in all its connected groups, whose combined influence will flip *their* neighboring groups, who flip their neighbors, and so begins a network-wide cascade, be it a business, a city, or a nation.

To borrow an analogy from Duncan Watts, the physicist turned sociologist, think of it like this. Imagine a forest with a busy road cutting through it. Every day, a few people toss cigarettes out of their car windows, but most of those embers never make it out into the trees. However, a few do. They bounce on the asphalt and tumble into the brush, but when they make it that far they always fizzle out in the dampness. Each cigarette has the potential to set off a blaze that could cascade across the entire forest, but the timber isn't vulnerable. Then a drought sets in. Great swaths of land grow parched, and the trees in those places begin to die and crumble. The same number of people carelessly toss cigarettes into the same forest, but still, most of the time, nothing happens. Yet if one should land on a dry patch among some crisp straw, the fire will spread and eventually engulf a dead tree, and then it will spread to its neighbors. If the fire grows strong enough, it will dry out the area around it as it expands, making previously resistant areas just as vulnerable as naturally dry ones.

Before long, the entire countryside is on fire for miles. Once a patch of forest is vulnerable, the spark that sets off the blaze could be as small as a single cigarette, or it could be as large as a lightning bolt, or a bomb, or a trash fire, but if the conditions aren't right, if some portion of the system isn't vulnerable, these far-more-influential catalysts have no better chance of starting the inferno than a tiny ember. But once those conditions are met, all it takes is a spark.

The fact that the state of the network determines whether global cascades are possible explains not only why some ideas catch on and others do not, but why some ideas appear over and over again and go nowhere until one day they change everything. Just like the cigarettes that landed in the forest a thousand times until one day they caused a massive fire, the same kind of shock can strike a system a billion times, then on strike one billion and one it happens to hit a percolating vulnerable cluster. Events like Stonewall, for example, happened every day in San Francisco, Los Angeles, Chicago, New Orleans, and in small towns all across America. Then one day, as the story goes, in a bar in New York, one woman's defiance set off a global cascade that would lead to one of the fastest about-faces in public opinion in recorded history, and the Supreme Court changing the marriage laws of an entire nation.

Societies aren't fixed. Large social systems, though they seem stable, are always changing in subtle ways that are imperceptible to the people living within them.

Even if thresholds remain constant in a way that prevents a cascade from building momentum within a single group, all manner of circumstances can affect the average number of connections between groups, altering the conditions in ways that randomly create percolating vulnerable clusters. Any society can, without its knowledge, change from one in which a global cascade is impossible to one in which it could happen at any time. Repeated shocks to the system that before seemed futile now have the potential to change the world.

Change can creep along with no signs of meaningful progress for decades. It makes the status quo seem like it was unanimously agreed upon, stable and eternal. It makes mind change seem impossible—until one day, a lucky strike causes so much change that everyone's thresholds are met within a percolating cluster. Then the culture-wide spread begins. A social change cascading this way will reach everyone except those who have difficult-to-meet thresholds or who are part of a cluster that is disconnected from the network, like a cult, an insulated religion, or a remote community.

The rush to end slavery, the cascade of changed minds concerning same-sex marriage, the rapid shift in marijuana laws, the volcanic spread of protests to end police brutality—these are just a few examples from American history. Critical junctures across the globe have routinely changed our concept of right to wrong, true to false, commonplace to taboo, and vice versa. From the appearance of the domestication of animals to the theory of evolution, from the Copernican Revolution to the Protestant Reformation, from the Industrial Revolution to the French Revolution to the end of the Cold War, discontinuities and innovations have led to rapid, surprising, status-quo-shattering global cascades of change.

Since most people are in the fat part of the bell curve, neither early adopter nor holdout, changes like these seem to come out of nowhere. All they see are the middle dominoes. This has contributed to the belief that influencers must be the most important factor, as if they are vectors of disease in the viral spread of ideas. Some people seem more crucial to the spread of an idea than others—those people in the old Apple ads, the crazy ones, the tastemakers, trendsetters, thought leaders, and other influentials. Get those people to change their minds, the old thinking goes, and everyone else will fall in line. The old advice was that anyone looking to get information or behaviors to spread should seek out the ultra-connected nodes in a network, the people that others look to for guidance on how to think and act. In reality, though, anyone can start a cascade.

For an idea to spread across a network in such a way that it flips almost everyone from thinking in one way to thinking in another, you don't need thought leaders or elites. The crucial factor is the susceptibility of the network. If there are enough connected people with low thresholds across groups, any shock—any person—can start a cascade that will flip the majority of the population.

As Watts says, you don't need an atom bomb to start an avalanche. Once the conditions are met, any bump will do.

———

In his book *The Day the Universe Changed*, science historian James Burke wrote, "We are what we know, and when the body of knowledge changes, so do we."

Throughout our history, evolving moral values, the sequential impact of discovery, increasing contact between nations and groups, surprising innovations, and the accelerating rate of invention have all continuously and relentlessly updated the beliefs and attitudes populating the models we have used to define reality itself.

As individuals and as entire cultures, we move from paradigm to paradigm—models that explain reality for as long as we can hold on to them. Because of this, Burke told me, "at any given time, we're in a box which defines the world and tells us what it is. These definitions constrain what we think, and also what we think we *can think*." Before Copernicus, the heliocentric model was inconceivable. The Earth was the center of the cosmos. When Copernicus produced evidence this was incorrect, at first it seemed like error, and so it went into abeyance. To resolve the problems, a new, better model was necessary, and that meant the old model would have to go. "That was a real mess," said Burke, "because if the Earth wasn't the center of everything, then it wasn't the center of God's attention, and if we weren't the center of God's attention— help!"

In the 1990s, Americans were not only opposed to same-sex marriage but the very idea of homosexuality. Today, that attitude for most people is as ridiculous as the belief that geese grow on trees.

We've left a trail of dozens of discarded models of reality, shared beliefs, moral high grounds, and superseded scientific theories that were each once the final word. By today's standards, we were wrong, and we were not only blind to our wrongness—we believed we were right. Being wrong, we think, is always a thing of the past. Today, we think, and will continue to think, we have finally arrived at certainty.

Every era, every culture, believed it knew the truth, until it realized it didn't; then when the truth changed, the culture changed with it. People can seem myopic and perpetually ignorant, but I prefer to see how marvelous we are at changing our minds in big ways. The fact that you don't believe geese grow on trees or that you *do* believe that the Earth goes around the sun is a fact shows that our models of reality— our knowledge, beliefs, and the attitudes they support—are fungible.

Most shocks are absorbed. Most cascades never escape their local clusters. Yet every stable system is punctuated by random, routine, global cascades that seem so sudden and unexpected that we pick them apart in retrospect and try to pin their sources on amazing, incredible, visionary people or world-shaking, life-changing, essential inventions instead of the real cause—those occasions when the excitability of the nodes was just right, the density of the connections was all lined up, and a shock that on any other day would go nowhere ends up going everywhere.

Duncan Watts told me that as far as mainstream thinking is concerned, most people strongly reject the notion of randomness. They'd rather believe the world turned out the way it did because that's the way it was supposed to turn out.

"We don't want to learn it because we just don't like the lesson," he said. "This is something I struggle with, because I think it is debilitating, really, this insistence on being able to tell a good story about things. It is deeply ingrained, but I think it's very misleading." I told him I would try to change people's minds by reseeding the network. Who knows? Maybe it will take this time. Which is the point—persistence plus luck is what changes minds, not genius. The ideas that change the world are the ones in the heads of people who refuse to give up.

We've seen many ways to get people through the natural mind-change process—and we've seen the persuasion techniques that deliver the best results. We've learned to counter the effects of tribal psychology; create better online worlds to tap into what gave us the ability to change our minds in the first place; use the genetic gifts of assimilation and accommodation, reasoning, elaboration, perspective-taking, and social learning that give argumentation the power to change the minds of people bound within SURFPADified and tribal ideologies. Scaled up, these paths to change disturb the status quo when the network effects we've discussed create the conditions that make cascades of change unpredictable. But no status quo is eternal. Every system occasionally grows fragile. The key to changing a nation, or a planet, is persistence.

At any one time, for any given system, thousands of us are banging away at it hoping to make the difference that changes the world, but no one knows where the vulnerable cluster is at. No one can will the system to cascade for them.

The system must become vulnerable. When it is, with so many people banging away, it is inevitable that someone will start the cascade that changes everything, but that someone isn't preordained. You need no special privilege to start striking at the status quo, because no one is in control. What you *are* in control of is whether or not you stop striking. And if the change you want to make is big, you may need to strike all your life. All throughout the struggle for racial equality in America, people who struck at the status quo had to pass their hammer down to fresh arms. Because once that struggle began, there was always someone hard at work, looking for the vulnerable cluster. The cascades that led to change weren't constant, but they *were* inevitable. The key is to never put that hammer down.

The people who change the world are the people who persist, people like Dave Fleischer, who has overseen an effort to knock on more than thirteen thousand doors, and he is still knocking. Often but not every time, a knock leads to a change. He is sure of this, and the research backs him up—maybe not this knock, but eventually that rapping on the door will shatter the status quo and change everything.

CODA

N   ear the end of writing this book, I was invited to the Gather
       festival in Sweden to interview Mark Sargent, a prominent flat-
Earther, in front of a live audience.

I was invited because I had contributed to the documentary *Behind
the Curve*, an exploration of motivated reasoning and conspiratorial
thinking told through the lives of people who have formed a community around the belief that the Earth is flat.

The documentary was popular on Netflix at the time, and I invited
the producers on my podcast to discuss the science, both planetary and
social, that their film explored. The organizers of Gather listened to
the podcast and then offered an invite to both me and Mark, the flat-
Earther whom the documentary follows most closely, to have a chat
on stage.

Like most conspiracy theorists, flat-Earthers are usually reasonable, intelligent, scientifically curious people. They love their families, they hold down jobs, they pay their bills, and so on. In other words, they aren't crazy or stupid. So what leads reasonable, intelligent, scientifically curious people to believe the Earth is flat? At its core, the phenomena of both believing in a flat Earth and forming a community around that belief are driven by the same absolutely normal, absolutely common-to-the-human-experience psychological mechanisms we've learned about throughout this book—which led to subcultures like anti-vaxxers, moon landing hoaxers, evolution deniers, 9/11 truthers, Sandy Hook truthers, birthers, QAnon followers, anti-maskers, ivermectin eaters, and Pizzagate.

Whatever model you subscribe to as a flat-Earther, the binding idea is that there is a mysterious powerful *them* who at some point learned the Earth was flat—either through seeing it from space or from exploring to the farthest edges of the disc—and now they are covering it up for some reason.

Flat Earth is a compelling conspiracy theory because it explains all other conspiracy theories. This is why we faked the moon landing. This is why we cover up aliens. This is why Kennedy was assassinated. This is what the Deep State is all about. That's not to say there aren't schisms within the community; there are camps, like denominations within a religious belief system. Some believe it's more like a snow globe with a hyper-advanced projection of space and the sun and the moon playing on the inner surface to trick us. Some have built intricate old-fashioned orreries with gears and mechanical arms to demonstrate how the disc flips through space, producing night and day. Some believe aliens made the disc; others, gods.

For most people, these disagreements are manageable, because at the end of the day, it's the notion of a powerful *them* hiding the *truth* that motivated them to dig deeper, find one another, and form a community. They can all agree on that. Then group psychology took over; now they are bound by tribalism and reputation management, signaling to one another by committing to the central dogma that, no matter what, the Earth is not a globe.

Beneath that dogma is a value that expresses itself in attitudes. Flat-Earthers don't distrust the scientific method, just the institutions that use it; so they often use the scientific method to test their hunches. When they perform experiments and the results suggest that their hypothesis is incorrect or provides evidence for a competing hypothesis, they dismiss that evidence as anomaly.

It's likely that over time they'll follow the same course of mind change that occurred throughout scientific history, the path of superseded theories in chemistry and physics and psychology and astronomy and so on. They will move through Piaget's stages of assimilation and accommodation until they reach one of Kuhn's paradigm shifts. The explanatory model will hold until enough anomalies make it clear that a different set of explanations is needed to make sense of things.

This is why we invented science in the first place. Science is smarter than scientists, and the method is what delivers results over time. But for it to work, you must be willing to say you are wrong. And if your reputation, your livelihood, your place in your community are at stake, well, that can be hard to do.

In my interview with the producers of *Behind the Curve*, I argued that observing how curious, logical, intelligent people get led astray by their own psychological mechanisms—aided by the conspiracy-friendly algorithms of Google and YouTube, and the tribal and identity-stoking context of social media—shows how we are all prone to this kind of thinking. It provides the humility and empathy I think we need in these contentious times.

It's useful to think of confirmation bias as the goggles we put on when we feel highly motivated by fear, anxiety, anger, and so on. In these states we begin looking for confirmation that the emotions we feel are justified. Why would we do that? I compare it to camping in a remote area; when we hear a strange sound we take out the flashlight and, from our tent, search the trees for confirmation that the emotions we feel are justified.

People who are vaccine-hesitant, for example, feel all these feelings for different reasons, but the resulting behavior is the same. From the safety of their devices, they search the internet for confirmation that their attitudes and emotions are reasonable. Outside the internet, in the woods, the search for confirmation would result in disconfirmation or nothing or some innocuous false positives. On the internet, however, confirmation is guaranteed. Even if 99 percent of the information available is disconfirmatory, if you are searching for that 1 percent, you *will* find it.

We do this because we are social primates who gather information in a biased manner for the purpose of arguing for our individual perspectives, in a pooled information environment, within a group that deliberates on shared plans of action toward collective goals. We are lazy, because we expect to off-load the cognitive labor to a group deliberation process in which every flashlight looking at the forest adds something to the resulting argumentation before planning our shared decision on how to proceed based on shared motivations.

So when interacting with someone who is vaccine-hesitant, you'll get much further if you frame it as respectful collaboration toward a shared goal, based on mutual fears and anxieties, and demonstrate you are open to their perspective and input on the best course of action.

Imagine you both heard a strange noise; you are scared and searching with your own flashlights. You each have some hunches, but most importantly, you want to share input before, together, you reach a conclusion. Explore the reasoning behind their hunches with empathetic questioning and listening. Ask what justifies their confidence, and how. Then share the same.

———

When Gather invited me to talk with Sargent, I took it as an opportunity to demonstrate what I had learned from street epistemology and deep canvassing in front of an audience. I called Anthony Magnabosco and asked him to run through the technique again. Then I called the researchers who had studied technique rebuttal versus topic rebuttal, who told me that in such a shame-sensitive environment the best thing to do in front of an audience was to ask Sargent about his processing, not to refute his claims.

When we met, I found Sargent charming and silly. I told him not to worry: I wouldn't be making fun of him. I had no desire to make him seem foolish. He said he didn't mind if I did and told me about a commercial he had done for a sports betting app in Australia. He told the camera it made betting so easy, even he could do it in his head. The ad ends by saying, "It's foolproof!"

Onstage, I asked about his life before flat Earth, where he grew up, what he did for a living. He told me he had once been a chef at a Mediterranean restaurant in Seattle. But after breaking all the records in a computer pinball game, the company hired him as a ringer, going around to arcades, promoting the machines as an unbeatable champion. He traveled around the country and "made the games look better than they were."

I said it seemed like that might have planted a seed, a sense that there really were hidden forces at work pulling the wool over people's eyes.

"Yes, I was part of a conspiracy," he said. "A video game conspiracy."

I mentioned that he had also already been famous once, and it must feel good to be famous again, traveling the world giving lectures about flat Earth, appearing in documentaries and commercials, and so on. He said it did.

I asked how he came to believe in a flat Earth, and he told me he was never the "sort of person who closed the drapes" and lived in fear. He just found conspiracies interesting but at some point ran out of conspiracies to research. He got bored, but when he found a YouTube video about flat Earth, it just made sense to him. "I remember getting a visceral response. I got flushed. Which was weird."

He looked up everything he could find to shoot down the theory, but the more he looked, the more he became convinced. There's an enormous amount of content online, he said, and after nine months of consuming it, he made a video of his own, running through the clues he thought were most compelling. It went viral, and a million views later he was receiving emails and invitations. Soon he found his way into the community, and over time he rose through the ranks to become a spokesperson. He now speaks around the world, and this year alone he had been to Australia, London, Texas, and now here, in Stockholm, Sweden.

"Every day I wake up and try to destroy Flat Earth, and every day I fail," Mark told me. For him, it was all about research, all about connecting the dots. He felt like he was doing his due diligence, looking up facts that made sense. Some confirmed his hunches, some didn't, but it all pointed to the same conclusion. The only issue really was that once one becomes a flat-Earther, friends and coworkers tend to distance themselves. But since the community is so large now, so welcoming and friendly, it's not so bad. There's even a website for flat-Earthers who want to date but fear what will happen when they reveal their beliefs.

I asked Sargent what those beliefs were. He ran through the claims, then I verified I understood the claims, then asked for his reasoning. I listened, not challenging, and noted that the common theme for him seemed to be that science, as an institution, had leapt to conclusions too soon. There was still plenty we didn't know about space and time and the way planets form. He agreed.

"There are many mysteries of the universe to which we have only a few pieces of evidence," I said. "We don't have all the tools. Maybe we haven't done the work yet. It seems like a conception in Flat Earth is that scientists have answers for everything, but if I'm hearing you correctly, you are saying there's still a lot of room for mystery in this model as well."

"Yep," said Sargent. "I don't have all the answers. Not even close."

I asked, given that, how did flat-Earthers like him figure out the Earth was flat?

Mark picked up a small model that looked a bit like a snow globe, a flat disc of the continents covered with a glass dome, and showed it to the audience. "Can I prove this to you in a court of law right now? No. I can't." Then he picked up a small globe. "But can I create so much reasonable doubt in this that you have nowhere else to turn but to some model like that?" he asked, pointing at the snow globe. "All day long."

I asked if he held the flat Earth model to the same level of scrutiny he did the globe model, the kind of scrutiny a scientist would. He said the flat Earth movement was young; they still had a lot of work to do, playing catch-up with centuries of research defending the prevailing wisdom.

I suggested that if he agreed flat Earth is just one hypothesis among many, then it could be tested scientifically like any other hypothesis; but to have any reasonable scientific discussion, we must use some standard for our confidence. He said sure, and I asked what his confidence level was, zero to one hundred. He said ninety-nine. Then I asked, as Anthony had suggested, if he saw evidence that suggested to his satisfaction that the flat Earth model was incorrect, what would he do?

"Oh, I'd quit. I'd quit in a second."

Nearly an hour in at this point, I felt like that was a good place to stop, and we talked a bit about the experiments flat-Earthers had planned, including an expedition to the supposed South Pole. Then I thanked him, and we moved backstage.

Mark told me it was one of the best conversations he had ever had on the topic, and that night we went to a bar to drink and talk about Sweden. I said I'd like to keep having conversations like we had one day, but not today, and we ordered food.

ACKNOWLEDGMENTS

This book took a long time to write. The longer it took, the more the world changed. What seemed obvious became questionable, and what was questionable became obvious, and on it went until right about here. Along the way, I learned as much about how minds change from the journey to these final words as I did from the research behind them.

But I had a lot of help on this journey, and I fear I can never express the magnitude of my appreciation nor make appropriate use of the space available to acknowledge every person whose encouragement, criticism, and counsel made this project possible.

Without any doubt, I can say this would have never been more than a few unanswered questions without the input and inspiration of my wife, Amanda McRaney. Musing on the concepts in their infancy, you told me, "This sounds like a book," and as they multiplied, your ideas to add, subtract, and alter sections big and small are reflected throughout its pages. I'm in debt for life to your contributions and support. Thank you so very much.

I'm also tremendously grateful for my agent, Erin Malone Borba. You believed in and fought for this project from the beginning, and then again and again, unflinchingly, through a series of strange and unexpected twists of fate. You have been my champion since way back in the blogging days. It was your hand that pulled me into this world, and when I decided to take on an ambitious new adventure, you cleared the way. Thank you.

Niki Papadopoulos, you are rare an incredible editor who understands how to extract a book's true potential hidden inside a janky, unfocused manuscript. You saw the stifled humanity in the earlier versions and knew exactly how to rework the chapters to free its voice and mine. I owe a great deal to your vision and persistence. Thank you.

Trish Daly, your careful editing and insistence on not only adding what was clearly missing but cutting away the parts of the book that distracted and detracted from its story, purpose, and heart brought everything into focus. You were always willing to meet and chat when I was uncertain, and every time I came away feeling like I should have met with you sooner. Thank you.

Eamon Dolan, when I emailed you a thirty-thousand-word chapter about conspiracy theories, you called me, took a deep breath, and asked what the hell I was thinking. That call led to many others, and you guided the original idea from a convoluted rehash of previous work to something that was far outside my comfort zone when we first met. Thank you.

Misha Glouberman, you reached out near the middle, listened to my zealous rants about what, at the time, felt like insights, and carefully dismantled them one by one. I benefited from your expertise many times, and your friendship and feedback were invaluable to me as it all came together. Thank you.

Will Storr, I sent you an early manuscript that you returned with praise where it was worthy and criticism where it was not. Our conversations before and after lit fires that continue to burn in my head, and your amazing work researching and writing books about the unpersuadable and the stories we tell ourselves both challenged and inspired me. Thank you.

Hugo Mercier, this entire project is the result of how I had to change my own mind, about everything I had been writing, following our conversation about your research into arguing and persuasion and what happens in the brain when minds change. Thank you.

There are so many others. My parents Jerry and Evelyn McRaney, Alistair Croll, Joe Hanson, Dave Fleischer and the Leadership LAB, David Broockman, Joshua Kalla, Tom Stafford, Simon Sinek, Nick Andert, Caroline Clark, Daniel J. Clark, Karin Tamerius, Rob Willer, Sam Arbesman, Jonas Kaplan, Sarah Gimbel, Chenhao Tan, Gordon Pennycook, Andy Luttrell, Ada Palmer, David P. Redlawsk, Peter Ditto, Anthony Magnabosco, Charlie Veitch, Megan Phelps-Roper, Zach Phelps, Robert Burton, Stephen Lewandowski, David Eagleman, Lilliana Mason, Donald Hoffman, Duncan Watts, Dan Kahan, Steven Novella, Brendan Nyhan, Jason Reifler, Nathan Fischer, Deborah Prentiss, the late Lee Ross, Melanie C. Greene, Richard Petty, Pascal Wallisch, Jay Van Bavel and the social scientists at NYU, Rory Sutherland and the team at Ogilvy Change, to name a few.

And then there is the great science historian James Burke, whose series I watched on PBS as a child. Early on, *Connections* and *The Day the Universe Changed* set me up for a lifetime of curiosity about how and why things came to be, why they aren't different, and how they might change in the future. I could thank James for that alone, but I've been immensely lucky to get to know him over the years and even work on a few projects together. For a historian, James is surprisingly optimistic about where our species may be headed over the next five hundred years. So I must credit James for continuously steering me away from cynicism as I shared with him bits and pieces of the book and discussed the big ideas. Thank you.

In *Connections*, James offered an "alternate view of history" in which great insights took place because of anomalies and mistakes, because people were pursuing one thing, but it led somewhere surprising or was combined with some other object or idea they could never have imagined by themselves. Innovation took place in the spaces between disciplines, when people outside of intellectual and professional silos, unrestrained by categorical and linear views, synthesized the work of people still trapped in those institutions, who, because of those institutions, had no idea what one another was up to and therefore couldn't predict the trajectory of even their own work, much less history itself.

In *The Day the Universe Changed*, Burke said knowledge was invented as much as it was discovered, and new ideas "nibble at the edges" of common knowledge until values considered permanent and fixed fade into antiquity just like any other obsolete tool. My favorite line from the book has to do with imagining a group of scientists who live in a society that believes the universe is made of omelets and goes about designing instruments to detect traces of interstellar egg residue. When they observe evidence of galaxies and black holes, to them it all just seems like noise. Their model of nature cannot yet accommodate what they are seeing, so they don't see it. "All that can accurately be said about a man who thinks he is a poached egg," joked Burke, "is that he is in the minority."

The influence on this book should be obvious. I learned that when the environment changes, minds must change to accommodate, resisting and relenting in turns on a meandering, revisionary path to provisional epiphany. But it goes deeper than that. Burke once told me that our system of knowledge and discovery had never been able, until recently, to handle more than one or two ways of seeing things at a time. In response, we have long demanded conformity with the dominant worldview or with similarly homogeneous ideological binaries; but that was all going to change once the internet was in everyone's pockets.

For much of his career, James created documentaries and wrote books aimed at helping us to make better sense of the enormous amount of information that he predicted would one day be at our fingertips, and it was this bit of advice he offered at the end of *Connections* that I carried with me through every chapter:

"Recognize within yourself the ability to understand anything, because that ability is there, as long as it is explained clearly enough. And then go and ask for explanations. And if you are thinking right now, 'What do I ask for?' Ask yourself if there is anything in your life that you want changed. That's where to start."

NOTES

INTRODUCTION

xv **same-sex marriage, abrupt:** Benjamin I. Page and Robert Y. Shapiro, *The Rational Public: Fifty Years of Trends in Americans' Policy Preferences* (Chicago: The University of Chicago Press, 2005).

xvii **"a successful intentional effort":** Daniel J. O'Keefe, *Persuasion: Theory and Research* (Newbury Park, CA: Sage Publications, 1990).

xvii **"better viewed as coercive":** Richard Perloff, *The Dynamics of Persuasion* (New York: Routledge, 2017).

CHAPTER 1: POST-TRUTH

3 **or had lost someone that day:** "9/11 Conspiracy Road Trip," *Conspiracy Road Trip*, BBC, 2011. https://www.bbc.co.uk/programmes/b014gpjx.

4   **described him as a "known anarchist":** Mark Hughes, "Royal Wedding: Masked Anarchists Thwarted by Police," *The Telegraph*, April 29, 2011. https://www.telegraph.co.uk/news/uknews/royal-wedding/8483761/Royal-wedding-masked-anarchists-thwarted-by-police.html.

7   **He titled it:** Charlie Veitch, "No Emotional Attachment to 9/11 Theories—The Truth Is Most Important," YouTube, June 29, 2011. https://www.youtube.com/watch?v=ezHNdBE5pZc.

8   **that's like exchanging the belief:** Aodscarecrow, "Why Charlie Veitch Changed His Mind on 911–1/3," YouTube, July 1, 2011. https://www.youtube.com/watch?v=SavpCQlu2GA.

9   **"all this horrible stuff":** Interview with Stacey Bluer on March 7, 2016.

9   **so he left the community:** Anti New World Order, "Alex Jones Says He Knew Charlie Veitch Was an Operative a Year Ago," YouTube, July 26, 2011. https://www.youtube.com/watch?v=02ybVM8jmus.

10   **eliminating all superstitions:** Interview with George Lowenstein and David Hagmann, April 3, 2017.

11   **called the information deficit model:** George Lakoff, *The Political Mind: A Cognitive Scientist's Guide to Your Brain and Its Politics* (New York: Penguin Books 2009); "At the Instance of Benjamin Franklin: A Brief History of the Library Company of Philadelphia," Library Company. http://librarycompany.org/about/Instance.pdf; *How to Operate Your Brain*, directed by Joey Cavella and Chris Graves, performed by Timothy Leary, Retinalogic, 1994.

11   **professionals like journalists:** Paul McDivitt, "The Information Deficit Model Is Dead. Now What? Evaluating New Strategies for Communicating Anthropogenic Climate Change in the Context of Contemporary American Politics, Economy, and Culture," *Journalism & Mass Communication Graduate Theses & Dissertations* 31 (2016). https://scholar.colorado.edu/jour_gradetds/31.

11   **"Truth is dead. Facts are passé":** "'Post-truth' Named 2016 Word of the Year by Oxford Dictionaries," *The Washington Post*, November 16, 2016. https://www.washingtonpost.com/news/the-fix/wp/2016/11/16/post-truth-named-2016-word-of-the-year-by-oxford-dictionaries/?utm_term=.f3bd5a55cb2f.

11   **"killing people's minds":** Allister Heath, "Fake News Is Killing People's Minds, Says Apple Boss Tim Cook," *The Telegraph*, February 10, 2017. https://www.telegraph.co.uk/technology/2017/02/10/fake-news-killing-peoples-minds-says-apple-boss-tim-cook.

12 **"beyond debate, discussion, or argument"**: Nick Stockton, "Physicist Brian Greene Talks Science, Politics, and . . . Pluto?" *Wired*, May 8, 2017, accessed March 4, 2022. https://www.wired.com/2017/05/brian-greene-science -becames-political-prisoner/.

12 **Zuckerberg was sitting before Congress**: "The Key Moments from Mark Zuckerberg's Testimony to Congress," *The Guardian*, April 11, 2018. https://www.theguardian.com/technology/2018/apr/11/mark-zuckerbergs -testimony-to-congress-the-key-moments.

12 **"lost their ability to support consensus"**: William Davies, "The Age of Post-Truth Politics," *The New York Times*, August 24, 2016.

12 **The New Yorker examined**: Elizabeth Kolbert, "Why Facts Don't Change Our Minds," *The New Yorker*, February 19, 2017.

12 **The Atlantic announced**: Julie Beck, "This Article Won't Change Your Mind," *The Atlantic*, March 13, 2017.

12 **"Is Truth Dead?"**: *Time*, April 3, 2017.

CHAPTER 2: DEEP CANVASSING

15 **to see it in action**: Much of the material in this chapter comes from interviews with David Fleischer and others at the LAB. The team also provided written material and video archival footage, and allowed me to spend time at their facilities as well as take part in training and canvasses. While there, I interviewed other visitors and the scientists studying the LAB. I visited three times between 2016 and 2018.

16 **first covered the research**: Lynn Vavreck, "How Same-Sex Marriage Effort Found a Way Around Polarization," *The New York Times*, December 18, 2014.

21 **52 percent voted to ban**: "The California Proposition 8 Initiative Eliminates Right of Same-Sex Couples to Marry," Ballotpedia, 2008. https://ballotpedia .org/California_Proposition_8,_the_%22Eliminates_Right_of_Same-Sex _Couples_to_Marry%22_Initiative_(2008).

21 **called The Prop 8 Report**: "The Prop 8 Report," The Prop 8 Report. http://prop8report.lgbtmentoring.org.

21 **Fleischer wanted to know who**: Ta-Nehisi Coates, "Prop 8 and Blaming the Blacks," *The Atlantic*, January 7, 2009. https://www.theatlantic.com /entertainment/archive/2009/01/prop-8-and-blaming-the-blacks/6548.

22 **no right to object:** This ad is often referred to as *The Princess Ad*. YesOnProp8 called it "It's Already Happened." It can be viewed on YouTube on their channel: https://www.youtube.com/user/VoteYesonProp8.

23 **reconsidering their vote:** Details of the lead-up to the vote came from *The Prop 8 Report* and interviews with Dave Fleischer.

40 **after their social networks:** Donald P. Green and Alan S. Gerber, *Get Out the Vote: How to Increase Voter Turnout* (Washington, DC: Brookings Institution Press, 2015).

41 **after just one conversation:** Michael LaCour and Donald Green, "When Contact Changes Minds: An Experiment on Transmission of Support for Gay Equality," *Science* 346, no. 6215 (2014): 1366–69. doi:10.1126 /science.1256151.

41 **you could change their minds:** Benedict Carey, "Gay Advocates Can Shift Same-Sex Marriage Views," *The New York Times*, December 11, 2014. https:// www.nytimes.com/2014/12/12/health/gay-marriage-canvassing-study-science. html; "The Incredible Rarity of Changing Your Mind," *This American Life*, January 31, 2018. https://www.thisamericanlife.org/555/the-incredible-rarity -of-changing-your-mind; Robert M. Sapolsky, "Gay Marriage: How to Change Minds," *The Wall Street Journal*, February 25, 2015. https://www.wsj .com/articles/gay-marriage-how-to-change-minds-1424882037; "Article Metrics and Usage Statistics Center," *Article Usage Statistics Center*. http://classic .sciencemag.org/articleusage?gca=sci%3B346%2F6215%2F1366.

42 **that *Science* quickly provided:** You can read their report here: *Irregularities in LaCour* (2014), http://web.stanford.edu/~dbroock/broockman_kalla_aronow _lg_irregularities.pdf.

43 **agreed to be researched:** The details of the retraction come from interviews with Donald Green, Josh Kalla, David Broockman. I also interviewed Michael LaCour, but only before the news of the alleged fraud became public, so he did not comment on it. Green spoke to me on the phone the week of the retraction, because I had already been in contact with him after visiting the LAB for the first time. LaCour has not made any public statements after initially defending himself.

45 **that would take generations:** Betsy Levy Paluck, "How to Overcome Prejudice," *Science* 352, no. 6282 (2016): 147. doi:10.1126/science.aaf5207.

45 **paper was published in *Science*:** David Broockman and Josh Kalla, "Durably Reducing Transphobia: A Field Experiment on Door-to-Door

Canvassing," *Science* 352, no. 6282 (2016): 220–24. doi:10.1126/science
.aad9713.

45 **"No, Wait, Short Conversations":** Ed Yong, "No, Wait, Short Conversations
Really Can Reduce Prejudice," *The Atlantic*, April 7, 2016. https://www
.theatlantic.com/science/archive/2016/04/no-wait-short-conversations
-really-can-reduce-prejudice/477105.

45 **wrote *The New York Times*:** Benoit Denizet-Lewis, "How Do You Change
Voters' Minds? Have a Conversation," *The New York Times*, April 7, 2016. https://
www.nytimes.com/2016/04/10/magazine/how-do-you-change-voters-minds
-have-a-conversation.html.

46 **more effective than traditional canvassing:** Andy Kroll, "The Best Way
to Beat Trumpism? Talk Less, Listen More," *Rolling Stone*, September 15, 2020.
https://www.rollingstone.com/politics/politics-news/2020-presidential
-campaign-tactic-deep-canvassing-1059531.

47 **no awareness of their own flips:** T. J. Wolfe and M. B. Williams, "Poor
Metacognitive Awareness of Belief Change," *Quarterly Journal of Experimental
Psychology* (2006), U.S. National Library of Medicine, accessed November 27,
2021. https://pubmed.ncbi.nlm.nih.gov/28893150/.

48 **"Flip-flop, flip-flop!":** You can still buy the flip-flops sold outside the convention
through online retailers. They are now considered "presidential memorabilia."
The attack ads, produced by the Club for Growth PAC, are available on YouTube.

50 **their opinions became less extreme:** Philip M. Fernbach, Todd Rogers, Craig
R. Fox, and Steven A. Sloman, "Political Extremism Is Supported by an Illusion
of Understanding," *Psychological Science* 24, no. 6 (2013): 939–46. doi:10.1177
/0956797612464058.

50 **encouraged analogic perspective taking:** Virginia Slaughter and Alison
Gopnik, "Conceptual Coherence in the Child's Theory of Mind: Training
Children to Understand Belief," *Child Development* 67, no. 6 (1996): 2967–988.
doi:10.2307/1131762.

51 **learn how others saw:** A. M. Leslie, O. Friedman, and T. P. German, "Core
Mechanisms in 'Theory Of Mind,'" *Trends in Cognitive Sciences* 8 (2004): 528–33.

51 **but, until prompted, never considered:** Lara Maister, Mel Slater, Maria V.
Sanchez-Vives, and Manos Tsakiris, "Changing Bodies Changes Minds: Owning
Another Body Affects Social Cognition," *Trends in Cognitive Sciences* 19, no. 1
(2015): 6–12. doi:10.1016/j.tics.2014.11.001; Andrew R. Todd, Galen V.
Bodenhausen, and Adam D. Galinsky, "Perspective Taking Combats the Denial

of Intergroup Discrimination," *Journal of Experimental Social Psychology* 48, no. 3 (2012): 738–45. doi:10.1016/j.jesp.2011.12.011.

CHAPTER 3: SOCKS AND CROCS

57 **"the debate that broke":** "What Color Is the Dress? The Debate That Broke the Internet," New Hampshire Public Radio, June 17, 2021. https://www .nhpr.org/2015-02-27/what-color-is-the-dress-the-debate-that-broke-the -internet#stream/0.

57 **"the drama that divided":** Terrence McCoy, "The Inside Story of the 'White Dress, Blue Dress' Drama That Divided a Planet," *The Washington Post*, October 25, 2021. https://www.washingtonpost.com/news/morning-mix/wp /2015/02/27/the-inside-story-of-the-white-dress-blue-dress-drama-that -divided-a-nation.

57 **was preparing for her daughter:** I first learned about the backstory of *The Dress* from an interview with Pascal Wallisch. A complete account can be found here: Claudia Koerner, "The Dress Is Blue and Black, Says the Girl Who Saw It in Person," *BuzzFeed News*, February 27, 2015. https://www .buzzfeednews.com/article/claudiakoerner/the-dress-is-blue-and-black-says -the-girl-who-saw-it-in-pers#.idKqgP3G2.

58 **32.8 million unique views within:** Adam Rogers, "The Science of Why No One Agrees on the Color of This Dress," *Wired*, February 27, 2015. https://www .wired.com/2015/02/science-one-agrees-color-dress.

58 **Actress Mindy Kaling:** Mindy Kaling (@mindykaling),"IT'S A BLUE AND BLACK DRESS! ARE YOU FUCKING KIDDING ME," Twitter, February 26, 2015, https://twitter.com/mindykaling/status/571123329 328914433.

60 **none knowing what it does:** Jakob von Uexküll, *A Foray into the Worlds of Animals and Humans: With a Theory of Meaning*, trans. Joseph D. O'Neil (Minneapolis/London: University of Minnesota Press, 2010).

60 **"What is it like to be a bat":** Thomas Nagel, "What Is It Like To Be a Bat?" *Philosophical Review* 83 (1974): 435–50.

62 **see how they would react:** Colin Blakemore and Grahame F. Cooper, "Development of the Brain Depends on the Visual Environment," *Nature* 228, no. 5270 (1970): 477–78. doi:10.1038/228477a0.

64 **reality they've always known:** Information about brain plasticity in this chapter came from an interview with David Eagleman about his book: David Eagleman, *Livewired* (Toronto: Anchor Canada, 2021).

65 **"effects of the stone upon":** Bertrand Russell, *An Inquiry into Meaning and Truth* (Hoboken, NJ: Taylor and Francis, 2013).

68 **"business about seeing puzzling enough":** Ludwig Wittgenstein, *Philosophical Investigations* (Oxford, UK: Blackwell, 1953).

72 **the ambiguity *never registered*:** Pascal Wallisch, "Illumination Assumptions Account for Individual Differences in the Perceptual Interpretation of a Profoundly Ambiguous Stimulus in the Color Domain: 'The Dress,'" *Journal of Vision* (April 1, 2017). https://jov.arvojournals.org/article.aspx?articleid =2617976; Pascal Wallisch and Michael Karlovich, "Disagreeing about Crocs and Socks: Creating Profoundly Ambiguous Color Displays," arXiv.org, August 14, 2019. https://arxiv.org/abs/1908.05736.

78 **to see them as gray:** "Exploring the Roots of Disagreement with Crocs and Socks," *Pascal's Pensées*, accessed November 27, 2021. https://blog.pascallisch .net/exploring-the-roots-of-disagreement-with-crocs-and-socks.

81 **"than at any point in":** "Political Polarization in the American Public," Pew Research Center, April 9, 2021. https://www.pewresearch.org/politics/2014/06 /12/political-polarization-in-the-american-public.

81 **differing interpretations of reality itself:** Mara Mordecai and Aidan Connaughton, "Public Opinion about Coronavirus Is More Politically Divided in U.S. than in Other Advanced Economies," Pew Research Center, October 28, 2020. https://www.pewresearch.org/fact-tank/2020/10/28/public-opinion-about -coronavirus-is-more-politically-divided-in-u-s-than-in-other-advanced -economies.

83 **a frame contest:** Erik C. Nisbet, P. S. Hart, Teresa Myers, and Morgan Ellithorpe, "Attitude Change in Competitive Framing Environments? Open-/Closed-Mindedness, Framing Effects, and Climate Change," *Journal of Communication* 63, no. 4 (2013): 766–85. doi:10.1111/jcom.12040.

83 **it's because of X:** Leo G. Stewart, Ahmer Arif, A. Conrad Nied, Emma S. Spiro, and Kate Starbird, "Drawing the Lines of Contention," *Proceedings of the ACM on Human-Computer Interaction* 1 (2017): 1–23. doi:10.1145/3134920.

85 **"into the mind of others":** Blaise Pascal, *Pensées* (New York: P.F. Collier & Son, 1910), 12–13.

CHAPTER 4: DISEQUILIBRIUM

92 **"matter that carries information":** Steven Pinker, *How the Mind Works* (London: Penguin Books, 2015).

94 **adjust our predictions going forward:** Mark Humphries, "The Crimes against Dopamine," *The Spike*, June 23, 2020. https://medium.com/the-spike /the-crimes-against-dopamine-b82b082d5f3d.

95 **by making it more predictable,** Michael A. Rousell, *Power of Surprise: How Your Brain Secretly Changes Your Beliefs* (Lanham, MD: Rowman & Littlefield, 2021).

95 **we didn't know we didn't:** Stanislas Dehaene, *How We Learn: The New Science of Education and the Brain* (London: Penguin Books, 2021).

96 **create and interact with knowledge:** Jean Piaget, *Principles of Genetic Epistemology* (London: Routledge, 2011).

97 **through the use of propositions:** Robert M. Martin, *Epistemology: A Beginner's Guide* (London: Oneworld, (2015); Noah M. Lemos, *An Introduction to the Theory of Knowledge* (Cambridge, United Kingdom: Cambridge University Press, 2021).

98 **as knowledge, philosophically speaking:** Nassim Nicholas Taleb, *The Black Swan* (Tokyo, Japan: Daiyamondosharade, 2009).

100 **exactly like being right:** Kathryn Schulz, *Being Wrong: Adventures in the Margin of Error* (New York: HarperCollins, 2011).

101 **hatch, dangle, detach, and fly:** Ray Lankester, *Diversions of a Naturalist*, 3rd ed. (Methuen & Co.: London, 1919).

102 **fell from the goose tree:** Edward Heron-Allen, *Barnacles in Nature and in Myth* (London: Milford, 1928).

103 **"resemblance to a bird":** Sir Edwin Ray Lankester, *Diversions of a Naturalist* (New York: Macmillan, 1915).

104 **In 1949, two psychologists:** Jerome S. Bruner and Leo Postman, "On the Perception of Incongruity: A Paradigm," *Journal of Personality* 18, no. 2 (1949): 206–23.

105 **subsequent runs of the experiment:** Leo Postman and Jerome S. Bruner, "Perception Under Stress," *Psychological Review* 55, no. 6 (1948): 314–23. doi:10.1037 /h0058960.

107 **"are rabbits afterwards":** Thomas S. Kuhn, *The Structure of Scientific Revolutions* (Chicago: The University of Chicago Press, 2015).

108 **"an effort of assimilation":** Jack Block, "Assimilation, Accommodation, and the Dynamics of Personality Development," *Child Development* 53, no. 2 (1982): 281. https://doi.org/10.2307/1128971.

109 **"When there is a balance":** Jonathan Y. Tsou, "Genetic Epistemology and Piaget's Philosophy of Science," *Theory & Psychology* 16, no. 2 (2006): 203–24. doi:10.1177/0959354306062536.

111 **new beliefs and a new:** Richard G. Tedeschi and Lawrence G. Calhoun, "Posttraumatic Growth: Conceptual Foundations and Empirical Evidence," *Psychological Inquiry* 15, no. 1 (2004): 1–18. doi:10.1207/s15327965pli1501_01.

112 **gives a sense of belonging:** Colin Murray Parkes, "Bereavement as a Psychosocial Transition: Processes of Adaptation to Change," *Journal of Social Issues* 44, no. 3 (1988): 53–65. doi:10.1111/j.1540-4560.1988 .tb02076.x.

114 **"can you get there":** Reynolds Price, *Whole New Life: An Illness and a Healing* (New York: Plume, 1995).

115 **forgotten without a conclusion:** David Eagleman, *Incognito: The Secret Lives of the Brain* (Edinburgh: Canongate, 2016).

117 **doomsday cult in Chicago:** Leon Festinger, Stanley Schachter, and Henry W. Ricchen, *When Prophecy Fails: A Social and Psychological Study of a Modern Group That Predicted the Destruction of the World* (New York: Harper & Row, 1956).

117 **four fake politicians across:** David P. Redlawsk, Andrew J. W. Civettini, and Karen M. Emmerson, "The Affective Tipping Point: Do Motivated Reasoners Ever 'Get It'?" *Political Psychology* 31, no. 4 (2010): 563–93, 2010. doi:10.1111 /j.1467-9221.2010.00772.x.

120 **should the anomalies accumulate:** Julia Galef, co-founder of the Center for Applied Rationality, deserves credit for the term *abeyance* being used in this way. I first heard of abeyance when she used it during an interview on her show, *Rationally Speaking,* as she described how we set aside anomalies in science and in life itself.

CHAPTER 5: WESTBORO

125 **obnoxious and rabid hate group:** "Westboro Baptist Church," Southern Poverty Law Center, https://www.splcenter.org/fighting-hate/extremist-files/group /westboro-baptist-church.

125 **group of radical Christian hatemongers:** Andrew Lapin, "A Properly Violent 'Kingsman' Takes on a Supervillain With Style," NPR, February 12, 2015. https://www.npr.org/2015/02/12/384987853/a-properly-violent-kingsman-takes-on-a-supervillain-with-style.

126 **ride home from a bar:** Melanie Thernstrom, "The Crucifixion of Matthew Shepard," *Vanity Fair*, January 8, 2014. https://www.vanityfair.com/news/1999/13/matthew-shepard-199903.

126 **church carried signs that read:** Alex Hannaford, "My Father, the Hate Preacher: Nate Phelps on Escaping Westboro Baptist Church," *The Telegraph*, March 12, 2013. https://www.telegraph.co.uk/news/religion/9913463/My-father-the-hate-preacher-Nate-Phelps-on-escaping-Westboro-Baptist-Church.html.

126 **he had been in hell:** "Perpetual Gospel Memorial to Matthew Shepard," Westboro Baptist Church Home Page. https://www.godhatesfags.com/memorials/matthewshepardmemorial.html.

126 **The publicity led to local:** I read a number of older articles from local newspapers detailing the events of the drive. This article provides an overview written at the moment the church gained national attention: "Holy Hell: Fred Phelps, Clergyman, Is on a Crusade," *The Washington Post*, November 12, 1995. https://www.washingtonpost.com/lifestyle/style/holy-hellfred-phelps-clergyman-is-on-a-crusade/2014/03/20/af0a3e52-b06b-11e3-a49e-76adc9210f19_story.html.

126 **earned his associate's degree:** "Religion: Repentance in Pasadena," *Time*, June 11, 1951.

126 **By their own count:** A full list of Westboro's internal accounting of their picketing is available on their website, godhatesfags.com.

127 **in favor of Westboro:** Adam Liptak, "Justices Rule for Protesters at Military Funerals," *The New York Times*, March 2, 2011. https://www.nytimes.com/2011/03/03/us/03scotus.html.

128 **"I wasn't sure what":** Interview with Zach Phelps-Roper, February 13, 2016.

130 **called him and told him:** Mike Spies, "Grandson of Westboro Baptist Church Founder is Exiled from Hate Group," *Vocativ*, April 23, 2015. https://www.vocativ.com/usa/us-politics/westboro-baptist-church/index.html.

131 **Justin and Lindsey had traveled:** Justin and Lindsey are not their real names. These pseudonyms were taken from Megan Phelps-Roper's memoir, *Unfollow: A Memoir of Loving and Leaving the Westboro Baptist Church* (New York: Farrar, Straus and Giroux 2019).

138 **serve on Twitter's Trust:** Adrian Chen, "Unfollow: How a Prized Daughter of
the Westboro Baptist Church Came to Question Its Beliefs," *The New Yorker*,
November 15, 2015. https://www.newyorker.com/magazine/2015/11/23
/conversion-via-twitter-westboro-baptist-church-megan-phelps-roper.

140 **retweeting her and making fun:** The details of Megan's story here
and throughout the rest of this chapter are a combination of her
account from my interview with her and recollections from her memoir,
Unfollow.

150 **Four of Fred Phelps's children:** The details of the excommunication and
conversion of Fred Phelps came from my interview with Zach Phelps-Roper. The
number of people who have left Westboro varies somewhat across sources, but
the numbers here reflect what I consider to be the consensus. More details
available within this article, whose author I interviewed about Zach's sister
Megan leaving the church: Adrian Chen, "Conversion via Twitter," *The New
Yorker*, March 10, 2018. https://www.newyorker.com/magazine/2015/11/23
/conversion-via-twitter-westboro-baptist-church-megan-phelps-roper.

152 **"I hope they can find":** "I Am Zach Phelps-Roper. I Am a Former Member
of the Westboro Baptist Church. Ask Me Anything!" Reddit.com. https://
www.reddit.com/r/IAmA/comments/2bvjz6/i_am_zach_phelpsroper_i_am
_a_former_member_of_the.

CHAPTER 6: THE TRUTH IS TRIBAL

156 **Charlie Veitch as my guide:** "Manchester Blue Tit," Faunagraphic, accessed
November 28, 2021. https://www.faunagraphic.com/manchester-blue
-tit-print.

158 **join the conversation happening:** Charlie Veitch, "Charlie Veitch on Alex Jones
Show (May 2009)," YouTube, October 25, 2009. https://www.youtube.com
/watch?v=Pd_Erw91uyE.

159 **what happened in their brains:** Much of this material comes from interviews
with neuroscientists Sarah Gimbel and Jonas Kaplan about their paper: Sarah
Gimbel, Jonas Kaplan, and Sam Harris, "Neural Correlates of Maintaining One's
Political Beliefs in the Face of Counterevidence," *Scientific Reports* 6, no. 1
(2016). doi:10.1038/srep39589.

161 **felt at odds with the group:** S. E. Asch, "Effects of Group Pressure on the
Modification and Distortion of Judgments," in H. Guetzkow, ed., *Groups,
Leadership and Men* (Pittsburgh, PA:Carnegie Press), 177–190.

161 **electricity up to lethal doses:** Stanley Milgram, "Behavioral Study of Obedience," *The Journal of Abnormal and Social Psychology* 67, no. 4 (1963): 371–78. doi:10.1037/h0040525.

161 **took over a summer camp:** Muzafer Sherif, *The Robbers Cave Experiment: Intergroup Conflict and Cooperation* (Norman, OK: University Book Exchange, 1961).

162 **garbage from a few days:** I wrote about the Robbers Cave experiment in my book *You Are Now Less Dumb* and was reminded of it as an example of tribal loyalty when I interviewed political psychologist Lilliana Mason about her book, *Uncivil Agreement: How Politics Became Our Identity* (Chicago: University of Chicago Press, 2018).

163 **overestimated the true number:** Henri Tajfel, "Experiments in Intergroup Discrimination," *Scientific American* 223, no. 5 (1970): 96–102. doi:10.1038 /scientificamerican1170-96.

165 **"social death is more frightening":** Interview with Brooke Harrington conducted August 2021.

166 **fused with group identity:** Interview with Dan Kahan on December 4, 2017.

166 **why this was a mandatory:** "Cultural Cognition Project—HPV Vaccine Research," The Cultural Cognition Project. http://www.culturalcognition.net /hpv-vaccine-research.

168 **His credentials, of course, never changed:** Dan M. Kahan, "The Politically Motivated Reasoning Paradigm, Part 1: What Politically Motivated Reasoning Is and How to Measure It," in *Emerging Trends in the Social and Behavioral Sciences, eds. Robert Scott and Stephen Kosslyn* (Hoboken, NJ: John Wiley and Sons, 2017).

168 **a very rational decision:** Interview with Dan Kahan on February 11, 2018.

169 **"face that kind of pressure":** "Cultural Cognition Project—Cultural Cognition Blog—Who Distrusts Whom about What in the Climate Science Debate?" The Cultural Cognition Project. http://www.culturalcognition.net/blog/2013/8/19 /who-distrusts-whom-about-what-in-the-climate-science-debate.html.

169 **willing to share their beliefs:** David Straker, *Changing Minds: In Detail* (Crowthorne: Syque, 2010).

170 **all the other emotional trappings:** Straker, *Changing Minds.*

171 **those who wish to signal:** Anni Sternisko, Aleksandra Cichocka, and Jay J. Van Bavel, "The Dark Side of Social Movements: Social Identity, Non-Conformity,

and the Lure of Conspiracy Theories," *Current Opinion in Psychology* 35 (February 21, 2020): 1–6. https://www.sciencedirect.com/science/article/pii /S2352250X20300245.

172 **detect "dangerous coalitions":** Jan-Willem van Prooijen and Mark van Vugt, "Conspiracy Theories: Evolved Functions and Psychological Mechanisms," *Perspectives on Psychological Science* 13, no. 6 (2018): 770–88. https://doi.org /10.1177/1745691618774270.

174 **aren't looking for a particular:** Computathugz, "Truth Festival|TruthSeekers |FreeThinkers," Truth Juice, September 19, 2014. http://www.truthjuice.co.uk /non-truthjuice-festivals.

174 **form the word *LOVE* with:** DunamisStorm, "The TruthJuice Gathering 2011 (Andy Hickie—Universal Mind)," YouTube, May 31, 2011. https://www.youtube .com/watch?v=UUssKyamG-Q.

174 **"infinite, fractal," and "holographic":** Truth Juice Films, "Truth Juice Summer Gathering Pt2," YouTube, September 22, 2010. https://www.youtube.com/watch ?v=LBYKqzdDCxk.

175 **"slave-work-money-gift" paradigm:** Charlie Veitch, "Kindness Offensive/Love Police SUNRISE FESTIVAL COMPETITION 2011," YouTube, January 7, 2011. https://www.youtube.com/watch?v=xD2PO4ECu8U.

176 **reminding ourselves of our deepest values:** Geoffrey L. Cohen, David K. Sherman, Anthony Bastardi, Lillian Hsu, Michelle Mcgoey, and Lee Ross, "Bridging the Partisan Divide: Self-affirmation Reduces Ideological Closed-Mindedness and Inflexibility in Negotiation," *Journal of Personality and Social Psychology* 93, no. 3 (2007): 415–30. doi:10.1037/0022-3514.93.3.415; Kevin R. Binning, Cameron Brick, Geoffrey L. Cohen, and David K. Sherman, "Going Along versus Getting It Right: The Role of Self-integrity in Political Conformity," *Journal of Experimental Social Psychology* 56 (2015): 73–88, 2015. doi:10.1016 /j.jesp.2014.08.008.

176 **When those conditions were met:** David K. Sherman and Geoffrey L. Cohen, "The Psychology of Self-Defense: Self-Affirmation Theory," *Advances in Experimental Social Psychology* 38 (2006): 183–242. doi:10.1016/s0065 -2601(06)38004-5.

177 **We can feel safe to change our minds:** Brendan Nyhan and Jason Reifler, "The Roles of Information Deficits and Identity Threat in the Prevalence of Misperceptions," *Journal of Elections, Public Opinion and Parties* 29, no. 2 (May 2017): 1–23. doi:10.1080/17457289.2018.1465061.

178 **together on the ride back:** Sherif, *The Robbers Cave Experiment*.

178 **in the modern world:** Interview with Tom Stafford on September 13, 2016.

CHAPTER 7: ARGUING

184 **a woman named Jane:** Mark Snyder and Nancy Cantor, "Testing Hypotheses about Other People: The Use of Historical Knowledge," *Journal of Experimental Social Psychology* 15, no. 4 (1979).

185 **back to the experimenters:** I interviewed psychologist Peter Ditto about his experiment, which is available here: Peter Ditto and David F. Lopez, "Motivated Skepticism: Use of Differential Decision Criteria for Preferred and Nonpreferred Conclusions," *Journal of Personality and Social Psychology* 63, no. 4 (1992): 568–84. doi:10.1037/0022-3514.63.4.568.

186 **we step off and go:** Daniel Gilbert, "I'm O.K., You're Biased," *The New York Times*, April 16, 2006. https://www.nytimes.com/2006/04/16/opinion /im-ok-youre-biased.html.

188 **out of one's head and:** Jonnie Hughes, *On the Origin of Tepees: The Evolution of Ideas (and Ourselves)* (New York: Free Press, 2012).

189 **signal to the people:** Dan Sperber, Fabrice Clément, Christophe Heintz, Olivier Mascaro, Hugo Mercier, Gloria Origgi, and Deirdre Wilson, "Epistemic Vigilance," *Mind & Language* 25, no. 4 (2010): 359–93. doi:10.1111 /j.1468-0017.2010.01394.x.

190 **could benefit the group:** Much of this chapter comes from an interview with Hugo Mercier about his paper with Dan Sperber, "Why Do Humans Reason? Arguments for an Argumentative Theory," *Behavioral and Brain Sciences* 34, no. 2 (2011): 57–74. doi:10.1017/s0140525x10000968.

192 **the most reasonable justification:** Hugo Mercier and Dan Sperber, *The Enigma of Reason* (Cambridge, MA: Harvard University Press, 2017).

193 **they couldn't justify doing otherwise:** Christopher K. Hsee, "Value Seeking and Prediction-Decision Inconsistency: Why Don't People Take What They Predict They'll Like the Most?" *Psychonomic Bulletin & Review* 6, no. 4 (1999): 555–61. doi:10.3758/bf03212963.

193 **But they didn't, because they couldn't:** Eldar Shafir and Amos Tversky, "Thinking Through Uncertainty: Nonconsequential Reasoning and Choice," *Cognitive Psychology* 24, no. 4 (1992): 449–740. doi:10.1016/0010-0285(92) 90015-t.

194 **in the study, though:** Emmanuel Trouche, Petter Johansson, Lars Hall, and Hugo Mercier, "The Selective Laziness of Reasoning," *Cognitive Science* 40, no. 8 (2015): 2122–136. doi:10.1111/cogs.12303.

197 **where individual reasoning fails:** Tom Stafford, *For Argument's Sake: Evidence That Reason Can Change Minds* (Amazon Digital Services, 2015).

197 **lazy reasoning, disagreement, evaluation, argumentation, truth:** David Geil and Molly Moshman, "Collaborative Reasoning: Evidence for Collective Rationality," *Thinking & Reasoning* 4, no. 3 (1998): 231–48. doi:10.1080 /135467898394148.

198 **individuals become less likely to contradict it:** Cass R. Sunstein, "The Law of Group Polarization," University of Chicago Law School, John M. Olin Law & Economics Working Paper No. 91. doi:10.2139/ssrn.199668.

199 **arguments from third parties:** Mercier and Sperber, *The Enigma of Reason*, 307.

199 **high anxiety and intense outrage:** Robert C. Luskin, Ian O'Flynn, James S. Fishkin, and David Russell, "Deliberating Across Deep Divides," *Political Studies* 62, no. 1 (2012): 116–35. doi:10.1111/j.1467-9248.2012.01005.x.

199 **consensus on inferences and shared goals:** Stafford, Tom. "A Lens on the Magic of Deliberation," *Reasonable People* (blog), September 1, 2021. https://tomstafford.substack.com/p/a-lens-on-the-magic-of-deliberation.

CHAPTER 8: PERSUASION

202 **homesickness set in:** Frank Capra, *The Name Above the Title: An Autobiography* (New York: Bantam Books, 1972).

202 ***This,* he proclaimed, is why:** *Prelude to War*, directed by Frank Capra. United States: Special Services Division, 1942.

203 **showcased the courage:** Carl Hovland, Irving Lester Janis, and Harold H. Kelley, *Communication and Persuasion: Psychological Studies of Opinion Change* (Westport, CT: Greenwood Press, 1982).

205 **so they could pass their college courses:** Interview with psychologist Richard Petty on July 8, 2018.

206 **impact the message had:** Harold Lasswell, "The Structure and Function of Communication in Society," in *The Communication of Ideas*, ed. L. Bryson (New York: Institute for Religious and Social Studies, 1948).

207 **neutral or negative evaluation:** Joel Cooper, Shane J. Blackman, and Kyle Keller, *The Science of Attitudes* (New York: Psychology Press, 2016).

210 **more arguments, better policy:** Richard E. Petty, John T. Cacioppo, and David Schumann, "Central and Peripheral Routes to Advertising Effectiveness: The Moderating Role of Involvement," *Journal of Consumer Research* 10, no. 2 (1983): 135. doi:10.1086/208954.

210 **whether a celebrity endorsed:** Petty, Cacioppo, and Schumann, "Central and Peripheral Routes."

212 **until they cross the "confidence gap":** Alice H. Eagly and Shelly Chaiken, *The Psychology of Attitudes* (Belmont, CA: Wadsworth Cengage Learning, 2010).

213 **"ELM has this lofty premise":** Interview with Andy Luttrell conducted in January 2022.

214 **make a persuasive message:** Much of this section comes from *The Science of Attitudes* by Joel Cooper, Shane Blackman, and Kyle Keller, which provided an overview of attitude change research that I then tracked down and read.

215 **a failure into a success:** G. Tarcan Kumkale and Dolores Albarracín, "The Sleeper Effect in Persuasion: A Meta-Analytic Review," *Psychological Bulletin* 130, no. 1 (2004): 143–72. doi:10.1037/0033-2909.130.1.143.

217 **any person-to-person message:** Francesca Simion and Elisa Di Giorgio, "Face Perception and Processing in Early Infancy: Inborn Predispositions and Developmental Changes," *Frontiers in Psychology* 6 (2015). doi:10.3389/fpsyg.2015.00969.

217 **the less guarded we become:** Susan Pinker, *The Village Effect: How Face-to-Face Contact Can Make Us Healthier and Happier* (Toronto: Vintage Canada, 2015).

CHAPTER 9: STREET EPISTEMOLOGY

241 **and they resolve their ambivalence:** William Richard Miller and Stephen Rollnick, *Motivational Interviewing: Helping People Change* (New York: Guilford Press, 2013).

241 **neatly organized into one of two:** Philipp Schmid and Cornelia Betsch, "Effective Strategies for Rebutting Science Denialism in Public Discussions," *Nature Human Behaviour* 3 (2019). https://www.nature.com/articles/s41562-019-0632-4.

242 **very idea of certainty itself:** Interview with Robert Burton conducted May 2021.

243 **trapped in a neurological prison:** Robert Alan Burton, *On Being Certain: Believing You Are Right Even When You're Not* (New York: St, Martin's Griffin, 2009).

249 **component that evokes mental imagery:** Melanie C. Green and Jenna L. Clark, "Transportation into Narrative Worlds: Implications for Entertainment Media Influences on Tobacco Use," *Addiction* 108, no. 3 (2012): 477–84. doi:10.1111 /j.1360-0443.2012.04088.x.

251 **I had spent the most time with around the campfire:** Nathan Fischer is a pseudonym.

CHAPTER 10: SOCIAL CHANGE

259 **but it hadn't happened yet:** Marvin Harris, *Our Kind: Who We Are, Where We Came From, Where We Are Going,* (New York: Harper Perennial, 1991).

260 **that led to this very sentence:** Kim Ann Zimmermann, "Pleistocene Epoch: Facts About the Last Ice Age," *LiveScience*, 2017. https://www.livescience.com /40311-pleistocene-epoch.html.

260 **"high-frequency environmental change":** The material concerning the Ice Age's impact on cultural evolution came from an interview with Peter J. Richerson on December 20, 2016.

261 **evolutionary dance floor ever since:** Peter J. Richerson and Robert Boyd, *Not by Genes Alone: How Culture Transformed Human Evolution* (Chicago: The University of Chicago Press, 2006).

263 **patiently ran through the science:** Lesley Newson and Peter J. Richerson, "Moral Beliefs about Homosexuality: Testing a Cultural Evolutionary Hypothesis," *ASEBL Journal* 12, no. 1 (2016): 2–21.

265 **Research at the University of Wisconsin:** Christie F. Boxer, Mary C. Noonan, and Christine B. Whelan, "Measuring Mate Preferences," *Journal of Family Issues* 36, no. 2 (2013): 163–87. doi:10.1177/0192513x13490404.

265 **divorce rates for first marriages:** Virginia Pelley, "The Divorce Rate Is Different than You Think," *Fatherly*, February 18, 2022, accessed March 4, 2022. https://www.fatherly.com/love-money/what-is-divorce-rate-america/.

267 **mind about same-sex marriage:** "Transcript: Robin Roberts ABC News Interview with President Obama," ABC News, May 9, 2012. https://abcnews .go.com/Politics/transcript-robin-roberts-abc-news-interview-president-obama /story?id=16316043.

268 **an issue that would affect:** Ro Suls, "Deep Divides Between, Within Parties on Public Debates about LGBT Issues," Pew Research Center, October 4, 2016. http://www.pewresearch.org/fact-tank/2016/10/04/deep-divides-between -within-parties-on-public-debates-about-lgbt-issues; "Two in Three Americans Support Same-Sex Marriage," Gallup, May 23, 2018. https://news.gallup.com/poll /234866/two-three-americans-support-sex-marriage.aspx.

268 **Bush his second term:** Carolyn Lochhead, "Gay Marriage: Did Issue Help Re-elect Bush?" *SFGate*, January 23, 2012. https://www.sfgate.com/news /article/gay-marriage-Did-issue-help-re-elect-Bush-2677003.php.

268 **ban same-sex marriage across:** Elisabeth Bumiller, "Same-Sex Marriage: The President; Bush Backs Ban in Constitution on Gay Marriage," *The New York Times*, February 25, 2004. https://www.nytimes.com/2004/02/25/us/same-sex -marriage-the-president-bush-backs-ban-in-constitution-on-gay-marriage.html.

269 **offered to perform the ceremony:** Matt Viser, "New 'Cottage' at Maine Compound for Jeb Bush," *Boston Globe*, May 23, 2015. https://www .bostonglobe.com/news/nation/2015/05/23/jeb-bush-having-new-house-built -for-him-family-compound-maine-even-prepares-for-campaign/mrVSwhPY kanfgL6nA4fRVK/story.html.

269 **"Why don't you guys":** David Carter, *Stonewall: The Riots That Sparked the Gay Revolution* (New York: Griffin, 2011).

269 **a push by leaders in:** Carter, *Stonewall*.

270 **professional understanding of:** Mark Z. Barabak, "Gays May Have the Fastest of All Civil Rights Movements," *Los Angeles Times*, May 20, 2012. http://articles.latimes.com/2012/may/20/nation/la-na-gay-rights-movement. 201 20521; "So Far, So Fast," *The Economist*, October 9, 2014. https://www.economist .com/briefing/2014/10/09/so-far-so-fast; Reihan Salam, "That Was Fast: Not Long Ago, Same-Sex Marriage Was a Cause Advanced by a Handful of Activists. Now It's the Law of the Land. How Did That Happen?" *Slate*, June 26, 2015. http://www.slate.com/articles/news_and_politics/politics/2015/06/supreme _court_gay_marriage_decision_why_politicians_and_judges_moved_so.html; Matt Baume, "Gay Marriage Timeline for the US," About.com. This website is now offline, but cached versions can be found through Google.

270 **using their new lines of communication:** E.J. Graff, "How the Gay-Rights Movement Won," The American Prospect, June 7, 2012. http://prospect.org /article/how-gay-rights-movement-won.

270 **preventing similar cases from:** Molly Ball, "How Gay Marriage Became a

Constitutional Right," *The Atlantic*, July 1, 2015. http://www.theatlantic
.com/politics/archive/2015/07/gay-marriage-supreme-court-politics
-activism/397052.

272 **far from such sociological:** Gordon Allport, *The Nature of Prejudice*
(Oxford, UK: Addison-Wesley, 1954).

273 **designated driver at least:** "Designated Driver Campaign: Harvard Center
Helped to Popularize Solution to a National Problem," Harvard School
of Public Health, June 1, 2010. https://www.hsph.harvard.edu/news/features
/harvard-center-helped-to-popularize-solution-to-a-national-problem; "Harvard
Alcohol Project: Designated Driver," Harvard School of Public Health, May 20,
2013. https://www.hsph.harvard.edu/chc/harvard-alcohol-project.

274 **generated by the institution of slavery:** Kwame Anthony Appiah, *The
Honor Code: How Moral Revolutions Happen* (New York: W. W. Norton & Co,
2011).

275 **"Solemn gentlemen went to":** Steven Pinker, *The Better Angels of Our Nature:
Why Violence Has Declined* (New York: Penguin Books, 2012).

276 **"our relationship to gay people":** Derek Penwell, "How Did We Learn to Love
Gay People So Quickly?" *The Huffington Post*, December 7, 2017. https://www
.huffingtonpost.com/derek-penwell/how-did-we-learn-to-love-gay
-people-so-quickly_b_2980858.html.

276 **"Compared to so many issues":** "How Unbelievably Quickly Public Opinion
Changed on Gay Marriage, in 5 Charts," *The Washington Post*, June 26, 2015.
https://www.washingtonpost.com/news/the-fix/wp/2015/06/26/how
-unbelievably-quickly-public-opinion-changed-on-gay-marriage-in-6-charts
/?utm_term=.8283bd8a4590.

276 **"fastest flip of a":** Among those I interviewed who verified this were political
scientists Brendan Nyan, Josh Kalla, and David Broockman, and psychologists
David Redlawsk and Jason Reifler.

276 **About 86 percent of people:** Frank Langfitt, "The Fight to Change Attitudes
toward Covid-19 Vaccines in the U.K.," NPR, April 19, 2021, accessed March 4,
2022. https://www.npr.org/2021/04/19/988837575/the-fight-to-change
-attitudes-toward-covid-19-vaccines-in-the-u-k.

276 **"added to people's skepticism":** Frank Langfitt, "The Fight to Change Attitudes
toward Covid-19 Vaccines in the U.K.," NPR, April 19, 2021. https://www.npr.org
/2021/04/19/988837575/the-fight-to-change-attitudes-toward-covid-19-vaccines

-in-the-u-k. Greg Satell, *Cascades: How to Create a Movement That Drives Transformational Change* (New York: McGraw-Hill Education, 2019).

277 **"thresholds of resistance":** Mark Granovetter, "Threshold Models of Collective Behavior," The American Journal of Sociology 83, no. 6 (May 1978): 1420–43.

280 **imagine three groups of people:** Greg Satell, *Cascades: How to Create a Movement That Drives Transformational Change* (New York: McGraw-Hill Education, 2019).

283 **all it takes is a spark:** Clive Thompson, "Is the Tipping Point Toast?" *Fast Company*, January 2, 2008. https://www.fastcompany.com/641124/tipping -point-toast.

285 **models we have used:** James Burke, *The Day the Universe Changed* (Boston: Little, Brown, 1995).

286 **"if we weren't the center":** Interview with James Burke on September 9, 2016.

CODA

289 **around the belief that:** David McRaney, "YANSS 151—What We Can Learn about Our Own Beliefs, Biases, and Motivated Reasoning from the Community of People Who Are Certain the Earth Is Flat," You Are Not So Smart, July 22, 2019. https://youarenotsosmart.com/2019/04/09/yanss-151-what-we-can -learn-about-our-own-beliefs-biases-and-motivated-reasoning-from-the -community-of-people-who-are-certain-the-earth-is-flat.

INDEX

Italicized page numbers indicate material in photographs or illustrations.